The Color Mac®

Design Production Techniques

Marc D. Miller and Randy Zaucha

AAZ4985

The Color Mac: Design Production Techniques

© 1992 Marc D. Miller and Randy Zaucha

Library of Congress Catalog No.: 92-71248

ISBN: 0-672-30025-7

94 93 92   4 3 2 1

Interpretation of the printing code: the rightmost double-digit number is the year of the book's printing; the rightmost single-digit number the number of the book's printing. For example, a printing code of 92-1 shows that the first printing of the book occurred in 1992.

To Richard and Fiora Miller (a.k.a. Dad and Mom)

Miss Kimberly Eckardt, and to All Artisans of Color

Publisher	Mike Britton
Associate Publisher	Karen A. Bluestein
Managing Editor	Neweleen Trebnik
Development Editor	Stuart J. Torzewski
Production Editor	Cheri Clark
Copy Editor	Julie Sturgeon
Editorial Production Coordinator	Karen Whitehouse
Cover Designer	Katherine Hanley
Designer	Scott Cook
Color Scanning and Separations	Marc D. Miller Randy Zaucha
Photographs	Fashion photos by Ahmet Sibdialsau, Click Image, NY, NY Scenic photos by Jeff Reinking, Seattle, WA Other photos by Marc Miller and Randy Zaucha Back cover photos by Ana Guerrero
Production Team	Beth J. Baker, Scott Boucher, Michelle Cleary, Kate Godfrey, Debbie Hanna, Phil Kitchel, Barry Pruett, Linda Seifert

Composed in Wiedemann, Helvetica, and
MCPdigital by Hayden

About the Authors

Marc D. Miller

Marc D. Miller is an instructor at The Graphic Arts Institute of Northern California in San Francisco. He has been in the art, printing, and pre-press world for more than 12 years in what he likes to call the "imaging profession." He speaks frequently on the changing traditions of print production, color theory, digital output options, and image manipulation. In lectures, he often presents the concept of digital expressionism as a general term for the many incarnations of art produced using a computer.

Working as a consultant for printing and pre-press companies, Marc bridges the gap between digital imaging and traditional printing technology. His skills and background in photography, graphics design, and photo retouching add dimension and depth to the issues of professional printing and color reproduction.

Marc earned a degree in Commerce & Engineering from Drexel University in Philadelphia, where he concentrated on computer technology and mechanical engineering. He has worked extensively for several photography studios, including Crane Photography of Philadelphia. Marc is based in San Francisco and Philadelphia and consults in Europe— when not producing digital color output for his company, Creative Endeavours.

Randy Zaucha

Randy Zaucha's eight years of graphic arts schooling started in high school and continued through undergraduate school at Illinois State University and graduate school at Rochester Institute of Technology. Since college, he has accumulated 15 years in the printing trade in various positions. Randy is a journeyman color scanner operator with both time "on the bench" and positions as a color scanner trainer, demonstrator, and troubleshooter for two major scanner/pagination system manufacturers. He has more than five years of pagination and image retouching experience.

Recently, Randy wrote and published *The Scanner Book for Color Imaging*, describing how to color-separate various types of original copy brought in for reproduction. Currently, Randy works as a freelance color consultant and gives seminars and classes on color in the field and at The Graphic Arts Institute of Northern California.

We Want to Hear from You

What our readers think of Hayden is crucial to our sense of well-being. If you have any comments, no matter how great or how small, we'd appreciate your taking the time to send us a note.

We can be reached at the following address:

Mike Britton
Hayden
11711 N. College Ave.
Carmel, IN (yes, Indiana—not California...) 46032
(317) 573-6880 voice
(317) 573-2583 fax

The authors can be reached at the following addresses:

Marc D. Miller
C/O Graphic Arts Institute
665 3rd Street
San Francisco, CA 94107

Randy Zaucha
C/O Blue Monday Publishing
Box 295
2440 16th Street
San Francisco, CA 94103

Acknowledgements

During the course of writing this book we discovered that apart from its computer graphics definition, the word pixelated means "somewhat strange and mischievous or mentally unbalanced". An interesting discovery, since we spend much our time swimming in the wonderful world of color and pixels where the term means something quite different. But many times during the course of this journey we have encountered the non-graphics definition of pixelated. Our trip was by no means undertaken alone, in fact during our travel we encountered many craftspeople with whom we shared our mission. To those persons who helped us through those pixelated moments we thank you. Although we probably may miss mentioning someone this is not intentional, but we would like to mentioned specifically, and in no particular order, the following persons for aiding in our endeavour.

For their generosity we thank all of our friends and family, including: Dan Primeaux; Ana Guerrero; Michael Carling; Meta Whaley; John Derry of Fractal Design; George Putkey; Edgar Guttzeit; Rick Belemy of Color Services, Seattle; Steve Guttman of Adobe; Matt Keefe, Jeff Raby, Jill Qualls, of TX in San Francisco for the wonderful transparency output; Karen Rosen; Tom Slick Donohue; Charly Frech; Angi Ebert; Tina Schleicher; Ryan Miller; Ida Maddesi for all the great pasta; Scot "Scooter" Miller; Chris Anne Bradley; Joseph "J.R." Rance jr.; Penny Chase of Agfa Corporation; Rebecca Field; Merril Sheilds of Octogon Graphics in San Francisco for the use of your toys; Chelsea Sammel; Hagiet Cohen; Larry Cohn; L. Brouwers; Ivor Chazan; Roger Stephenson of DuPont; Jeff Reinking; Marcus D'Martialé of Pixelated Productions; Ahmet Sibdialsau; Scott at Prentice Hall for the late night software delivery; Kurt Schwent of Storm Technologies; Peter Sylvester; Robert Santucci of Romar Productions; Ned and many others......

We would like to extend a very special thanks to the the staff and crew of the Graphic Arts Institute in San Francisco, and especially to its director Steve Whaley. Without his encouragement, faith, skill and generosity we would not have produced this book. A simple acknowledgement is far from adequate except to add out heartfelt thanks and appreciation.

Marc D. Miller & Randy Zaucha
San Francisco, CA
June, 1992

Foreword

It is quite amazing to go back just 15 years to see how finished art was assembled for color publications. Traditionally, art directors and designers were not taught how to typeset or perform color separations. These tasks were undertaken by experienced and capable specialists.

In those days, if you counted the number of times someone rekeyed an original and then edited the copy, you would not be surprised if it took seven or eight passes before the copy was final. That was when galleys of type came in rolls, which then were cut into columns and pasted to the finished art board. A necessary precaution was usually a prayer that the editor would not find a typo or change the design, because that would mean lifting all the mechanicals and repasting them (a messy, time-consuming, and somewhat risky process).

The advantages of electronic page layout were obvious immediately: no galleys of type, no wax, no press-on type, no tape, no X-acto knives, and infinitely editable copy and elimination of much of the hand stripping associated with tints and colored copy. Electronic page layout was exciting and challenging. Exciting because the new electronic tools put controls in the hands of the creator. Challenging because the creator also assumed responsibility for the production of the finished page—a process for which most designers and artists had not been trained.

Just as desktop publishing illustrated the potential lack of training and relevant skills associated with typesetting, so desktop color publishing already has brought attention to a new set of production skills that the graphic designer may be only partially prepared to address. A designer may be an expert in selecting color to communicate a message, but ensuring that color appears correctly on a page is another story.

For those claiming that while the technology exists to do commercial color on the desktop, but not the skills—this book goes a long way in closing the knowledge gap. With extensive knowledge in traditional color techniques, Marc Miller and Randy Zaucha have produced an excellent guidebook to assist the newcomer to color publishing by presenting the information in a relaxed, informative manner. Although the concepts presented are technically complex, any color aspirant should be able to follow the book as it presents techniques in a simple, practical style. Perhaps the greatest strength of *The Color Mac* is the manner in which it offers specific instructions and goals within the context of broad theoretical considerations.

For example, for "memory colors" (those colors that people picture in their minds, such as the red in an apple), Randy and Marc provide specific CMYK percentages that you can use to create a deep realistic red. They suggest that you memorize the combination of percentages of common colors in order to present color while maintaining clarity and vibrance.

Just as the page layout revolution created an instant demand for typesetting knowledge and skill, the shift to color highlights has created demands for new skills required by Mac users wanting to take advantage of the low cost and flexibility associated with color use in electronic publishing. Skills in color scanning for separation are quite different from those required for scanning for position only.

Desktop color is not difficult, but different. This means it is time to go back to school...or better yet, read this book.

Howard Barney
John Stewart
Barneyscan Corporation

Contents

Introduction

*If you want to hit the mark you need to aim a little above
the target; [because] every arrow that flies feels the pull
of earth.*

—Henry David Thoreau

Learning to play good music is analogous to learning to produce quality color. A teacher presents the fundamentals. You practice many hours; you eventually play flawless Mozart or create best quality color. By the very nature of your endeavor, you realize that simply knowing the basics does not mean you can play the music of the masters in two days or produce quality color digital images without training. Sure, you can program an instrument to play Mozart, or you may know software packages that manipulate color images. But what if someone requests Igor Stravinsky or Oscar Peterson? What do you do—run out and buy the new Stravinsky software? What happens when you have other requests, or you when want to improvise and create your own music or digitized images? With practice and experience, you can play the masters and more. The same is true of creating best quality color.

As a result of teaching people about color, we have learned that good craftsmanship comes from knowing the basics. We wanted to produce a simple introductory text for our students that would familiarize them with the fundamentals of digital imaging and the craft of producing color. We wrote this book with the idea that knowing the underlying basics of color and digital imagery gives you—the craftsperson—a more solid base from which to seek out and eventually create your own digital-image environment. *The Color Mac* provides such a foundation of information from which to build your craft and develop expertise.

This book presents information in such a fashion that the reader is well-instructed on the basics, but not so inundated with detail that he feels unable to deviate from specific instructions and explore uncharted territory. Actually, the reader is invited and encouraged to build on basic color-production instructions and expand the possibilities. We simply give the reader the road map from which to choose a path to reach the destination. Because these roads are well-traveled by us, we want to help others avoid many of the roadblocks we have encountered in the past.

Since its introduction, the Macintosh has emerged as an indispensable tool in the professional world of color images and graphics. The Mac provides access to a world of color that at one time was available only on very expensive (and therefore unattainable) workstations. During the Mac's inception, the idea of "good-enough color" was coined to establish the Mac in a highly competitive color-reproduction market. Although most of the early color produced from the Macintosh was only "good enough," the concept of good-enough color no longer is necessary to compensate for this early growth stage. The Macintosh now can produce high-quality professional color if you apply the proper techniques.

Learning about color is as important as learning about how to operate the programs that work with color. Software programs change; the basics of color do not. A software package's true worth is not how good the program's shortcuts are, but, more important, the program's capacity to enable you to override its attributes and apply your enhancements and knowledge to a particular situation. The more you learn about color and the craft of color reproduction, the more control you can exercise in choosing the direction you want to go with this knowledge.

In a highly competitive environment, what separates good color from great color is not what hardware or software you use, but *how* you use your tools to produce color. The Mac is a "do it" tool, an intuitive tool, a fun tool, and the Mac wants you to do it yourself. Don't allow the freedom to learn and explore provided by the Mac to be compromised by believing those who say that excellent color is too difficult to learn. You must make an effort and you may want to reach only certain levels. As with most good investments, however, the rewards are greater than you imagine. The Mac presents you with the vehicle to learn and excel. Believe you can, and don't be intimidated by the subject matter or the so-called experts.

More and more, people are realizing the intrinsic value of understanding their craft or profession. Knowing your craft is at the core of achieving any success in that craft. The future of digital imaging and color reproduction lies in learning not only programs but the fundamentals from which these programs operate. The evolution of image software programs is the result of the user's ability to design his or her own work environment, customized to fulfill specific needs. The people who excel know the basics of the color and imagery they want to produce. Learning how the Macintosh can quickly and efficiently link processes that before were separate is the true power of digital technology. The Macintosh is an important tool for the craft of digital imaging and color. As computer technology changes the way we do things, the need to develop craftsmanship is imperative.

We hope you enjoy traveling the roads of color and discovering some of the wonder and fascination that we have experienced working with color. The most important concept to understand, however, is that the Macintosh does not produce color—you do. The process and need for craftsmanship in every walk of life is one of the most powerful lessons computer technology can give us. As computer technology changes the way we arrive at a conclusion, the need to develop craftsmanship is imperative. And so we introduce you to the craft of color.

Marc & Randy

What Are Pixels?

The question "What are pixels?" can elicit many kinds of answers. Pixels have been part of how we create images for longer than many people realize. The very word "pixel" conjures an understanding of something familiar, yet elusive. The glossary description of a pixel says it is a discrete unit or element of an entire image. Discrete means a unit or an element that cannot be fractionalized or broken down into smaller elements. But what does that mean and how does it apply to modern digital images? Enigmatic as a pixel may be, understanding a pixel's function is critical to your ventures into digital images.

The Picture Element

The word *pixel* comes from a combination of two words: *picture* and *element*. The first two letters of each word separated by an *x* has resulted in a word that has become a cornerstone of digital imagery. The *x* in the middle is actually helpful in understanding the concept of picture elements. Because pixels are located on a grid, x and y coordinates describe the location of any picture element. In other words, an *x* and a pixel both can mark a specific spot. We discuss this later. You sometimes hear persons working in the field of video use the word "pel" rather than pixel, but more and more, "pixel" is supplanting this term.

Every type of drawing, painting, photograph, or image uses some variation of picture elements (pixels). One of the more obvious examples is the wonderful art created with the mosaic technique and style. If you have seen a mosaic, you may have noticed that the image is composed of tiles arranged in intricate patterns depicting a variety of people, places, and things. What are the characteristics of a mosaic? Each tile is a separate individual unit. Each tile or element also occupies a specific location-area relative to other tiles or elements. Each element also has some value of color.

Unlike real estate, which thrives on location, location, location, a pixel or picture element is dependent on discrete individual units, location-area, and color value. Regardless of how simple or elaborate the image system, if you apply the rules, you will find that the rules work. Before you apply the rules to digital images, try some common and familiar image systems. Try needlepoint. Does needlepoint involve individual units that can't be divided? Yes, within the cloth grid each stitch is a separate element. The size of the stitches may vary, but you always have an individual stitch that cannot be divided into half a stitch. The location-area of each stitch relative to other stitches makes up the image on a grid of holes. The value of the stitch is the various colored threads. Even if you use only black threads and no other color, each element has a value. Needlepoint is a fairly uniform system. You also find a uniformity with digital computer systems.

But do the three guidelines hold for something that is not as uniform, such as photographic film? Light-sensitive grains or crystals make up a photograph, so there *are* individual units, as you can see in figure 1.1. The crystals are not necessarily placed uniformly on the film, but each crystal or grain does have a location-area. And whether you use color or black-and-white film, each grain or crystal has a value. So we find that—perhaps without even realizing it—

something as common as taking a picture, which presumably we all have done, uses the concept of picture elements or pixels.

Fig. 1.1.
The grains of film as shown also are the pixels of photography.

Digital Pixels

How do pixels relate to working with digital images? When you begin to recognize how to assemble images, you are in a unique position of understanding ways to manipulate these images. Your ability to create an image is directly proportional to understanding the system that produces those images. You begin to explore ways of creating images, not guessing or hit-or-miss. Exploring and experimenting can expose unique aspects of an image system. But unless you discover the basic parts that make up the image system, the exercises are pointless. When you understand these basics, you are placed firmly in command of creating images how, where, and when you want. Pixels are at the core of image manipulation regardless of whether that image system is needlepoint, painting, photography, digital imagery, or a combination of systems. Each of these systems requires a basic understanding of picture elements.

Discrete Unit

We'll apply the pixel guidelines of discrete unit, location-area, and value to computer graphics. In digital images a picture element is indeed discrete. A pixel cannot be divided into half pixels. An individual pixel can be described by its aspect ratio. The aspect ratio is the proportion of the horizontal edge divided by the vertical edge. The aspect ratios of all pixels used in a specific digital system are the same. You will not find a digital system that mixes pixels with different aspect ratios. The Macintosh system works exclusively with square pixels, as shown in figure 1.2. A square pixel has an aspect ratio of one.

Other computer systems, which include video, work with pixels that have other aspect ratios and in some cases use three-sided (triangular) pixels. If you exchange images between systems that do not have the same pixel aspect ratios, you need to compensate for the difference or the image appears distorted. The most common way is to stretch an image's picture or image aspect ratio to match the aspect ratio of the system on which you are working. An image's aspect ratio is the proportion of the number of horizontal pixels divided by the number of vertical pixels, as shown in figure 1.3. The image aspect ratio is not necessarily the same as the pixel aspect ratio.

Fig. 1.3.
The total number of pixels across (900) divided by the total number of pixels down (600) is 900:600 or 1.5:1.

For example, if you import an image from a system that uses a pixel aspect ratio of two to one (2:1) into the Mac environment, you need to stretch the image aspect ratio 200 percent horizontally to retain the proper proportions of the image. Later in this chapter we cover in greater detail how to work with pixels that have different aspect ratios. The mathematical implications of square pixels are simple. Square pixels provide a perfect symmetry that is instinctively easy to grasp. Because each side of the pixel is equal, the nonmathematician can begin to comprehend the

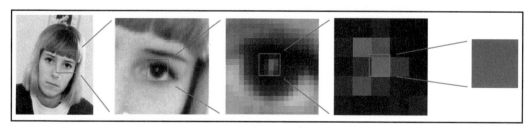

Fig. 1.2.
A square pixel.

computations that produce the seemingly fantastic effects of digital computer graphics. Square pixels work like a jigsaw puzzle in which all the pieces fit easily with little worry about how the sides of the pieces relate. All the inner pixels are touched on four sides by another pixel. Pixels on the outer border of an image are touched on three sides, and the corner pixels are touched on two sides.

Location-Area

The location of a pixel is based on a centuries-old system developed by the mathematician and philosopher René Descartes. This system is known as the *Cartesian coordinate system*. Those of you who gave any thought, in those tiresome high-school geometry classes, to the usefulness of math now have a vindicated, smiling geometry teacher. Graphics, by its very nature, is a two-dimensional system and Cartesian coordinates aptly describe any graphics you encounter. Although some of today's computer graphics are highly complex and intricate, digital image origins are simple and basic. You don't need to become a mathematician to grasp the concepts of digital graphics because you already use the core concepts every day. The Cartesian system, as shown in figure 1.4, consists of two axes: x on the horizontal plane crossing perpendicular to y on the vertical plane.

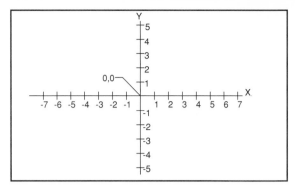

Fig. 1.4.
The Cartesian coordinate system with the origin of 0,0 located at the center.

Each axis has a zero point. The zero point can be placed anywhere but is most useful placed where the x and y axes intersect. Every pixel can be identified individually using Cartesian coordinates. Figure 1.5 shows the location on a grid or map of a certain pixel with the x,y coordinates 440,98.

Fig. 1.5.
A grid or bitmap of pixels in which a single pixel is identified by the coordinates 440,98.

Each pixel has a unique location-area, and only one pixel can occupy a single set of coordinates on each grid or map of pixels. This map of pixels is better known as a bitmap; the images these pixels describe are called bitmap images. With this map you can adjust any or all of the pixels you encounter. When you begin image retouching, you will think you literally can move pixels. But on each unique bitmap, you can reassign only the value of a pixel, not a pixel's location-area. Changing the value of a pixel or a group of pixels to match another pixel group gives the appearance of moving those pixels. The perceived movement is very much like department store lights that seem to move, when in fact, the lights simply blink on and off, never leaving their fixed locations.

Bitmap images also are known as raster images. Raster lines commonly are used in video to describe the rows of pixels in an image because video images display pixels line by line.

Value

The value of a pixel is based on the number of bits of information the pixel contains. The number of bits of information also is known as bit resolution or pixel color resolution. Figure 1.6 illustrates how bits are used in digital image systems.

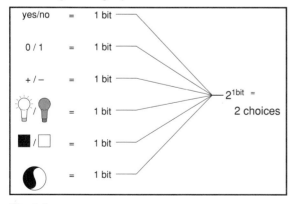

Fig. 1.6.
The binary system is the basis for all modern computing.

The binary code that is the basis of all modern computing is the method used to ascribe value to a pixel. The simplest pixel has two choices: on or off; yes or no; black or white. The total number of choices is two raised to the power of one. The two is the base number system, and one is the exponent and indicator of the number of bits of color value per pixel. A pixel with two raised to the power of one is a one-bit pixel, and the images described by a map of these one-bit pixels is called a one-bit image. A bit of information is the binary choice of zero or one, on or off, as mentioned. Adding more bit (on, off) choices to a system increases the number of potential combinations. The chart in figure 1.7 illustrates how the choices of pixel values increase as you increase the number of bits (on, off choices) per pixel.

The most common and established pixel value system is the 24-bit color system. As the chart in figure 1.9 shows, 2 raised to the power of 24 results in a total possible choice of 16,777,216 colors—a few more than your crayon box offers. In fact, the human eye cannot distinguish the subtle variations of many of the millions of colors. Although 24-bit color does not encompass the entire range of color we can see with our unaided eyes, it comes close.

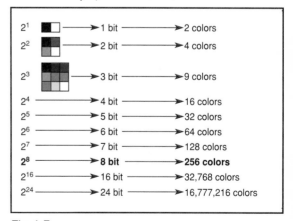

Fig. 1.7.
The total number of color choices increases as the number of bits increases.

In a digital color system, each pixel is described by combining the primary colors of red, green, and blue (RGB). Red, green, and blue take advantage of the triple nature of color. White light, as you know, is a combination of all colors in the spectrum. This spectrum is divided into three parts of red, green, and blue. It may be more accurate to divide the color spectrum into more than three parts, but the complexity of such a system does not justify the gains in color range. Trichromatic color systems, of which RGB is a member, is the minimum color system that produces the largest color range. Trichromatic color is a universally accepted process of producing color whether in photography, television, printing, or digital computer graphics. This communality links all modern image systems. We discuss how later.

Each RGB color shares equally the total 24 bits (on, off choices), so each has a value range of 2 raised to the power of 8, resulting in 256 levels or choices for each color of red, green, and blue. Every pixel in a 24-bit image has a separate value of RGB combined to establish a final composite value of color. (See figure 1.8.) You can adjust one, two, or all three color values of a pixel to create a new pixel value, which you will do when color-correcting images in the RGB color space. The total number of unique color combinations is 16.7 million, as mentioned previously.

When you work with printing colors, a 32-bit color system applies. In printing, each picture element is described by a combination of cyan, magenta, yellow, and black (CMYK). Although including a fourth channel to a trichromatic system seems to defeat the purpose of minimizing the number of color channels, you will discover that the addition of a black channel is necessary to compensate for deficiencies in printing inks. Because the printing process does not have the same range of color possibilities as digital pixels, you cannot deduce that the total range of color for 32 bits is 4,294,967,296 colors. We discuss the range of print colors later. For now, you should understand that the black channel produces an additional 8-bit system for a total of 32 bits, as shown in figure 1.9.

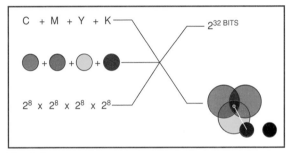

Fig. 1.9.
In a 32-bit system, cyan, magenta, yellow, and black each have 8 bits of information.

To conclude the investigation into what pixels are, our Macintosh pixels do fit the guidelines of what makes a pixel. A discrete unit made of square picture elements, a unique location-area described by a bitmap, and value described by a combination of red, green, and blue define Macintosh picture elements.

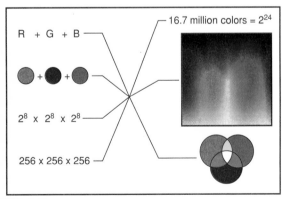

Fig. 1.8.
In a 24-bit color system, red, green, and blue each have 8 bits of color information.

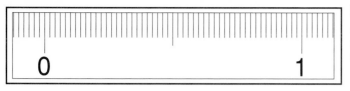

Fig. 1.10a.
Slicing one inch into 100 equal parts gives a resolution of 100 elements per inch.

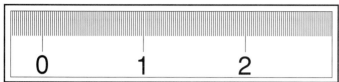

Fig. 1.10b.
Slicing one centimeter into 100 equal parts gives a resolution of 100 elements per centimeter.

Concepts of Resolution

Now that you know what a pixel is, you need to understand how pixels are used to describe images. As mentioned before, pixels exist on a grid or bitmap and are components and elements of an image. The quantity or number of picture elements, better known as resolution, is critical to the detail and quality of an image. The resolution of an image equals the number of pixels per unit of measure, as illustrated in figures 1.10a and 1.10b. Remember that within image systems resolution is universal. Every image system requires a certain number of picture elements to describe an image. Resolution is a way of describing bitmap images, which in turn are made of pixels. In fact, a criterion for an image *is* the number of pixels, or the resolution.

Bitmap images are considered resolution-dependent because how continuous an image appears depends on the number of pixels or resolution of an image. A continuous image is one in which you cannot see the individual pixels that make up the image. If your resolution is less than required, you will begin to notice individual pixels in the form of jagged edges, called *jaggies*. In any type of output, having visible individual picture elements is called *pixelization*. As shown in figure 1.11, typically, the higher the resolution (the more pixels per unit of measure), the less likely you will see the individual pixels, and therefore the image blends into a continuous smooth image.

Fig. 1.11.
The more resolution in an image, the more continuous the image appears.

Fig. 1.11a.
Image at 300 pixels per inch.

Fig. 1.11b.
Image at 150 pixels per inch.

Fig. 1.11c.
Image at 50 pixels per inch.

The examples of needlepoint and photographic film can illustrate the concept of resolution. On a pattern that measures 10 by 10 inches, the resolution of the needlepoint would be equal to the number of stitches (pixels) per inch. If there are 20 stitches per inch, there would be a total of 200 stitches in each direction. The same applies to film grain. You often have heard about very fine-grained film. Saying that the film is fine grained is no different than saying that the resolution of the film is high or that the number of grains (pixels) per millimeter is large. Fine-grained films are considered higher quality because the images appear sharper, better defined, and more

continuous. If the resolution of an image is too low, the individual picture elements become visible. An enlarged photograph can appear grainy because the number of grains per inch is low. Unless you want the grain for visual effect, this graininess illustrates the concept of ineffective resolution. Effective resolution in both cases results in an image that appears to be one continuous tone and not groups of identifiable picture elements.

There are three important types of digital resolution: bit resolution, image resolution, and device resolution.

Bit Resolution

We previously discussed bit resolution in describing the value of a pixel. Bit resolution relates to the amount of color information stored in each pixel. Typically, the range is between one and 32 bits per pixel.

Image Resolution

Image resolution refers to the total number of pixels of a particular image. The unit of measure is left up to the user. Think of images in terms of the total number of pixels horizontally and vertically, and you will avoid confusion when referring to the size of an image. Communicating the total number of pixels of an image provides every person with all the information needed to apply his or her own preferred physical measuring units. The output method you choose determines the physical size of the image. For example, as shown in figure 1.12, you can tell others you need an image 634 pixels wide and 468 high more easily than telling them you need an image 317 pixels per inch for a 3-inch-by-2-inch frame. This example is even more difficult if the person who creates the image works with units other than inches, such as millimeters. More than a few unnecessary calculations and conversions are sidestepped simply by using pixels. If a person is given the proper number of pixels, that person does not need to know the final physical size. Pixels provide a universal and effective method of communicating image size. A useful symbol to use for pixels is "*pxs.*"

Fig. 1.12.
This image, 951 pxs across and 634 pxs down, has 317 pixels per inch (ppi) and 12 pixels per millimeter (ppcm).

Device Resolution

Because images are displayed with a variety of output systems, it is important to consider the output resolution available from each device. Each output device has a specific resolution it can produce. Meeting the requirements of a device's resolution is critical to producing the highest quality image. The number of pixels you should have in an image is directly proportional to the output you choose. The three most common output devices are monitors (video), halftone plotters (imagesetters), and film or transparency recorders.

The higher the resolution of an image, the more continuous an image appears. Bitmap images commonly are referred to as continuous tone images, or CT images. When the resolution of the image matches the output device properly, you cannot see the picture elements that make up the image. The image appears as a continuous tone to the unaided eye. When pixelization occurs, you know that the number of pixels in your image does not meet the minimum required number for your chosen output device. Images with a small number of pixels often are referred to as low-resolution or lo-res images. High-res or high-resolution images are images that contain large numbers of pixels.

Monitor Resolution

A monitor screen has a fixed resolution and in most cases is 72 or 80 pixels per inch (ppi). The very common Apple 13-inch color monitor, which actually has an image area of slightly more than 11 inches diagonal, has a screen resolution of 640 pixels across and 480 down. An image which matches that number of pixels across and down displays as a continuous image without any noticeable pixels. If you simply want to view the highest quality image to the *full* size of a monitor, your image need be only 72 pixels per inch. This number matches the resolution of the monitor one to one. Less than 72 ppi results in pixelization. More than 72 ppi will not improve the image because the additional pixels cannot be displayed.

Imagesetter (Halftone Plotter) Resolution

The most common use of digital images is output to halftone film separations. There are two items to consider regarding image resolution when producing halftone film: the resolution of the plotter or image-setter and the line screen ruling you are using to print the image.

11

The higher the resolution of the imagesetter, the more accurate the halftone dot, and as a result the image-setter dots can reproduce a higher quality image.

Imagesetter resolution often is described as dots per inch (dpi). The term dpi can be misleading and often is mixed incorrectly with other descriptions of resolution. The potential quality level of an imagesetter is described by the number of imaging elements per inch (epi). These imaging elements are grouped to create dots.

The term "dot" has been overused. A dot refers to a halftone dot or a printer's dot, not to pixels and not to the imagesetter elements that make up and describe a halftone dot. (See figure 1.13.) The quality or resolution of a halftone dot is directly related to the number of elements the imagesetter can use to produce that dot. The more elements per inch, the higher the resolution of the imagesetter and the more accurate the dot. The more accurate the dot, the higher the quality of the reproduced image. The higher quality image is more pleasing to your clients. Chapter 12 discusses epi in greater detail.

A line screen ruling of halftone dots sometimes mistakenly is used as a way of describing digital pixel resolution. Because screen ruling actually relates to lines of halftone dots used in printing rather than digital images, you should address a line screen ruling as part of output. Too often the mixture of digital resolution and printing halftone resolution has caused confusion. For clarity's sake, digital image resolution always will be referred to as pixels per inch (ppi) and never as dots per inch (dpi). Dots per inch or lines per inch (lpi) describe the line screen frequency. In a 133-line screen, each line contains 133 dots per inch. The terminologies of dpi and lpi complement one another. The chart in figures 1.14a through 1.14d describes each term. Screen ruling and halftone dots are discussed further in Chapter 15.

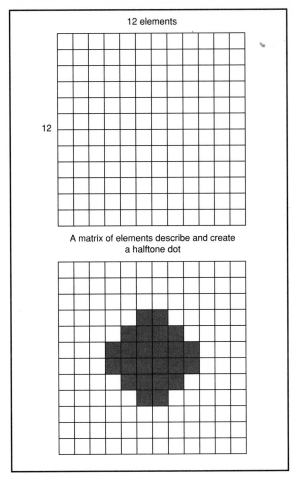

Fig. 1.13.
The elements of an imagesetter create halftone dots.

Remember that every image system has some kind of picture elements used to describe an image. Typically, high resolution produces a more continuous-looking image. When an image is going from one image system to another, the resolution of each system is critical in achieving the highest quality image possible.

Halftone dots used in printing are the picture elements of printing. Photographic grains are the picture elements of photographs and transparencies. Screen or monitor elements are the pixels of video. When bringing an image into these systems, you carefully must consider the required resolution for each system. The special needs for each output are discussed later.

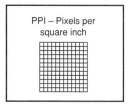

Fig. 1.14a.
Pixels per inch (ppi).

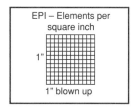

Fig. 1.14b.
Elements per inch (epi).

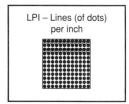

Fig. 1.14c.
Lines per inch (lpi).

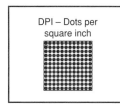

Fig. 1.14d.
Dots per inch (dpi).

Sampling and the Relationship to Output

When the resolution of an image does not meet your established needs, you can increase the effective amount of resolution. Scaling, sampling, resampling, up-sampling, down-sampling, and "resing"-up (or down) all are common terms used for increasing or decreasing the number of pixels in an image and, accordingly, its resolution to meet reproduction requirements. When changing the resolution of an image, you either add or subtract pixels from the bitmap of an image. Subtracting or scaling down an image is an easy process. You simply decide what your effective resolution should be and throw away the picture elements you don't need. (See figure 1.15.) If you have matched the required resolution for your output device properly, you should have an image that appears continuous regardless of how many pixels you discard. You do not gain any quality by using more pixels than required by your chosen output method. Using more pixels than needed also unnecessarily contributes to increasing the size of the file. This point is illustrated in Chapter 4.

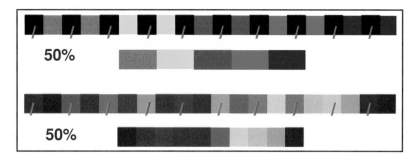

Fig. 1.15.
Down-sampling an image by 50 percent discards every other pixel.

Adding pixels or up-sampling or scaling-up or resing-up an image to increase an image's resolution is a more involved matter. Although most software handles this process very well, you need to understand the implications of creating new pixels and the different methods available. Slicing one inch into 100 equal samples, as shown in figure 1.16a, means there are 100 pieces per inch. Up-sampling is simply the process of slicing that inch into more pieces. Slicing that same inch into 200 pieces means that you have up-sampled or scaled the original by double. There are now 200 pieces per inch, as shown in figure 1.16b.

Whenever you create new pixels by scaling an image, pixels that already exist in the bitmap image are used as reference. The new pixels created are based on these existing pixels. Mathematical algorithms are used to create these new picture elements. Every piece of software uses similar algorithms, but each is unique in deciding how to achieve higher resolution. ColorStudio and Photoshop both have excellent sampling algorithms.

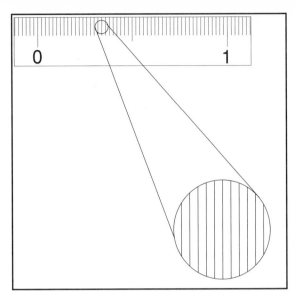

Fig. 1.16b.
One inch sliced into 200 pieces.

Replication and Interpolation

There are two specific methods of up-sampling or creating new pixels: replication and interpolation. Very often the concept of scaling or creating new picture elements is lumped under the title of interpolation. This labeling is misleading and incorrect.

Replication literally replicates or duplicates existing pixels. If you have one red pixel, replication simply creates another red pixel group equal in value to the original. Although this duplication does increase the resolution of the image, it does not appreciably affect how continuous an image appears. In fact, when you replicate images, you may see the effects of pixelization. Replication is very useful when you are working with flat solid colors or images that do not contain critical tones like flesh tones and blends. Replicating pixels also is extremely quick to process. If

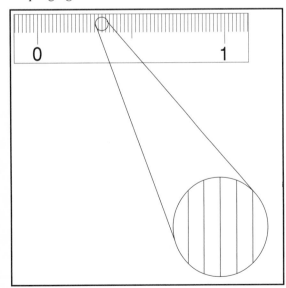

Fig. 1.16a.
One inch sliced into 100 pieces.

working with flat solid colors or images that do not contain critical tones like flesh tones and blends. Replicating pixels also is extremely quick to process. If your results do not require a high-quality, continuous tone, replication can be an extremely useful way to meet the resolution requirements of your chosen output. (See figures 1.17a and 1.17b.)

Interpolation is a more complicated method of creating new picture elements. Interpolation, rather than simply duplicating existing pixels, considers the individual pixel and also the surrounding pixels in determining values of new pixels. In a basic sense, interpolation averages existing pixels to create new pixels.

There are two types of interpolation: linear and bicubic. Linear and bicubic interpolation refer to the types of mathematical algorithms used to determine the value of the new pixels. *Linear* interpolation is faster to process, but *bicubic* is considered higher

quality. In most cases, the gain in quality is much better than the sacrifice of processing speed. (See figures 1.18a through 1.18d.) Increasing resolution by interpolating picture elements yields a more continuous tone image than replicating. Two important issues are associated with interpolation: the processing time to interpolate pixels is much longer than with replication, and excessive interpolation results in an image that appears very soft and out of focus. Later we discuss methods in image retouching that compensate for this softness, but there is no substitute for having your image at the proper resolution without any interpolation or replication. You should recognize that digital scaling is not a complete panacea for correcting images that do not have the correct resolution. Interpolating pixels should be done sparingly and with special consideration to the desired quality of image output.

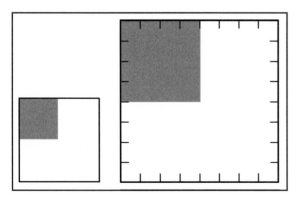

Fig. 1.17a.
2x2 pixels replicated 400 percent to 8x8 pixels.

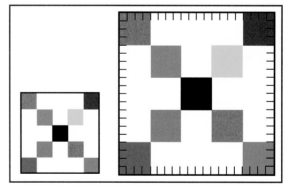

Fig. 1.17b.
5x5 pixels replicated 400 percent to 20x20 pixels.

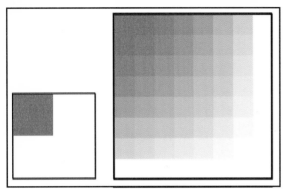

Fig. 1.18a.
Linear interpolation by 400 percent: 2x2 pixels interpolated to 8x8 pixels.

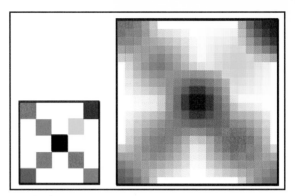

Fig. 1.18b.
Linear interpolation by 400 percent: 5x5 pixels interpolated to 20x20 pixels.

If scaling is used properly, the result can be exceptional and extremely effective. There are guidelines you might want to consider when scaling a bitmap image by either replication or interpolation. The diagrams in figure 1.19 illustrate some of the results of replication and interpolation. In general, replication is most useful if you have straight vertical or horizontal lines. And as mentioned previously, flat single-colored areas are best replicated. Diagonal lines, circles, or curves accentuate the jagged edges when replicated. These jagged edges commonly are referred to as jaggies. Interpolation with its processes of averaging is most useful when you are scaling

curves and diagonal lines because the averaging process tends to soften and smooth out the edges. Smoothing out edges too much is not always desirable and may create an out-of-focus look. When you are working with blends of color and tone, interpolation is a great benefit. Images with graduated color blends of tone and organic images like clouds are perfect examples of the type of image that can be scaled as much as you like with interpolation. With no edges to consider, you get a softening effect from interpolation that actually can add to the overall effectiveness of an image.

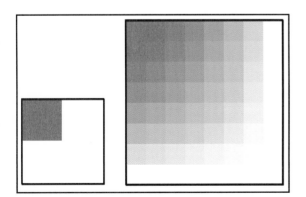

Fig. 1.18c.
Bicubic interpolation by 400 percent: 2x2 pixels interpolated to 8x8 pixels.

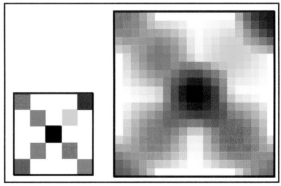

Fig. 1.18d.
Bicubic interpolation by 400 percent: 5x5 pixels interpolated to 20x20 pixels.

Fig. 1.19.
Replication produces better horizontal and vertical lines; interpolation, better curves and diagonal lines as well as organics and blends.

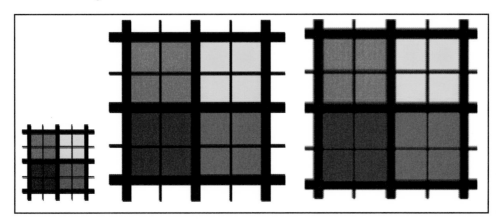

Fig. 1.19a.
Lines. Original replication interpolation.

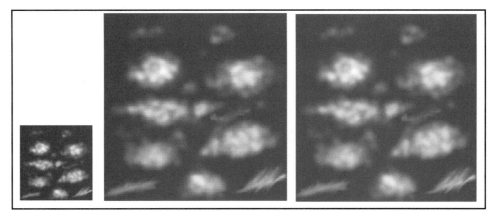

Fig. 1.19b.
Clouds. Original replication interpolation.

Fig. 1.19c.
Blends and tones. Original replication interpolation.

When replicating or interpolating, scale to a whole, round number when possible. If you need to scale something 190 percent, you can scale by 200 percent and then scale down. The reason is simple mathematics. When you give the software program easy-to-digest figures, the software quickly can create new pixels with a degree of uniformity. You find it easy to quickly calculate 200 percent of a number by doubling the number. You find it harder and slower to calculate 187 percent of that same number. Program software is no different.

Recall that digital bitmap is very uniform and scaling an image by 50, 150, 200, or 400 percent is relatively easier than scaling by more complex numbers. It is good to reiterate that these are only guidelines and not rules. Obviously, there are times when you need to scale an image a specific amount and the power of the Macintosh is here for that purpose. Only you can decide what methods to use and how appropriately they meet your needs.

File Sizes and Storage

A pixel bitmap is stored as an image file. After you have determined the resolution for your image, you will need to put the image in a digital format that can be saved for future use. Each file format has unique aspects, and Macintosh software can work with a great variety of file formats. Refer to Chapter 4, "Digital Image Files," for more about file storage.

Different Types of Pixels

As mentioned before, some digital systems do not use square pixels. The most notable are Commodore Amiga systems, IBM PCs that use Truevision, and Vista color video boards that produce broadcast NTSC and PAL video. Amiga systems use pixels with aspect ratios of 1.45:1. The pixel aspect ratio for TARGA files created from the PC is 1:0.97. When you import an image file from these systems into the square pixel environment of the Macintosh, you need to compensate for these differently proportioned pixels. These pixels are not inferior in quality to square pixels; they often are used in the video profession. The difference is corrected easily and is not a serious problem.

You first notice that the images you bring in from these systems appear out of proportion, usually squeezed horizontally. You see this most noticeably if the image contains circular objects. A person's face or a round ball appear tall and stretched in the vertical direction. Because you have substituted differently proportioned picture elements, the distortion makes perfect sense. Because you cannot change the proportions or aspect ratio of the square Macintosh pixels (nor would you want to), the only logical step is to stretch the image horizontally to counter the vertical distortion. This is achieved by up-sampling the image in only the horizontal direction until the proportions of the image appear as they did on the system on which they were created. You can modify an image visually until you achieve the look you want. Drawing perfect circles in the image before you transfer the file to the Macintosh is a good visual method of determining how much to stretch an image.

A more exact and direct method of stretching is taking the aspect ratio of the pixel you are importing and increasing the image horizontally by that amount. For example, if you imported an image from an Amiga system, you would stretch or up-sample the image by approximately 125 percent in the horizontal direction. Of course, if you prefer you also can down-sample the image in the vertical direction to meet the required image aspect ratio. In the case of the Amiga systems, you down-sample vertically 80 percent. Both methods achieve the same result in appearance, but whenever you down-sample an image, you discard information that you may want to retain. Figures 1.20a through 1.20c illustrate the need to compensate for pixels of different aspects ratios other than the 1:1 used on the Mac.

Fig. 1.20a.
Pixel aspect ratio 1:1.45.

Fig. 1.20b.
When you stretch the image horizontally 125 percent, the image appears true to its original shape.

Comparing Bitmap Images to Object Images

Any discussion about pixels and bitmap images would not be complete without a comparison of bitmap images to object images.

Objects are described by a series of points using mathematical formulas to connect them. Unlike pixels, which are discrete units, object points are not

Fig. 1.20c.
Corrected aspect ratios.

discrete. Objects are used for line drawing, and files that contain objects sometimes are referred to as linework files. A simple object such as a circle can be described as $x^2 + y^2 = z^2$. (See figures 1.21a, 1.21b and 1.21c.)

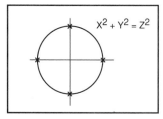

Fig. 1.21a.
The formula for a circle.

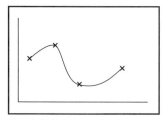

Fig. 1.21b.
A series of points linked by a line is the basis of PostScript.

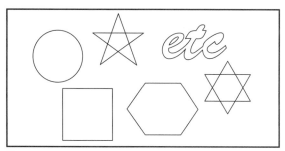

Fig. 1.21c.
A series of PostScript objects.

As objects become more complex, so do the formulas or languages that describe them. The most common object-based language is PostScript. The quality of output from objects is high, and the lines and curves are sharp, well-defined, and continuous. Objects are considered resolution independent because they do not depend on any specific amount of resolution to produce the final printed size. You easily can resize or scale them without losing quality in output. Because type size needs to be changed frequently, PostScript is popular in typography.

When objects are used to define more elaborate color (other than simple spot color), continuous color tones, or blends, there are disadvantages. (See figure 1.22.) The complexity of describing color with objects can make the size of the file containing the information large. This increases the processing time required to output. Steps or banding readily can be seen in many blends created with objects. Most retouching programs now allow the option of combining objects with a bitmap to take advantage of a bitmap's superior handling of color. In Chapter 13, we discuss how this is done.

In the next chapter you find the basic color theories regarding digital images. How color is defined and the relationship of different color spaces to one another are important in controlling and altering the appearance and perception of an image.

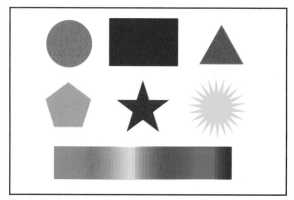

Fig. 1.22.
Flat color is easier to produce than elaborate blends, which are more complicated to produce with objects.

CHAPTER 2

Colors and Tones

Seeing Color

Colors inextricably are part of your daily life. People perceive colors in many different ways. Color is light energy. Light energy exists in the form of waves and particles. Waves exhibit different lengths or frequencies measured in nanometers, which are one thousand-millionth, (10^{-9}), of a meter. A light wave's length determines what color the light wave is perceived as. The range of light you can see with your unaided eye, known as the visual spectrum, is 400 to 700 nanometers (nm). (See figure 2.1.) This range of color is your starting point for understanding color. Light-wave lengths above 700nm are infrared energies. Lengths below 400nm are ultraviolet energies, X rays, and gamma rays.

You perceive the differences in wave energy (color) through your optical receptors: your eyes. The retinas in your eyes contain two main types of light-sensitive cells known as rods and cones. Cones perceive the hues of color or the length of a light wave, and rods perceive the value, strength, and relative brightness of a light wave.

There are three types of color-sensitive cones. Cones are receptive to the wavelengths of red, green, and blue light energy. Each type of cone is most sensitive to one band of red, green, or blue light energy but also is receptive to the wavelengths of the other two colors. Each type of cone is not receptive to one of the three colors exclusively because the cones do not necessarily contain only red, green, or blue absorbing pigments. Light reaching the cones triggers an electrical signal that is sent to the brain, processed, and interpreted as a portion of the visual spectrum. Genetically, every person exhibits slight variations of light-wave sensitivity. Physiological differences help explain why two people can look at the same object and perceive different color values. Color blindness is the result of chemical imbalances in the cones of the retina. (See figure 2.2.)

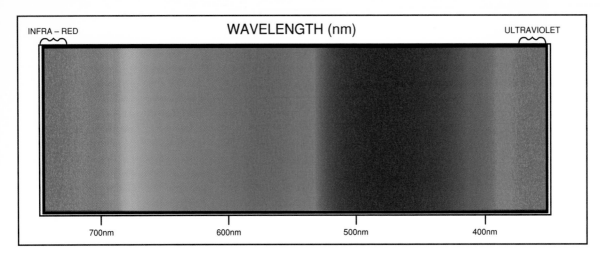

INFRA – RED

WAVELENGTH (nm)

ULTRAVIOLET

700nm   600nm   500nm   400nm

Fig. 2.1.

You can remember the visual spectrum of colors using the anagram of red, orange, yellow, green, blue, indigo, violet—better known as Roy G. Biv.

All perceived color, in a basic sense, is an interpretation of a red, green, and blue (RGB) color gamut. Gamut literally means the total range of possibilities. Color gamut, or simply gamut, is a frequently used term in color reproduction meaning a range of color. Because the cones in the retina are receptive to RGB, even the biological gamut of color is based on an RGB color space. This physiological interpretation offers the primary reason that colors on a computer monitor or television are combinations of red, green, and blue. Because your eyes perceive red, green, and blue, it makes sense that monitors have a basis in the RGB color system.

Color cannot be sliced into digestible sections easily. You need to understand that color, in nature, exists in overlapping, almost fluid, waves. Also understand that red, green, and blue contain portions of one another mixed together. The colors red, green, and blue are not sliced perfectly into three parts. There is a transition from one color to another, and opinions

vary regarding where one color begins and another ends. The general range of red, green, and blue are red areas, 580nm and greater; green areas, 490-580nm; and blue areas, less than 490nm. There are areas of transition from one color to another, such as blue-green (480-510nm), yellow-green (550-570nm), and yellow-orange (570-630nm). These transitional areas contribute to the differences of color perception from person to person.

Neutrality or neutrals represent equal values of perceived red, green, and blue. Neutrality means that no one color has more influence than another. Because the red, green, and blue are equal, they effectively cancel each other. Neutral colors also are known as grays. Gray colors are equally perceived values of RGB between white and black. White represents the maximum perceived value of RGB, and black represents the total absence of the light waves of red, green, and blue. (See figure 2.3.)

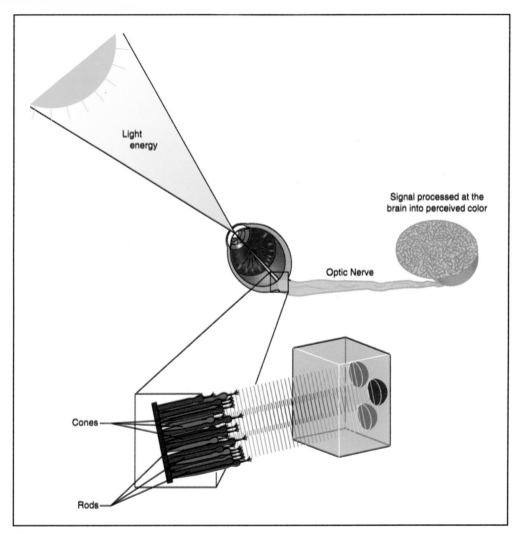

Fig. 2.2.
The rods and cones in the retina of the eye send signals to the brain perceived as color.

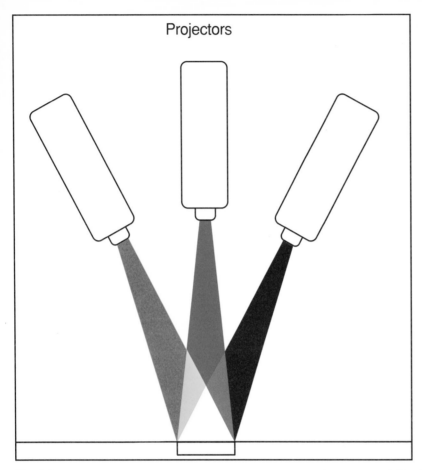

Projectors

Fig. 2.3.
The additive nature of light.

Understanding that color systems are not perfect helps your ability to deal with the inevitable variations in all color reproductions. If reproducing color were as simple as counting one, two, three, we would not need to discuss how to eliminate the variables.

Eliminating the variables or at least anticipating variable effects is what the craft of color reproduction is all about. For example, the red in a tomato typically reflects to your eyes the following portions of the visible spectrum: 50 percent of red, 30 percent of orange, 20 percent of yellow, 15 percent of yellow-green, 10 percent of green, 10 percent of blue-green, 5 percent of blue, and 5 percent of violet. Imagine how complex a color system would be if you needed to consider all these variables.

Because our eyes receive information within a red, green, and blue system, it is possible to create all visible color by using an RGB system. Remember that every created RGB system uses your eyes as the starting point. Each RGB color system exhibits limitations in trying to meet the standards your eyes have established. Because of the limited color gamut (color range) of phosphors on a monitor, or pigments in a transparency, or ink on paper, you need to consider each color reproduction process and compensate for deficiencies as much as possible. Your understanding of how color and color reproduction involve constant ebbs and flows is critical to your ability to use color effectively and grasp the craft of color reproduction. (See figure 2.4.)

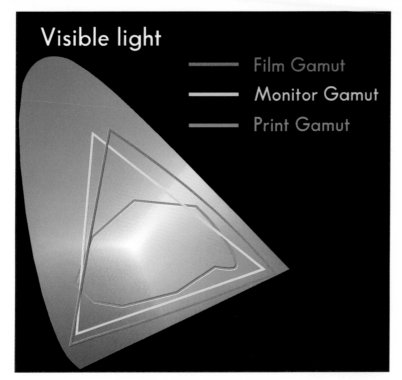

Fig. 2.4.
The color gamuts of life, monitors, transparencies, and print.

The Psychology of Color

Did you ever wonder why you feel calm in a bluish room?

Colors are associated with emotions. Although the specific reasons for this association are debatable, everyone is familiar with the related effects of color and the emotions. Colors that elicit a sense of speed or quickness, that tend to excite or give lively feelings, are considered warm or hot. Examples are yellows, oranges, and reds. Cool colors such as blue and violet produce feelings of calm or soothing cold and shade. Greens typically are considered nurturing colors. This idea is understandable because much of our lives depends on growth and green plants. Rooms in which you spend great amounts of time should have such colors as dark greens, browns, or beige.

A brightly lit room does not contribute to a romantic feeling. But soft lights give a sense of comfort and security because the effects of color are less dramatic and intense with dim lighting. Because you perceive less color in poorly lit conditions, the colors' effects are lessened. Understand that color affects your perception with more than qualitative logical percentages and values. Emotional responses to color contribute to the explanation of why judgments of color from one person to another can be different.

So far, we have discussed physiological and emotional influences on color perception. A third influence on color perception is the color reproduction method. You can have physical differences in color due to the reproduction methods and color gamut limitations of the type of output selected. The difference in the types of ink sets used from one printer to another is an example of how the physical reproduction of color can vary.

Besides the actual reproduction method used, the physical arrangement and lighting of color has dramatic effects. Dimly lit rooms and fluorescent or incandescent lights all can contribute to the way a color or colors are perceived. Viewing color in the proper or consistent lighting conditions also is important, and it is discussed in later chapters.

Because colors influence other colors, the best way to judge a color is to surround it or isolate it with a neutral color—white, gray, or black. Because there is no color to influence or to create a bias, you can assess the color accurately. Surrounding color can influence the perception of color, as figure 2.5 illustrates.

Although this example illustrates how surrounding color works, this example is not typical of a real-world situation. A better example involves how white golf balls with a red background appear pink and the same golf balls with a blue background appear bluish even though the color of the golf balls is identical in both images. (See figure 2.6.)

Awareness of the concept of surrounding color helps you understand the emotional effects of your color selection. The psychology of color is one of the most inexact sciences but also one of the most powerful. Color influences you greatly. Although mixing colors improperly won't cause a physical explosion like poorly mixed chemicals, poor color mixes can create the visual equivalent of grating fingernails on a slate blackboard. One of our favorites examples of a poor color mix, green surrounded by pink, is shown in figure 2.7.

Viewing two colors simultaneously influences their appearance. For example, if a yellow and a blue card are placed beside each other, the yellow card appears more yellow and the blue card seems bluer than if the cards are moved apart or viewed separately. (See figure 2.8.)

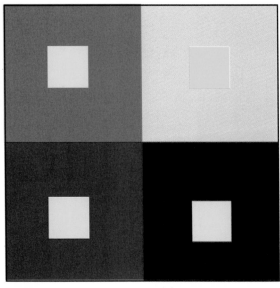

Fig. 2.5.
The yellow appears to be different in each case but is, in fact, the same value of yellow.

Fig. 2.6.
The color of the golf balls in each image is identical.

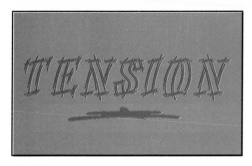

Fig. 2.7.
You can feel the tension of green type on a pink background.

Fig. 2.8.
Yellow and blue together look more intense than when separate.

Any featured color can be further intensified by using a complementary surround color. If a featured red area is surrounded by blue, the red has much more psychological impact than if it is surrounded by white or a warm color. This is because blue is a complementary color to red, so the blue surround intensifies the appearance of the red. (See figure 2.9.)

Fig. 2.9.
The red has more visual impact than the surrounding blue.

Green also is a complementary color to red. If you are so inclined, you may want to perform an experiment with color. Spend an entire day in a red-lit room, eating red food, while wearing red clothes. After being completely saturated with red, step onto a lush green lawn. The greens appear incredibly intense. This intensity, which might not last as long as the time you spent in the room, is partly a result of the green and blue cone receptors having little or no stimulation for an extended period. Although you may not work all the time in a red room, you may want to be aware of how surrounding colors in your environment can affect your perceptions of color.

The environment in which you live and work definitely affects how you perceive color. Whether you believe it or not, you also have your own established dispositions regarding color. You have colors that stimulate you in different ways, and you naturally have favorite colors. Because you have personal color preferences, you tend to skew any judgments of color reproduction toward your own preferences. Your personal bias is a strong influence on color reproduction. Although not quantifiable, your personal color biases contribute to problems with color reproduction. Awareness of a possible bias is a step in compensating for that particular bias.

Regardless of any real or imagined biases that may exist, our own visual system is very forgiving. Because your brain retains information about color, even if you see a color that is not exactly correct, your visual system compensates for any deficiencies. Unless you have something to compare colors to, isolated colors easily are enhanced by your memory bank of colors. A perfect example is television. When you watch persons on the screen, you accept that the color of their flesh is accurate. Unless the color changes radically—perhaps to a green—or a person stands near the television for comparison, you accept the color on the screen as representative. You actually add to that color from your past experiences.

Displaying a color image on a monitor is a reproduction method. As mentioned previously, RGB is the basic color system we perceive color with. It makes sense that we would try to create a system to match our way of perceiving as close as possible. Because reproduction methods cannot match exactly the RGB sensitivity of biological cones, it is impossible to reproduce color exactly to match your natural receptors.

The Additive Principle of Red, Green, and Blue

Red, green, and blue are called additive primary colors because if light from each of these colors is projected on each other, the result is all wavelengths of visible light, or white light. When you see each individual color, all you see is red, green, or blue. When the total visual spectrum from daylight is viewed on a piece of white paper, you really see an additive mixture of red light, green light, and blue light. Because white is all colors, all you need to produce any color is the ability to vary the proportions of red, green, and blue independently. Experiment with the variations of RGB color by using the Apple Color Picker in the Control Panel. You also can vary RGB with most image programs on the Macintosh. (See figure 2.10.)

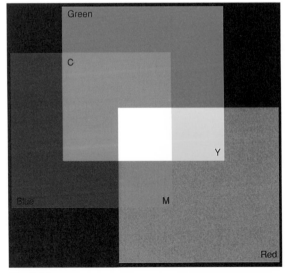

Fig. 2.10.
Red, green, and blue are additive primary colors.

The Subtractive Principle of Cyan, Magenta, and Yellow

In an additive color space, all color (white) is produced by mixing the primary colors red, green, and blue. Subtractive color produces white (all color) by the total absence of the subtractive secondary colors of cyan, magenta, and yellow (CMY). (See figure 2.11.) Blending the maximums of cyan, magenta, and yellow produces black. Although at first glance subtractive color seems very different from additive color, the two are directly inverse.

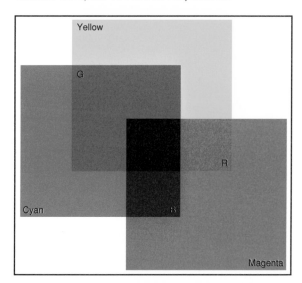

Fig. 2.11.
Cyan, magenta, and yellow are secondary colors.

Combining any two additive primary colors makes a subtractive secondary color. (See figure 2.12.) Combining any two subtractive secondary colors creates an additive primary color because the addition of red, green, and blue cancels producing white light. (See figure 2.13.) The third color excluded from these pairings is called the complementary color. (See figure 2.14.)

R = Red	R + G = Y
G = Green	
B = Blue	R + B = M
C = Cyan	
M = Magenta	G + B = C
Y = Yellow	

Fig. 2.12.
Two additive primaries make a subtractive secondary.

Y + M = R	or	(R+G) + (R+B) = R
Y + C = G	or	(R+G) + (G+B) = G
C + M = B	or	(G+B) + (R+B) = B

Fig. 2.13.
The addition of two subtractive colors results in a single additive primary.

Y	=	minus B
M	=	minus G
C	=	minus R

Fig. 2.14.
Subtractive colors subtract a primary color.

Subtractive color is used in reflective displays such as photography and printing. Combining varying intensities of cyan, magenta, and yellow dyes produces a wide range of colors. All you need to create a subtractive color reproduction is the ability to control the concentration of CMY dyes on film, transparency, or paper. This theory works well in controlled situations, but the practice of subtractive color reproduction is complicated. Impurities in the inks and dyes may absorb color when the color should be reflected to the viewer. This absorption creates darker areas in a color reproduction that are undesirable. Theory rarely lives up to its billing. Cyan, magenta, and yellow printing inks when added 100 percent should produce a pure black but instead create a muddy brown.

One compensation for the deficiencies found in inks and dyes is the creation of an artificial independent black to help achieve a real black. This is discussed in the following section.

A major disadvantage to additive color such as RGB is that reproducing color with RGB requires some kind of special device or projection to display the colors. Subtractive color does not need any special device such as a monitor to be viewed, but subtractive color does have reproduction difficulties, as mentioned, that need to be addressed.

This relationship is especially important when color separation results are being analyzed, because subtractive colors normally are used as printing ink colors. Chapter 5, "Color Spaces and Image Correction Methods," describes color correction techniques using additive and subtractive colors.

Introducing Black (K)

In photography, cyan, magenta, and yellow dyes are used without any need for other colors to achieve the desired color reproduction. In printing, an additional

color—black—is necessary to compensate for ink deficiencies. The letter K is used to avoid confusing B with the color blue. The use of four colors presents special concerns that are addressed in the chapters dealing with four-color printing. You can find a chart of the typical CMYK values for colored images in Appendix C, "CMYK Combinations."

Hue, Saturation, and Value (HSV)

Any color can be described by analyzing it in regard to three criteria: hue, saturation, and value (HSV).

Hue is the type of color being described, such as red, cyan, brown, and orange. The number of hues you can distinguish under ideal lighting conditions may be as high as 500. When looking at printing inks and monitors, the number of hues you can distinguish is determined by the properties of the pigments and phosphors that made the colors.

Saturation is the strength of a color or the amount of hue. For example, fire-engine red is more saturated than brick red. When you use printing inks, the maximum amount of saturation you can produce is printing a solid (100 percent) film of ink on the paper or substrate. Saturation also can describe the purity of a color. If saturation is at 100 percent, the color is considered pure, having no gray or neutral component (equal amounts of RGB or CMY). The lower the saturation, the closer the color is to gray. Zero or no saturation is a gray tone.

Value is the amount of relative brightness of the color, usually expressed as light or dark. Brightness is the degree of illumination in an area. As a color's value increases toward 100 percent, the color becomes whiter, and at 100 percent it becomes a white. Conversely, as a color's value drops to zero, this color becomes black. At a value of 50 percent, halfway between white and black, you have a color in balance tending toward neither black nor white. The color appears the most vibrant.

The hue, saturation, value color model is shown in figure 2.15.

You often hear HSV called HSB because value and brightness are similar. You may notice that on sunny days colors tend to be washed out, because the value of color is very high and is tending toward white. One of the best times to view color is during an overcast day when the daylight value is not as direct and bright. Take a walk after a rainstorm during the day, and notice how vibrant many colors appear. Furthermore, during the evening's starlight and moonlight, the colors in objects seem to disappear. At night the value is very low or tending toward black.

Based on the previously defined terms, a description of a bright, heavily saturated orange color is easy to understand and "see" without visually observing the color. Being able to understand a color verbally is useful when you discuss possible color adjustments with someone at a different location. Although we do not recommend that you rely exclusively on this method, HSV is another useful tool in communicating and understanding color.

Tone is a shade of color or a quality of color having some amount of value, whether colored or neutral (gray). All tones have density, the ability to stop or absorb light. All tones have a greater density than white, which has a density of zero. A tone that stops or absorbs all light is black.

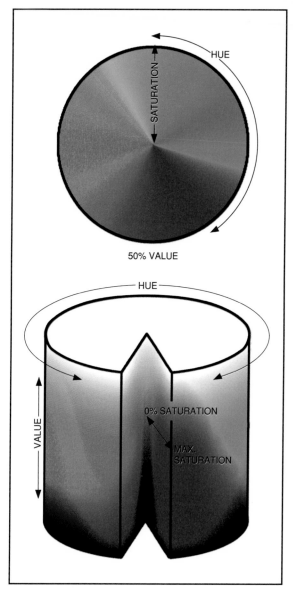

Fig. 2.15.
The HSV color model.

Figures 2.16a through 2.16e show an original image and the effects of varying amounts of saturation and value.

Fig. 2.16a.
Original image.

Fig. 2.16b.
Oversaturated image.

Fig. 2.16c.
Undersaturated image.

Fig. 2.16d.
High value.

Fig. 2.16e.
Low value.

The Properties of Monitors

A monitor is a source or projection of light energy. Reflective color is light energy whose light waves are bounced back or reflected to the viewer. The inks and dyes associated with reflective color absorb or reflect waves of color.

Most monitors that display images in computer graphics project beams of electrons onto a layer of fluorescent phosphors coating a glass screen. A cathode-ray tube (CRT), by varying voltages, emits streams of electrons with varying velocities. The velocity of the electron beams excites the phosphors, which glow to create the range of colors you perceive with your RGB cone receptors. The red, green, and blue beams are focused, bundled in triples, and converged so closely that your eye sees simply a solid color. The triple nature of color is verified in every modern color reproduction process. RGB, CYM, and HSV are called *trichromatic* color spaces because they need three components to produce a specific desired color.

The big display screens at major sports stadiums also use triples of RGB. From a distance the image has many different hues. But when you get close to the screen you see only the individual RGB bulbs.

Like every color reproduction system, monitors have deficiencies. The type and quality of the phosphors used to coat a glass screen create inherent color limitations. The physical size and weight of monitors is cumbersome. Light distortions at the outer curved edges of a screen contribute to color and viewing distortions. Prototype display screens that bundle tiny light-emitting diodes (LEDs) are in development. These LED systems, similar in concept to displays in laptop computers, are beginning to reach the same color quality achieved by CRT monitors. Although many issues still must be resolved and the implementation is far off, the physical savings of flat LED displays make them a promising innovation to color imaging.

Video Boards

Photo-realism greatly depends on the amount of color available in your color system. The Macintosh system processes color within its operating systems using 32-bit QuickDraw. With the exception of Photoshop, which was developed to work without QuickDraw, every color paint program on the Macintosh needs to have 32-bit QuickDraw in the system folder. To display color information on a monitor, you need a video board to translate the digital values into electric signals that send electrons to the screen.

When you are working with color photographs, 24-bit color displays are a necessity. You may work with 24-bit images using only an 8-bit display. But it is extremely difficult to "see" the full range of the color necessary to produce realistic images. Because 24-bit color contains more than 16 million color possibilities and 8-bit display shows only 256 of these colors, there is a huge difference in colors seen. Any cost savings you achieve by using an 8-bit video board does not justify the loss in color displayed.

A 24-bit color image requires an enormous amount of processing. Many video boards offer QuickDraw accelerators that help speed up processing time. In addition, many video boards now incorporate direct video input. Therefore, you can input video images directly into your image processing programs.

Convergence

How close the red, green, and blue electrons meet on the screen indicates the quality of display convergence. Perfect convergence or registration keeps unwanted halos of color from appearing. A halo is an unwanted border of color outlining the desired color. Lack of convergence, which exists most noticeably around edges of black type, contributes to a fuzzy, out-of-focus look. The focusing system in a CRT display literally must force the electron beams to come together, or converge. This task is difficult because the electrons have different charges and tend to repel one another. The overall sharpness and clarity of an image suffers when there is lack of proper focusing or registration. (See figure 2.17.)

Fig. 2.17.
Example of poor convergence.

The focusing system converges the electron source to a point on the screen. Not all points on the screen are an equal distance from the focusing lens. The best convergence occurs at the center of a screen. As you travel to the corners and edges, a less-focused image appears. This distortion occurs because the edges of the screen are not the same distance from the source as the center of the screen and therefore are not in perfect focus. High-precision quality displays diminish this problem by changing the methods of focusing. Creating screens with extremely curved surfaces compromises quality but alleviates the problem. All screens are curved to a certain extent. Convergence is one reason large-screened monitors are so long. The further the focusing lens is positioned from the screen, the less dramatically the screen needs to be curved.

Gamma

Every monitor has a certain associated brightness called *gamma*. Gamma is the slope or gradient of a line representing the brightness of a monitor. A gamma of 1.0 indicates a slope of 45 degrees, a gamma of 2.0 indicates a slope of 63 degrees, and so on. Having monitors set to the same gamma amount helps establish a consistency from screen to screen.

Most image programs enable you to adjust the gamma of the monitor, which typically is set from a value of 1.0 to 1.8 for computer graphics and 2.2 for video. (See figures 2.18a through 2.18f.) When the gammas are set, the white and black points stay anchored and the gamma curve bows out. You may have your own preferences, but you just need to keep a consistent gamma value set on your monitor. Changing the gamma changes the display of information but not the actual information. So although you may change your monitor gamma to make the image appear brighter, the actual digital information does not change. When you are judging images on various monitors, keeping the gamma constant ensures a level of consistence. Making your monitor too bright is not always advisable. Although the image looks vibrant on the screen, you may be creating biases that are unrealistic when you reproduce the image in print or on film. Consult with whoever produces your color reproductions, and try to match the gamma settings of their monitors.

Fig. 2.18a.
The original printed image and corresponding monitor gammas of 1.0, 1.4, 1.8, 2.0, and 2.2.

Fig. 2.18d.
Gamma of 1.8.

Fig. 2.18b.
Gamma of 1.0.

Fig. 2.18e.
Gamma of 2.0.

Fig. 2.18c.
Gamma of 1.4.

Fig. 2.18f.
Gamma of 2.2.

A popular Control Panel document is Gamma, by Knoll Software, which enables you to adjust the gamma of a monitor. Remember that changing the appearance of the image on the monitor does not change the file's image information. Therefore, changing the gamma of the monitor does not change the way the image reproduces. But changing the gamma is a useful way of adjusting the displayed image to match the output.

8-, 24-, 32-, 36-, and 48-Bit Color

As mentioned in Chapter 1, "What Are Pixels?" the bits indicate the number of color values a system can produce. For each 8 bits, 256 levels of electric signals are sent out by the electron guns. For photo-realistic images, a minimum of 24-bit color is required. Twenty-four-bit color gives 8 bits of information for each of the red, green, and blue guns. In 32-bit color, the additional 8 bits of information may exist for an alpha channel or a mask channel. The mask channel does not display color but is used to composite images. These channels need the 8 bits to store the mask information. CMYK color uses 32-bit color, 8 bits being distributed to each of the four colors.

As color systems become more sophisticated, the concept of 36- and 48-bit color is becoming more popular. These systems distribute 12 bits of information or 4,096 levels per red, green, and blue. Although this number makes the file size quite large, the increased color information is invaluable in many film-recording environments. The images are manipulated in a 36- or 48-bit environment and then converted to 24- or 32-bit by taking the best 8 bits of color, determined by the program. You occasionally may hear of high-end scanners that scan the "best eight." These scanners can scan 12 bits of color

information and then discard the 4 bits the program decides are not needed. Although this technology perhaps is far off for most retouching work, you should be aware of the eventual expansion into this area. In a 36- or 48-bit system, all the bits do not necessarily need to be used for color information. Multiple alpha and mask channels are extremely useful, especially for layering multiple images, typically done in video.

Introducing the Variations of Color Reproduction

As mentioned previously, many variations exist in color reproduction methods. Color reproduction is fluid and may differ from one process to another. Even matching color from the same reproduction method is difficult. Different printing shops offer various and different results. Even matching color from one monitor to another monitor is difficult. Color matching from one color system to another is troublesome because the only element you definitely can rely on is your own experience and knowledge. Several manufacturers have established standards for color matching. Each has its own bias and benefits. Establishing your own consistent environment ensures that your color accuracy is kept dependable and predictable.

Apple, Adobe, Letraset and Pantone, Kodak, Tektronix, and Trumatch are trying to establish standards. Because color is complex, there seldom is any real agreement, and it is unlikely there will be any. Conceivably, a handful of standards will emerge, but no single method is likely because so many different methods of color reproduction exist. When establishing a standard, you invariably omit something important from particular styles of color reproduction to simplify the process. Simplifying a process usually means limiting your choices. It is sufficient to be aware of the attempts at creating standards and, if you like, to choose one that fits your environment best.

A significant and useful standard is the color mixes from Pantone. A Pantone book consists of a full spectrum of colors, each numbered with mixtures of Pantone inks that compose them. Colors are communicated using the Pantone numbers, such as Pantone 150U. If the customer gave 150U as a spot color for a printed job, the printer would follow an ink mixing formula (using specially formulated Pantone inks) for 150U given by Pantone to make that color on the press. Sometimes the customer marks a Pantone color for a special area in a process four-color job. In the process color situation, the printer must be certain that the CMYK values will produce the equivalent color to Pantone 150U. (See figure 2.19.)

Typically, every printer determines its own process color mixes for Pantone colors and has no trouble matching the designated Pantone colors as long as the color desired is within the color gamut of the ink set being used.

There are few established standards regarding reproducing color from the Macintosh. To work effectively with color on the Mac, you must be thoroughly familiar with the basic principles and relationships of additive and subtractive color. To communicate color to others, you can and must use the terms hue, saturation, and brightness.

Regardless of the many useful and not-so-useful methods being touted today, if you know the basics, the control of color reproduction is in your hands. Many people will tell you that you do not need to know all the so-called complicated theories this book addresses and that their methods relieve you of the burden of color reproduction. Well, although some software may relieve you of some repetitive chores, often the software also relieves you of choices. When you limit your choices you limit your creativity. Your creativity then becomes directly proportional to what the program can do. Although you may decide some areas are better left to software, isn't it nice to know what the program actually is doing before you let the program make arbitrary decisions for you? A firm grasp of the basics enables you to choose intelligently what you need to work effectively.

The next chapter explores scanning and the different methods used to digitize color images.

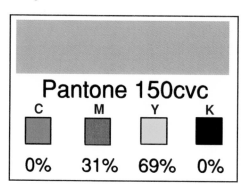

Fig. 2.19.
A Pantone CMYK color standard for 150U.

Scanning: Obtaining Color Pixels

I mages used in Macintosh image programs must be in a digital pixel format. You convert images to this format using specialized devices called scanners, digital still cameras, or video capture. Scanners sample an image one piece at a time, whereas still cameras and video receive all their data at once. The amount of image information taken in on scanners varies, but not on video and still cameras.

As previously mentioned, the amount of digital information input to the color system should be compatible with the amount of information needed at the output stage. Too little information results in a poor-quality image, and too much data wastes storage space and needlessly increases processing time.

This chapter analyzes the first part of a digital color system: the input stage. The devices that digitize images are examined and compared for quality of imaging, cost, and ease of use.

Drum Scanners

The *drum scanner*, or rotary drum scanner, is designated as such because it uses Plexiglas cylinders (called *drums*) to hold copy being scanned. (See figure 3.1.) The following section looks at this specialized tool for converting images into digital information formats.

Fig. 3.1.
A modern color drum scanner.

Characteristics of Drum Scanners

Since the 1970s, drum scanners have been producing the bulk of all color separations produced in the printing industry, which previously were made by photographic methods. With the advent of digital imaging systems in 1979, the scanner also became a digital input device that converted photographic images into bitmapped pixels.

Drum scanners are designed specifically to separate photographic images into RGB and CMYK color spaces. Input and output sizes vary from 8"x10" to 30"x40". Hardware configurations come in single all-in-one unit models and in modular form composed of two or three sections. Early models were analog machines with dozens of knobs and buttons; the latest models are digital with keyboard numeric control. Sampling speeds of 30 seconds per inch are typical,

and these scanners can produce screen rulings from 65 to 200 halftone dots per square inch. (For more on line screen rulings, see Chapter 15, "The Production of Four-Color Process Separations.") Optics and drive mechanisms meet strict manufacturing tolerances to ensure consistent sizing and image quality. Some scanners are used only as input devices, whereas others can separate and place the scans in a predetermined position on film for page assembly purposes.

Drum scanners perform two main functions: input and output. These functions can occur simultaneously, whether the output is to film or to a digital storage device. Input involves the sampling (scanning) of an original image. The analyzing section of the machine handles this task. Output to film is accomplished by imaging photographic film; the exposing section of the scanner handles this task.

Operating a scanner involves many steps that must be performed in a specific sequence. (See Chapter 16, "Digital Film Recording.") Training usually takes two to three weeks. Working in a high-speed production scanner shop requires highly experienced craftspeople to produce the highest possible quality and quantity. The knowledge of scanner operation, color theory, photography, and press conditions takes years to develop to a journeyman level.

Because a scanner makes reproductions of whatever it analyzes, items that are scanned are called originals, original copy, or just *copy*. Color copy that is transmissive (through which light can pass) is called a transparency, or *chrome*. Thirty-five-millimeter slides are examples of chromes. Any copy that is not transmissive is reflective. Reflective copy is scanned by using light reflected off the copy into the analyzing optics. Color prints commonly are called *C prints*, and drawings and paintings are called *art*. Copy that already has been separated and printed which is submitted to be scanned is called a *rescreen*.

Anything flexible enough to be wrapped around the drum scanner's input cylinder can be scanned, provided it is within the cylinder's size dimensions, is of uniform thickness, and is not more than an inch thick. Items that are not flexible need to be converted to a flexible medium such as a color print or transparency. In scanner shops, 35-millimeter slides usually are the most supplied image format.

How Drum Scanners Work

The drum scanner analyzes the copy being scanned by passing a beam of light through transmissive subjects (transparencies, slides) or reflecting off of opaque subjects (color prints, artwork). The light source must emit the complete visible spectrum of light so that all the possible colors of the original subject are transmitted to the scanner. The analyzing light source also should be of steady, stable illuminance. The most typical kinds of light sources are xenon and quartz halogen bulbs.

For transmissive subjects, the analyzing light is focused into a tiny beam of approximately .02mm. The beam passes through the Plexiglas cylinder and the transparency mounted on it. When the cylinder makes one complete rotation, the beam has sampled a vertical slice of the image. This scanned piece of image is called a *scan line*, which is a unit of information for the drum scanner. (See figure 3.2.) The amount of data in a scan line is discussed further in the section "Scanner Resolution."

Reflective subjects must have the analyzing light reflected off their surfaces. This light usually is beamed onto the copy from multiple directions using fiber optics to give an even illuminance of the reflective original.

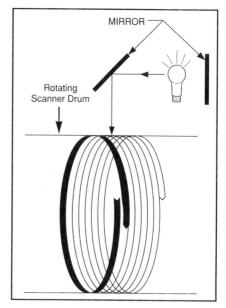

Fig. 3.2.
A scan line is made from a light spot on a rotating drum.

As the scan progresses, the cylinder continues to revolve, and the analyzing beam travels across the original subject and samples color information line by line. The beam passes through the drum and original, entering the analyzing head unit (which houses the scanner's optics) by going through a lens opposite the beam source. In the analyzing head, the color information in the light beam is split by mirrors and prisms into four beams. One beam goes through a red filter; another through a green filter; another through a blue filter; and the fourth through a red, green, or blue filter. The fourth beam is used for information pertaining to the sharpness of the image and has nothing to do with the actual color of the reproduction. Each of the first three beams represents the light from one-third of the visible spectrum because of the RGB filtering. (See figure 3.3.)

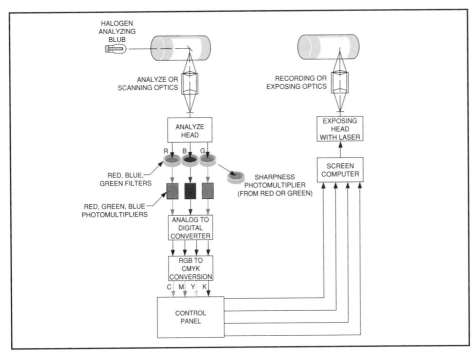

Fig. 3.3.
How color information goes through the drum scanner.

Each of the four beams now is channeled to a *photomultiplier* tube (called a PM), which is a photoelectric cell that emits electrons when stimulated by light. These PM tubes convert the light densities transmitted from the original copy into electrical signals representing color densities.

The information from the photomultiplier tubes goes into the scanner's color computer, which determines the red, green, and blue color space values of the image first. Then the computer assigns the cyan, magenta, yellow, and black values according to the printing conditions programmed into the scanner.

Next, the analog signal of the photomultipliers is converted to a digital signal by an analog to digital converter (A to D converter). Each scan line is assigned a number of picture elements determined by the dots-per-square-inch ratio of the line screen

ruling selected. Each picture element is assigned an 8-bit binary number that can represent 256 shades of gray from light to dark. Some of the latest scanner models can use a 10-bit binary number that can define 1,024 tonal steps. The number of steps represents the scanner's accuracy in reproducing the many subtle differences in the tones and colors of the original copy. More steps means that the scanner can produce an image which captures more fine detail and smoother color gradations.

The picture elements of the scan lines become pixel data when the scanner's input information is transferred to a color retouching or pagination system like the Macintosh. Pixel data of the converted image then can be stored for future use. Drum scanners are becoming a common fixture in many color Mac work environments.

CCD Scanners

The newest generation of scanners is the flatbed CCD type. First introduced to the printing industry in 1982, flatbed scanners hold originals in a flat template or glass slide for scanning. This configuration enables flatbed scanners to scan inflexible originals.

Characteristics of CCD Scanners

Besides the difference in the way flatbed and drum scanners hold original images, image data sensing is completely different also. A charge-coupled device (CCD) analyzes color information like the photo-multiplier tubes do on a drum scanner. The CCD linear array is a linear group of overlapping metallic electrodes (elements) layered over silicon crystal. Light striking the electrodes excites electrons, which react with the silicon crystal. An output amplifier picks up the electron signals and measures the light intensity from the electrode, which becomes the value of that picture element, or pixel.

CCD linear arrays can have a number of elements such as 1,024, 2,048, 4,096, or as many as 7,000. The CCD unit itself is one to two inches long, and each electrode is smaller than the diameter of a human hair.

Compared to photomultiplier tubes, the CCD linear array is more stable, but the PM tubes have a greater dynamic range when it comes to sensing light

densities. The extra dynamic range of the PM system gives the drum scanner the capability to produce higher quality images of superior tone and detail. (This information was taken from Gary G. Field's *Color Scanning and Imaging Systems*.)

The actual hardware is compact because of the CCD linear array size and because there is no need for an exposing section. The small dimension of CCD units has inspired the term *desktop* scanner because the entire unit can fit on a desktop.

Because flatbed CCD scanners are strictly input devices, all signals from them are digital. The CCD image file contains only RGB data. Conversion to CMYK values must be performed on a Macintosh using programs designed for RGB to CMYK translations.

Two areas in which drum and flatbed scanners differ the most is speed and cost. An 8"x10" final size scan from a 4"x5" original averages only two minutes on a drum scanner versus at least an hour to get film using a CCD device. The CCD method takes much longer because three steps must be taken to get to film: the scan (three passes to get RGB), translation of the CMYK files from the RGB data using software, and the imaging of the film on an imagesetter. CCD scanners may be slower than their powerful rotary drum counterparts, but at a tenth of the cost of a drum scanner, the CCD scanner is attractive to many people. Several models of CCD scanners that deliver excellent reproduction quality for the price are available for less than $20,000.

Training usually is accomplished in a day because the machines are simple to operate, but color theory and press condition knowledge still should be a part of the operator's skills.

Scanning with CCD Linear Array Scanners

A stable, even light source is necessary for illuminating the original copy held in the flatbed template. Xenon or quartz halogen bulbs normally are used for light sources.

The template holding the original copy slowly moves across the light source, and the color information from the original mirrors through a lens to the CCD linear array. Each format size has a separate lens to focus the color light data on the linear array. The number of pixels desired determines the number of samples taken.

Copy is scanned three times, one pass each for red, green, and blue information. Color data from the scans can be stored temporarily in a small one-image buffer housed in the scanner until it can be transferred to a Macintosh. The buffer on a scanner frees your Macintosh for other processing and permits you to retrieve your image at your convenience. Many other CCD scanners transfer file information to the Mac during scanning and tie up the Mac during the scanning process. (See figure 3.4.)

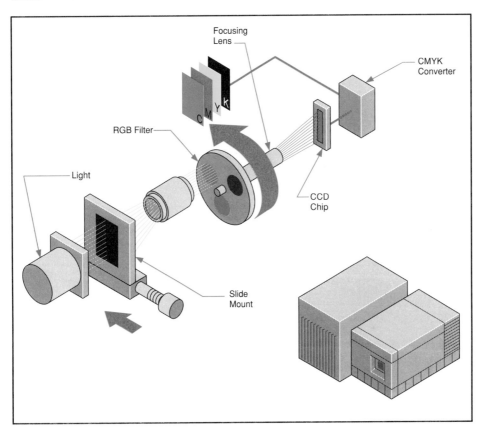

Fig. 3.4a.
Three Pass CCD Linear Scanner.

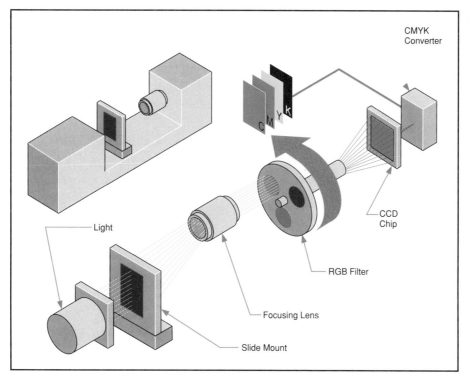

Fig. 3.4b.
Three Pass CCD Array Scanner.

CMYK Converter

CCD Chip

Light

RGB Filter

Focusing Lens

Slide Mount

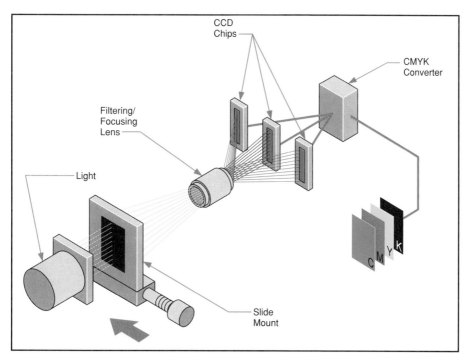

Fig. 3.4c.
Single Pass CCD Linear Scanner.

CCD Chips

CMYK Converter

Filtering/ Focusing Lens

Light

Slide Mount

Scanner Resolution

As mentioned in Chapter 1, "What Are Pixels?" device resolution pertains to the number of image elements per unit of measure. Scanners are categorized by their input resolutions, described as elements per inch (epi) or elements per millimeter (epmm), not dots per inch (dpi). Typical CCD scanner arrays can range from 2,048 to 4,096 total elements. This means that files created by CCD scanners are limited by the fixed number of elements. Image pixel resolution is adjusted by focusing the array over a small or large physical copy size with lenses. For example, a 2,048-element array focused over the width of a 4x5-inch copy produces more sampling per inch than if focused over the width of an 8x10-inch piece of copy. You should consider this difference when comparing scanners described as 300 to 600 epi. This designation means the scanner can produce input samples up to 300 to 600 samples or pixels per inch of copy. But as the copy size increases, the relative image resolution decreases because the sampling of the fixed CCD elements are spread over a greater distance. In comparison, high-end drum scanners can achieve sampling rates of up to 2,540 epi and are limited only by the precision and quality of the optics used to produce the digital scan, not by fixed elements. The more samples you scan from an image, the more image pixels you produce and the more accurate the digital reproduction is.

Digital Still Cameras and Video Captures

Electronic cameras (digital still cameras) use a CCD array to sample video analog data. The sampling is done using a single exposure, like a photographic camera. Image data is recorded on a reusable magnetic floppy disk at a fixed resolution, or a half resolution that doubles during the digitizing stage. Half resolution (field mode) doubles the number of frames you can store on one disk. Of course, image quality and sharpness is reduced because there is less information using half resolution.

The disk then is placed in a still video player, using a frame grabber. The individual frames from the camera's disk can be stored digitally as standard Mac file formats such as PICT and TIFF.

Video captures hold an individual frame of an analog video source. There are separate video capture boards and display and video capture board combinations. These video boards isolate frames of video information into standard Macintosh PICT files.

Specific Macintosh programs are designed to work with video sources. The quality of images from video sources is lower than from other scanned-image devices. You should consider the final use of the image when you are using video images for reproduction to mediums other than video. High-quality print applications require the resolution and quality of scanners; multimedia presentations work well with video source images. Additionally, video image sources increase the speed of bringing images online into the Macintosh environment. Because the photography and scanning operations are eliminated, you can enjoy significant time and cost savings.

You should select an input device for digitizing an original image based on the resolution capabilities of the output device used and the quality level desired. A complete range of input quality now is available to the Macintosh user from the high-end drum scanner to video capture sources.

The next chapter discusses storing digital images into a variety of file formats and the space needed to store digital images.

Digital Image Files

Storing Information

D igital files store the pixel information of an image. It is important to understand how you save an image. You store a two-dimensional matrix of pixels and their associated values into binary information called files. With the needlepoint example, the fabric holding the stitches is the file matrix. In photography, the photographic grains are held in a film emulsion mounted on an acetate base. Image storage on needlepoint or photographic film begins to reveal some of the implications of choosing the storage method. Just as the type of needlepoint pattern and type of film you use affect the final visual outcome, so can the type of digital files you choose affect the final production of your images.

Choosing a digital file format directly relates to what you want to do with an image. Regardless of your type of output, your storage disks have limited capacity. When you want to archive a set of images for future use, how much color quality you need and whether you want to use compression utilities are considerations that may influence your choice of a digital image file format. Macintosh image programs accept many file formats. Each program usually has an internal format as well as other formats, so images can be exchanged freely between different programs.

You have two issues to consider when dealing with digital image files: memory requirements and color information. The two issues are directly related. Among the new clichés of the '90s is the statement "I need more memory." As you begin to work more and more with color images, you will become intimately familiar with this statement. As they say, it comes with the territory.

The amount of color information stored on a file is the same as the color value of the pixels used in the image. In the case of an RGB color image, the information is stored as binary numbers indicating the value of each red, green, and blue component or channel. You can think of an image and the corresponding file as a collection of channels. In the case of a 24-bit RGB image, the red channel gives all the information regarding the red value of the pixels in an image; the blue channel, all the blue information; and the green channel, all the green information. A 32-bit CMYK file follows this pattern, except there are four channels of information, for the cyan, magenta, yellow, and black information.

Most retouching programs also contain alpha channels or mask layers. These additional channels are not used in describing the color of an image, but they may contain important information that can be used for masking, compositing of images, and transparency values in video. Chapter 8, "Merging and Collaging Images," discusses these channels further.

As mentioned in the first chapter, an image with 24-bit pixels is considered a 24-bit image, and the file containing this image is called a 24-bit file. An image with 8-bit pixels is stored as an 8-bit file, and so on. You usually can save a lower color information file into a higher one, but not the reverse. For example, you can store or save an 8-bit image in a 24-bit file format, but you cannot save a 24-bit image into an 8-bit format without losing color information. Depending on your needs, the loss of color information might be negligible.

The amount of color information, as mentioned previously, has an impact on the size of the file. Obviously, the more bits of information you have in any system, the more space you need to store that information. A pocket dictionary takes up less space than an encyclopedia, but the encyclopedia contains more detailed information in its system. Although digital systems may not seem physically large, the comparisons between files that contain detailed color information and file sizes are accurate. Trying to store a high-resolution 24-bit color image on a floppy is as cumbersome as trying to carry a heavy 24-volume set of books in your pocket.

The amount of storage space required for your images can be computed easily. You simply multiply the number of horizontal pixels by the number of vertical pixels. That calculation gives you the total number of pixels in the bitmap. You then multiply by three for 24-bit images, by two for 16-bit images, and by one for 8-bit images. The resulting number is close to the total size of a file, conveyed in bits of information. The following formulas show how easily you can compute the size of a file by entering the variable information.

pxs wide x # pxs high x 3 = file size of a 24-bit image

pxs wide x # pxs high x 2 = file size of a 16-bit image

pxs wide x # pxs high x 1 = file size of an 8-bit image

Storage mediums are measured in size by bytes, kilobytes (KB), and megabytes (MB). One byte is equal to 8 bits of information. One kilobyte is 1,000 bytes; one megabyte is 1,000 kilobytes; one gigabyte is 1,000 megabytes. These sizes are rounded off for easier negotiability, but the following equations give the specifics of how the bits and bytes work. It is fascinating how easy it is to find out how much space you may need for a given image and plan accordingly to meet those needs. Different file formats deal with ways of making the file sizes smaller, but this formula always gives you the near-maximum storage space a particular file requires.

8 bits	= 1 byte	
1,024 bytes	= 1 kilobyte	= 1,048,576 bits
1,024 kilobytes	= 1 megabyte	= 1,073,741,824 bits
1,024 megabytes	= 1 gigabyte	= 1,099,511,627,776 bits

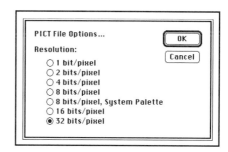

Fig. 4.1.
PICT file information.

File Types

Many different file types or formats are used on the Macintosh. We cover the most common type first and investigate the specific options of each.

PICT

PICT is Apple's internal format that is intended as a standard format for images in the Macintosh environment. Nearly every paint program on the Macintosh reads and writes to the PICT format. This compatibility enables you to exchange files freely between different Mac programs. The PICT format originally was only a one-bit-per-pixel format for MacPaint files. It later was modified to include up to 32 bits per pixel of color information. Sometimes you hear color PICT files referred to as PICT2 files. But it generally is accepted that when you refer to a PICT file you mean the PICT format that allows color information. Figure 4.1 shows the various options for saving a PICT file.

TIFF

The Tagged Image File Format (TIFF) is the most commonly used format and one of the most flexible formats. This format, introduced by Aldus Corporation, also is used extensively on the PC platform. Because you can save the file in an IBM PC format, you can pass the files from system to system with relative ease. Because TIFF is so flexible and is used by many different programs, there are some differences in how individual programs create TIFF files. This is becoming less and less the case as more programs move toward a more standard interpretation of the TIFF format. But you should be aware that images saved in older versions of TIFF may not work with some programs. Even so, most programs today accept the 5.0 version of the TIFF file format. The Crosfield StudioLink system, a high-end dedicated prepress system, now also reads in the TIFF format directly.

The Tagged Image File Format also takes advantage of LZW compression. This compression, developed by the team of Lempel, Ziv, and Welch (LZW), results in a smaller file size. It is important to recognize, however, that not all page layout and composition programs can read these LZW compressed files. If you are ever in doubt, do not use the LZW compression option a program may offer you. Always be aware of where you plan to transport your images because that affects your decisions on how to prepare your files.

EPS

The Encapsulated PostScript file format is used to export files to page layout programs. It originally was developed by Alsys to be used in object-oriented PostScript graphics. You can save an EPS or EPSF file as one composite file of RGB or CMYK images for output directly to color PostScript printers. You can save a full 32-bit separated CMYK file as a five-file EPS file. This format saves the color separation information in a separate file for each of the four process colors. The fifth file is a low-resolution PICT image, known as a PICT preview, used as a proxy for placement into a page layout program. The four other files are linked to this proxy; they always follow it wherever the PICT preview is saved. The diagram in figure 4.2 illustrates this concept.

EPS files are much larger than files in almost any other format. EPS files should be used primarily at the final stages of production to save storage space. The EPS format should be used mainly when you are dealing with full-color images. Because EPS files are very large, if you are working with gray-scale images, you should place the TIFF format into page layout programs to save valuable storage space.

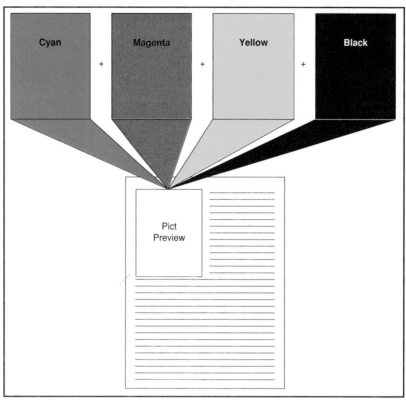

Fig. 4.2.
The five files of EPS format.

TARGA

The TARGA or TGA format was designed for and is a standard for programs using the Truevison TARGA and Vista video boards. Primarily used in the IBM PC world, this format is useful if you plan to transport your images into PC systems. Many Macintosh programs enable you to save and read an image in the TGA file format. When you do transport TGA files to other systems, you should remember that the filename must have a maximum of eight letters in the name plus a ".tga" suffix. An appropriate filename would be "maccolor.tga." When reading files from PC systems, be aware that there are several types of TARGA file formats, each of which has special considerations. You should refer to the system where the file was created to be certain.

Photoshop

This format is the default format used in Adobe's Photoshop image retouching program. Photoshop is a simple format that has no compression associated with the files. You can save the Photoshop format in a number of different color spaces from one to 32 bits. In addition to the 24 bits of color information, this format can save single or multiple 8-bit alpha channels for various image compositing purposes. Photoshop is a clean, quick saving and loading format. But if storage space is a consideration, choose a different file format. In most cases, you cannot use this format in a page layout program. If you plan to use the image in other Macintosh retouching programs, save the file in one of the previously mentioned file formats. The Photoshop format also can be read directly by the Scitex Visionary and VIP II system, a dedicated prepress system. You also may want to use the Scitex CT format mentioned later.

RIFF

The Raster Image File Format is the default format of Fractal Design's ColorStudio program. This image file format works with 32 bits of information and includes options for compressing the file to save storage space. In most cases, you would not use the RIFF format in a page layout program. RIFF is extremely useful in conjunction with ColorStudio because it can save space, but if you intend to use the image in other retouching programs, you need to save the image in one of the other formats.

Scitex CT (Continuous Tone)

This image file format is not a native Macintosh format. It is used to export 32-bit CMYK or gray-scale images into a format that the Scitex prepress workstation can read. Saving files into this format is a useful way of connecting the Macintosh to a dedicated prepress system used by many professional color separators. Many separators with Scitex systems have an extension to their workstations called Visionary, now known as VIP II. This extension links a Macintosh computer to a Scitex system and allows the free exchange of files from one system to another as long as they are saved in the Scitex CT format. If a separator does not have the VIP extension, you still have the option of exporting the Scitex CT file to a nine-track tape drive system attached to your Macintosh. The tape then can be read by tape drives linked to most Scitex systems. A nine-track tape can hold very large files, although you should be aware that saving to a nine-track tape can be time-consuming.

Crosfield CT (Continuous Tone)

Like the Scitex CT, the Crosfield CT format enables you to export files that can be read directly by the Crosfield workstations. The same options apply except that the dedicated system Crosfield uses to link the Macintosh is called StudioLink.

There are many more types of files that you can use on the Macintosh. Several other formats can be read from various programs into the Macintosh. In fact, the Macintosh, as a system, is not limited in any way by the types of files it can handle. The specific programs dictate what types of files can be imported.

The most useful programs can import a variety of file formats. Adobe's Photoshop provides the greatest number of options for importing different files into the Macintosh environment. Many of these formats are very specific and narrow in their scope and may be of limited use in a professional full-color environment. The previously mentioned formats for the time being are the most useful and effective when dealing with digital images on the Mac.

You also should note that there are a number of retouching systems that do not support any of these formats. When this is the case, you can use a RAW format within the Photoshop program. This file format is a generic format of literally *raw* pixel information. This format is extremely flexible and useful for exchanging images from obscure or dedicated image systems. When using any type of raw format, you always should know as much as possible about the pixel size of the image and the color system it is coming from or going to.

Compression

Now consider a topic that is one of the hottest issues currently discussed in the world of digital imaging: file compression. The idea of compacting or compressing a digital file to save storage space is nothing new. In fact, most of the listed file formats have some method of arranging the data to make the file as small as possible. Compression is a way of making the files as small as possible while retaining the integrity of the image and the image file. The implications are clear. If you can keep the important information that makes an image and decrease the amount of space required to hold it, you then can store more images. More important, the transportation of those images then would become faster and easier. How large an image

file can be is directly related to how fast a modem can send it to other systems. The amount of storage necessary for archiving then can be lowered substantially.

Lossy and Loss-less Compression

Compression algorithms or schemes can be classified as one of two types: *Loss-less* or *Lossy* (non-Loss-less). The two names describe exactly how the compression works. Loss-less compression schemes retain all the pixel information no matter how many times you compress and decompress the file. Lossy compression schemes lose pixel information from the original image. Consider frozen orange juice or instant coffee. Simply add water and you return to what you had before. But it isn't that simple. Just as the coffee and orange juice don't taste *exactly* as they would if they were made fresh, so a Lossy compressed file loses something when reconstituted or decompressed. In many cases, it meets our needs fine, but at times, there is no substitute for the real thing. You know the difference, but as you know, you can't always have freshly squeezed orange juice. Lossy compression is not without a sacrifice—the more you compress something, the more the quality and integrity of the image diminish. You always should be aware that compression carries with it a cost in quality that you may or may not want to pay.

Before reading about the specifics of each type of compression, consider how an image is saved as a file to understand how the image file can be compressed. This understanding gives you insight on when to use one compression scheme over another. This knowledge also will help you grasp how the map of a bitmap is defined.

Run-Length Encoding

Simple streams of pixel information are written sequentially, one right after another. From left to right, top to bottom, each pixel can be written into a raster file. Raster is a term often used in conjunction with bitmap images. Raster lines also are the linear arrays of pixels displayed on a monitor. A television displays with raster lines, scanning these lines across the screen from top to bottom. You often hear the term *raster* image intermingled with the term *bitmap* image; for the most part they are the same. Writing each pixel individually is an effective, predictable, and simple method, but the corresponding file is large. Unlike vector images, which store file information as formulas for connecting points, raster images save each picture element as an individual piece of information.

Run-length encoding (RLE) is a method of utilizing repeating patterns in a bitmap image to squeeze pixel information into smaller files. RLE works by providing a count and a value of a pixel. The count refers to the number of times the pixel's value should be repeated.

Imagine traveling from pixel to pixel on a raster line. When runs of the same color are encountered, *run-length* encoding writes to the file the number of pixels and the corresponding value. If an image has blocks of color, rather than wasting space by calling out the value of each of the pixels, RLE creates what can be considered packets of information. RLE involves no image degradation because it does not destroy information but only catalogs the pixel information differently.

The pixels of each packet have the same value and are adjacent to one another. Figure 4.3 illustrates the concept of RLE. The more similar or larger areas of solid color there is in an image, the smaller its total file size.

An image with a solid white background is a perfect example of an image that benefits greatly from RLE. An image with complex color blends and shifts benefits less from RLE. The two example images in figures 4.4a and 4.4b have the same number of total pixels, but their file sizes differ greatly because of the relative color complexity on the image with the larger file size. RLE usually deals with the separate channels of color information for each pixel. But RLE also works with multiple channels incorporating and coding the RGB values together. There are many other ingenious methods of nondestructive compression of files. Although discussing them all would be intriguing, it is sufficient to be aware of the basic concepts behind saving digital pixel information.

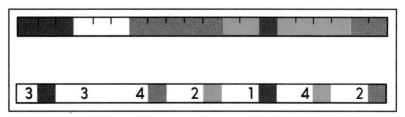

Fig. 4.3.
Run-length encoding groups similar pixels together.

Fig. 4.4a.
File size 2,219K.

Fig. 4.4b.
File size 1,643K.

Loss-less Compression

Loss-less compression, sometimes called *nondestructive compression*, does not compromise the quality of an image to attain a savings in file size. You can compress and decompress the files as many times as you want without losing any of the original pixel information. Although the space savings may not be as substantial as with some Lossy compression schemes, Loss-less ensures that you retain the quality of your original image. The two most commonly used Loss-less compression programs are Stuff-It Deluxe by Raymond Lau and Aladdin Systems, and Disk Doubler from Salient. Compressing files takes time, but each program compresses files and saves space sufficiently to warrant its use, especially when archiving images.

Lossy Compression

Lossy sometimes is called *destructive compression.* But *Lossy* sounds better because that title sounds as though it simply loses something without destroying it, when in fact, Lossy does just that. At the time of this writing, the Joint Photographic Expert Group (JEPG) has proposed a standard for compressing bitmap images using a Lossy compression scheme.

The JPEG compression scheme sections an image into 8x8 pixel areas. It uses an algorithm called the Discrete Cosine Transform (DCT) to average these 8x8 pixel blocks or cells into more manageable and predictable patterns. The predictability of these patterns makes it easier to save or encode the image file in a smaller amount of storage space.

Predictability, as you have seen, also is part of the explanation of how pixel information is saved when it is run-length encoded. JPEG compression enables you to decide by how much of a factor you want to compress an image. You specify the compression rate by a ratio number that varies between 1 and 250. The larger the number, the more compression will occur. The numbers do not relate directly to the amount of storage space saved but simply indicate an amount of compression that is occurring. A setting between 10 and 20 is recommended to keep the integrity and quality of an image used in a printing environment. For less critical output such as video, you can use a higher setting up to 100.

Remember, the more you compress an image with a Lossy scheme such as JPEG, the less quality you retain. The compression is intended to be used only at the ratio chosen during the first compression of a particular image. You can compress a file, decompress it, and then compress it at the same ratio as much as you like. But if you compress an already compressed file by using a higher ratio of compression, the quality deteriorates more rapidly than if you had chosen the higher ratio to begin with. Compressing a file that already has been compressed is not recommended. You can compress and recompress a file using different ratios, but remember your frozen OJ. If you were to continually hydrate and rehydrate the mix, back and forth, you eventually would end up with pale-colored water with no flavor or texture.

There is a cost of quality and speed when you compress something with a Lossy scheme. You should use Lossy compression schemes only after completing all necessary retouching of the image. Speed also is a consideration. Software implementation of JPEG compression and decompression can take an extreme amount of time. Specific, dedicated hardware chips added to the circuit boards of your Macintosh can compress images much faster than software alone. If you plan to use compression frequently, you may want to invest in such a chip, because a 40-megabyte image file can take up to an hour to compress with software alone. The chips take only seconds to minutes to implement the compression and decompression. These chips are licensed and marketed by C-Cube, EFI, and Micron Technologies.

Lossy types of compression can be a useful way of optimizing your available storage space, but remember: if you don't *need* compression don't use it. This is especially true for finely detailed, high-quality print images. You will find that storage mediums are making tremendous advances in their capacities to save larger amounts of digital information. The Lossy compression routines, for the most part, are geared toward sending digital information over phone lines. These little packages can be sent quickly and efficiently, then can be expanded at the destination point. Video images, for which the quality level is not as critical as with print, is a medium that takes best advantage of the file saving that Lossy compression affords. Even so, regardless of the medium you choose for output, it is important to be aware of the benefits and corresponding cost in regard to Lossy compression and to make your choices accordingly.

The images in figures 4.5a through 4.5d show examples of files that have used the JPEG Lossy compression scheme.

The next section discusses the concepts of digital image manipulation.

Fig. 4.5a.
No compression.

Fig. 4.5b.
Lossy compression good.

Fig. 4.5c.
Lossy compression bad.

Fig. 4.5d.
Lossy compression ugly.

Color

Introduction to Corrections

The majority of all image manipulations are color adjustments or color corrections. Color correction is usually the first and, oftentimes, the only *image processing* performed on an image. Image processing is a generic term used to refer to any type of procedure used on an image or images. Color corrections are performed for two reasons: first, to prepare the color information for reproduction, and second, to create visual effects not present in the original image.

In many color reproduction processes, color adjustments are necessary to ensure the best possible reproduction of color. This is because the original copy has been converted to a digital format (pixels) and then reconverted to an output format such as print separation films or photographic transparencies. The conversion processes take their toll on the accuracy of the color reproduced, so fine-tuning of color may be needed to ensure the best possible reproduction. For example, all digital files for output to a film recorder need to have a color correction made to the file to ensure proper reproduction of the tonal range of the original. (The specific corrections necessary are discussed in Chapter 17, "Video Output.") For many color-separated files destined for offset printing, color corrections are necessary based on the type of printer or type of inks or dyes used during the printing process.

Many manufacturers are presenting various color matching standards. Whatever form these matching systems take, at some stage they all involve color correction or adjustment to meet the needs of the output device being used.

The second most common use for color correction is adjusting the color in an image to create a desired visual effect. These visual effects vary from subtle to extreme, from helping an image look more real to making the image look more unreal. Common color corrections help make an image appear better lit or create an effect of new lighting. A typical color adjustment is called equalizing. An image is equalized when the darkest and lightest areas of the image are balanced or equaled to create an overall better-looking image.

Other visual corrections include removing color biases or *color casts* in an image. A color cast is an unnatural or unwanted bias of one color. A greenish face is an obvious color cast of green. Color corrections compensate for this unnatural bias by eliminating a portion of the color that causes the cast. (See figure 5.1.) In the case of a green face, removing green should bring the image closer to the preferred color.

Completely changing an original color to a new color is another visual way of color-correcting an image. For example, you may want to change the color of a sweater from green to blue or give a person with brown eyes blue eyes. (These are specific color corrections and they normally do not involve the entire image.) With all retouching, the best color corrections are the ones you do not notice. But color correction also is used to create extreme visual effects. Color corrections such as posterizing, solarizing, and arbitrary mapping represent only a few. These color adjustments rarely contribute to the realism of an image but rather offer unique visual effects that, if used appropriately, produce stunning results. (See figure 5.2f.)

Color corrections in most image retouching programs usually are accessed using two methods: sliders and curves. *Sliders* are a quick and easy way to access color corrections, but curves are a more comprehensive and flexible method. A program that links both offers the greatest amount of flexibility.

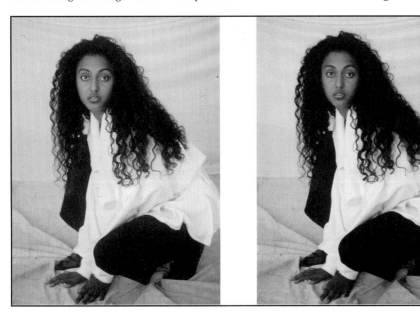

Fig. 5.1.
Removing green removes a green cast.

Fig. 5.2a.
Common types of color corrections. Original scan.

Fig. 5.2b.
Contrast color correction.

Fig. 5.2c.
Equalize color correction.

Fig. 5.2d.
Posterize color correction.

Fig. 5.2e.
Saturate color correction.

Fig. 5.2f.
Solarize color correction.

Color Curves

What Is a Color Curve?

A *color curve* is a visual linear description of the difference between an original input color value and any color changes or corrected output values you perform on your color systems. All colors in an image are described by a color curve. Any color adjustment you make in an image is represented or controlled by a color curve. Curves are a link to understanding color and tone corrections. Curves are precise and fluid and are an extremely flexible way of correcting color.

Figure 5.3 shows an x-axis and a y-axis with a line (curve) with a slope of one. The slope is the ratio between the value of x- and y-coordinates on the curve. A slope of one means the curve is at a 45-degree angle. The slope also is called the gamma, and the specific slope of any point along the curve is called the point-gamma. Gamma most often refers to contrast adjustments in mostly the middle part of the curve. The endpoints of pure white and black are fixed. You

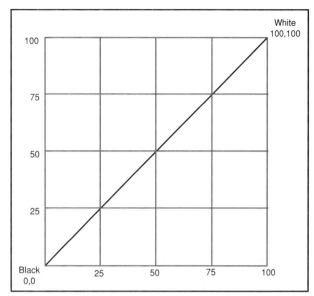

Fig 5.3.
A color correction curve.

read about gamma in Chapter 3, "Scanning: Object Color Pixels," as a description of the brightness of a monitor. The gamma of a monitor also is represented visually by a curve. (See figure 5.4.)

The curve indicates the colors of an image from white to black. One endpoint of the curve is pure white, and the opposite endpoint is pure black. The base visual effect of a curve is a straight line at an angle of 45

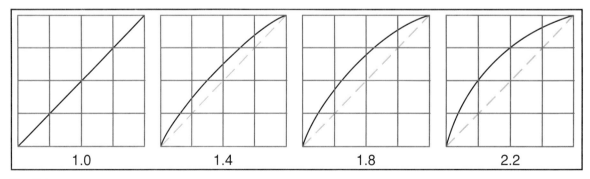

Fig. 5.4.
Examples of monitor gammas 1.0, 1.4, 1.8, 2.2.

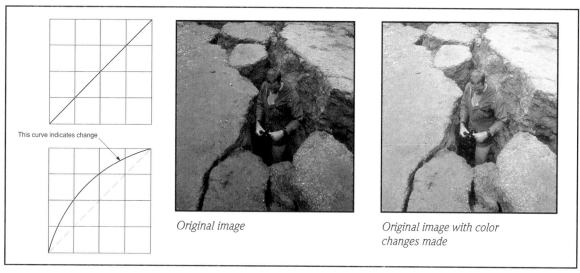

This curve indicates change

Original image

Original image with color changes made

Fig. 5.5.
The change in the curve corresponds to a color change in the image.

degrees, or a slope of one, and is unity or equilibrium. More precisely, if a point on the curve has the same x and y values, whatever value goes in also goes out. The curve (line) is a reference indicator for change. If the base curve is altered from its linear 45 degrees, the corresponding values of the image undergo a change. The curve shows this change by the distance of the new curve from the original 45-degree line. (See figure 5.5.)

How Does a Curve Work with an Image?

Because you know that all color is represented by the 45-degree curve, altering the curve adjusts color in an image. Modifying the basic 45-degree curve involves changing from the standard or original image. Curves represent changes in color.

The x-axis represents the input or original color. The y-axis represents the output or corrected color. When the curve is at a 45-degree angle, the x and y values are equal and so are the input and output values. The image indicates a steady state in which no changes are indicated. (See figure 5.6.)

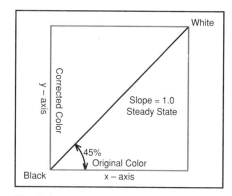

Fig. 5.6.
The basic parts of a curve.

Color images divide their color tone information into four parts, known as quartertones. (See figure 5.7.) The first quartertone is called the highlights. Highlights are the whitest or brightest parts of an image. The highlights range from the endpoint of pure white to the first 25 percent of color value. The second and third quartertones make up the midtones. The midtones of an image are typically areas of color between dark and light areas. The fourth quartertone is called the shadows. The shadows range from 75 percent value of color to pure black. These terms often are used in color correction; you should become familiar with the idea of quartertones to describe a color image. If a client asks you to lighten the shadows, your client wants the fourth quartertone adjusted.

For RGB color corrections, the endpoint where the x-axis and y-axis intersect indicates the darkest values in the image. The endpoint where the x-axis and y-axis are at their maximum value is the lightest part of the image. The dark areas and the light areas are better known as the shadows and highlights of an image and their endpoints as black and white.

As the curve is adjusted to the left, the image becomes brighter and whiter. The new RGB values are

indicated by the coordinates of the curve. The x-axis indicates the original value and the y-axis the new or corrected value. In figure 5.8a, the 50 percent value on the x-axis, when traced to the correction curve, corresponds to 80 percent. This is a change of 30 percent. As you know from Chapter 2, "Color and Tone," 100 percent RGB is white. Changing a 50 percent value of RGB to 80 percent brings that value closer to white, creating a lightening or brightening effect. Conversely, as the curve bows to the right, the image becomes darker or blacker. The same 50 percent value now comes closer to black because the y-axis value is now 20 percent. (See figure 5.8b.)

You may need time to grasp this idea fully, but the concept of curves is an important one and well worth the time needed to understand. By looking at a color image and its basic curve, compared to a modified image with its new curve, you begin to understand how curve shape describes color correction effects. You soon will discover the hidden power a curve can provide. Recognizing the shapes of curves also means understanding the corresponding color change. Certain curve shapes describe certain visual effects and color corrections. You have more power and control over an image by relating a visual color correction to a curve shape. A color correction of the image is depicted by the curve's shape. The power of curves enables you to be as broad or as specific as you need for any color correction or modification.

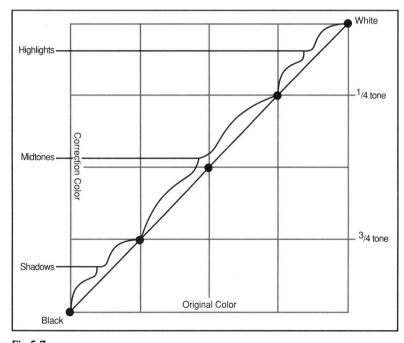

Fig 5.7.
Curves are divided into quartertones.

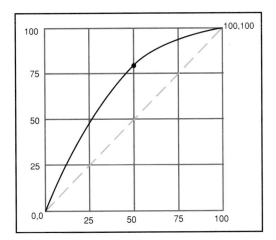

Fig. 5.8a.
Brighten color correction.

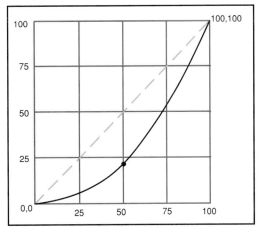

Fig. 5.8b.
Darken color correction.

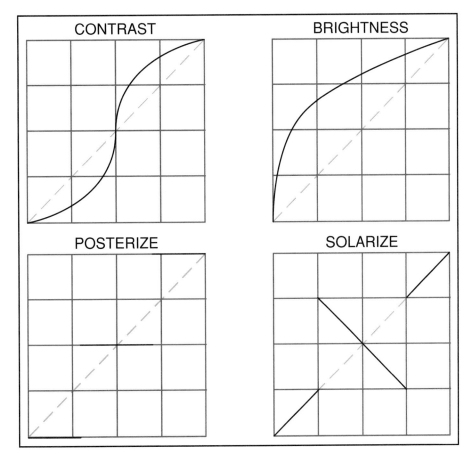

You can make color adjustments not only to the overall color in an image but to the specific red, green, and blue channels of the image. This allows for exact corrections and color adjustments. In Chapter 2, "Color and Tone," we specifically discuss the basics regarding adjustment of the RGB values. For now, see figure 5.9 for examples of color-correcting an RGB image using a curve.

Fig. 5.9.
Common RGB color correction curves.

CMYK Corrections

Color curves are used constantly in professional settings, especially with CMYK separations. (See figure 5.10.) It is important to understand that CMYK curves are a mirror of RGB color curves. Unlike RGB, the intersection of the x-axis and y-axis indicates the whitest values or highlights of an image, and the maximum values indicate the darkest areas or shadows. Using the same examples from the RGB

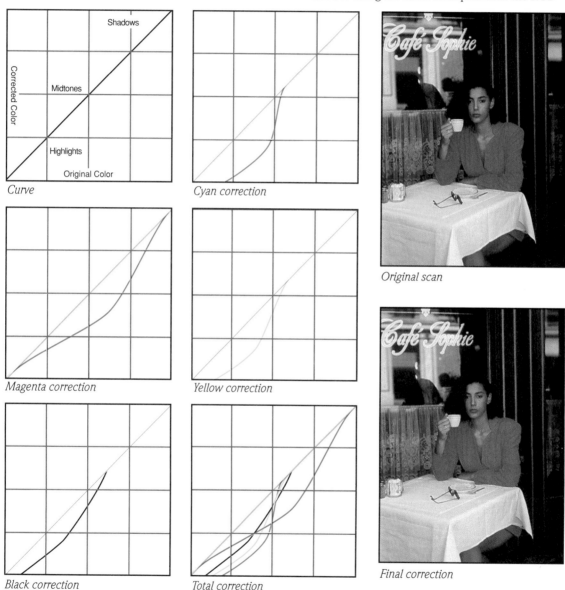

Curve

Cyan correction

Magenta correction

Yellow correction

Black correction

Total correction

Original scan

Final correction

Fig. 5.10.
CMYK color corrections.

curves, the CMYK curves are opposite in shape. Note that the image's color values change in a similar way but the curves are flipped. Also, the values used on a CMYK curve are solely percentages, whereas RGB curves use either levels from 0 to 255 or percentages. The percentages used by the CMYK curve correspond to halftone dots used for print output. This concept is discussed in Chapter 14, "The Basics of Four-Color Process Separations."

Sliders

Sliders also are used to make color adjustments. Sliders are represented differently than curves, but the result is the same. The graphic representations of a slider give quick access to a specific color adjustment. If you first understand color corrections with curves, using sliders is easy. If you learn only to use sliders, grasping color curve correction methods is more difficult. It is important to see how useful *both* sliders and curves are. Figures 5.11a through 5.11c show examples of popular slider color correction methods and their corresponding curve shapes. Knowing how to use both and using programs that link curves and sliders increase your control over an image color and give you more options to pursue.

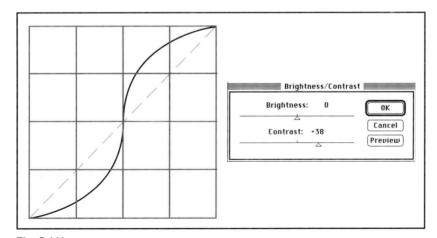

Fig. 5.11a.
Color levels slider and corresponding curve.

Fig. 5.11b.
Color brightness-contrast slider and corresponding curve.

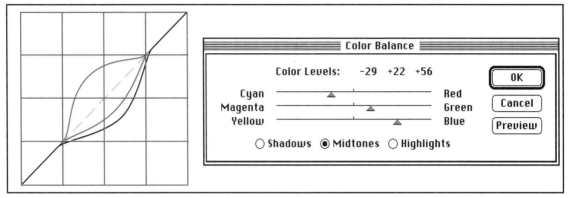

Fig. 5.11c.
Color balance slider and corresponding curve.

Many slider color corrections are a starting point from which more specific color correction can be achieved using a color curve. Obviously, you use the slider only if the slider control achieves your desired result. But when a slider control is linked to a color curve, you have more control than using a slider or curve individually.

Linking Sliders and Curves

There are no important color corrections that you cannot perform with a curve. The strength of the color curve in a program is critical to the control you have over making color corrections. Sliders are a great and easy way to perform a color correction, but linking a slider to the visual description of a curve is even more useful. Two perfect examples are contrast and posterize. The contrast curve is an S-shaped curve. By understanding how contrast works with a curve, you can use the slider with the understanding of what color corrections actually are happening to the image. After using a slider to achieve a certain

contrast, you can use the corresponding curve to fine-tune the correction to meet specific color adjustments.

Another good example is posterize. If you were simply to rely on a standard posterize effect, you would be able only to create very basic posterize effects. But by knowing that posterize is a flat curve with steps, you can create posterize effects in many different ways. (See figures 5.12a, 5.12b and 5.12c.)

Fig. 5.12a.
Original scan.

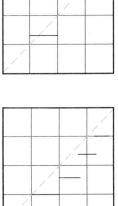

Fig. 5.12b.
A standard posterize.

Fig. 5.12c.
A custom curve posterize.

Basic Color Correction Guidelines

Regardless of whether you use sliders or curves or both, when performing a color correction you should be aware that more is less. The more color adjustment that is made to the original image, the less the image retains the original color values. In most cases, this change is fine, because you are performing the color correction for a reason. But you always should limit your color correction as much as possible. If you can get a scan that is exactly what you need, no color correction may be necessary. No correction means you can spend more time on other issues regarding the image. Also, in general, when large color corrections are made, maintaining detail in the image can be difficult. Often, detailed parts of an image are sacrificed to create the proper color. This loss may not be a problem, but no image processing is without sacrifice. If color correction is performed properly, the benefits far outweigh the sacrifices. But this cannot be stated enough: garbage in equals garbage out. Start with a high-quality image and you have more options to make the image higher quality. Start with a low-quality image and your options are few to make it even slightly better.

Preparing Images for Color Corrections

There is no substitute for a quality original. Do not become so reliant on your software program that you routinely accept low-quality originals. Good source material has more options and flexibility than originals that contain color casts, scratches, and exposure problems. Although it is true that many color corrections can be accomplished easily, if you tell a client that a major color adjustment is not a problem, the client is more inclined to stretch the boundaries of what is considered good source material. Proper color correction takes time, and that time should be charged to your client. But charging for any color correction becomes more difficult if you do not first establish with your clients the expected quality of the images they should provide. If you do not charge for the time, eventually you pay for that time. Unless you run a nonprofit business, this situation may eventually cut into your profit, and it always cuts into your operating budget.

For most color corrections, you can make a photograph darker more easily than you can make it lighter. So if you must choose between images that have been poorly exposed, you usually should choose the lighter one, because color-correcting that image to a normal appearance will be easier. (See figure 5.13.) The difficulty with dark images is that most underexposed images have a greater loss of detail. You can retrieve very fine detail from an overexposed image with proper color adjustments.

Fig. 5.13.
An overexposed image often is easier to correct.

Fig. 5.13a.
Overexposed image.

Fig. 5.13b.
Corrected version.

You cannot create detail with color corrections. If an image is missing some detail, you cannot create that detail unless you are willing to painstakingly draw it in. A favorite request is to bring out the face and head of someone in dark shadows. Although color correction may help the image, you cannot correct something that is not there.

Set Pure White and Set Pure Black

This color correction is available in Photoshop and ColorStudio. When set pure white and black are used, the endpoints of black and white are linearly adjusted. The density of the endpoints are corrected to white and black, neutralizing any casts. To use this color correction, you first need to choose an area that is supposed to be pure white but currently is not. If you choose a color that is 4 percent red, 6 percent green, and 10 percent blue and then use the "set to white" option, that color and any color of a lesser value automatically becomes set to pure white (RGB values become 0,0,0 percent). Conversely, when you choose a color that should be pure black, using the "set to black" option sets that color and any greater value to black (RGB values 100,100,100 percent). The color curve in figure 5.14 shows perfectly how this correction occurs for set white and black.

This correction works well if you have areas you know are supposed to be pure white or pure black. It is important to realize that not all images contain areas of pure white or pure black. Chapters 14 and 15, on color separation, go into greater detail about this process. It would be more useful for Macintosh image programs to have a "set to a specific value" option. So rather than setting to pure white, you

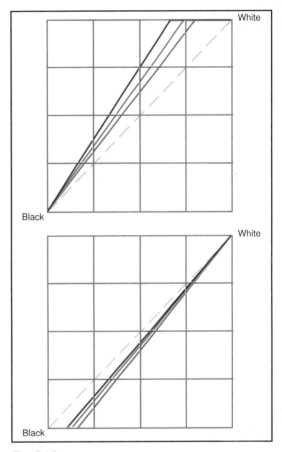

Fig. 5.14.
Set to white, black, and both.

could set a color to a specific value. Although this may not seem like a major concern, when you start to work with images that do not and should not contain pure white or black, you will find you need this option. Figure 5.15 shows an example of an image with neither pure white nor black but which, nonetheless, could benefit from a specific "set to" RGB value color correction. Figure 5.16 shows an example of a proposed RGB "set to a value."

Fig. 5.15.
The result of a "set to pure white" on an image with no white.

Fig. 5.15a.
Original image.

Fig. 5.15b.
"Set to pure white" done on image.

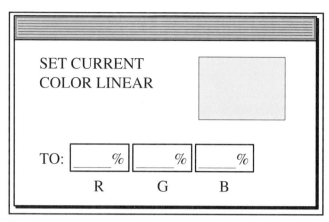

Fig. 5.16.
A proposed RGB "set to a value."

The Color Triangle

Few people know how to think in RGB or CMY. Therefore, it is helpful to use a simple diagram to assist in any color correction using either RGB or CMY color spaces. The diagram in figure 5.17 is a simple one that is easily drawn on notebooks, scratch paper, and tabletops. This diagram is a reminder of the relationships of RGB to CMY.

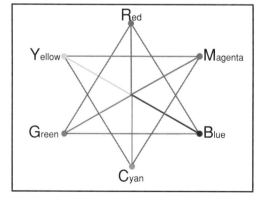

Fig. 5.17.
The color triangle of RGB and CMY.

Press operators, print buyers, and retouchers all are familiar with this triangle. The corners of one triangle are RGB and the corners of an inverted triangle are CMY. Although most programs enable you to correct only with RGB, it is useful to have the option to correct in the pure CMY as well. If you are going to make color corrections, you need to understand the relationship between RGB and CMY (see figure 5.18 and Chapter 2). An analogy to this limitation is a driver who knows only how to make right turns. The driver eventually gets to the destination, but adding a left turn to the repertoire enables you to arrive by the fastest, most direct route.

The triangle works in this way: the two primary colors that make up a side create the color between them. For example, blue, which is between cyan and magenta, is created by those two colors. The color that does not contribute to creating blue is yellow, which is directly opposite and which is called the complementary color. So if you want an image to be more blue, you can do two things: add magenta and cyan or remove yellow. In general, it is a good idea to

remove color to see whether that meets your needs before you add color. And you should perform one correction at a time rather than multiple corrections. This method avoids confusion while helping you to better understand color adjustment. Make an adjustment and decide from that point what is necessary; then move on to other adjustments if you feel that more are needed. (See figure 5.19.)

The remainder of the triangle works the same way. If you would like to decrease the amount of yellow in an image, you simply can decrease the yellow. You can achieve the same correction by decreasing the red and green (which make up yellow), or you can add blue, which is the complementary color to yellow. Even though the triangle does not take into consideration the additional black printer (used in CMYK), this correction method is always a useful guide. Many apprentice press operators and journeyman operators keep this simple reminder close at hand because the triangle of color correction is useful to their work.

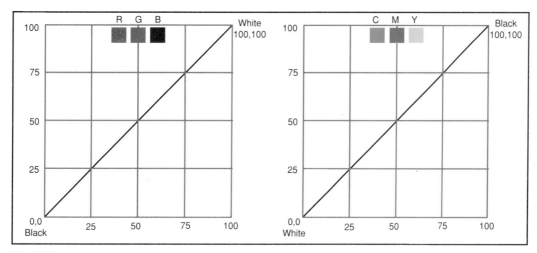

Fig. 5.18.
A comparison of RGB and CMY curves.

Fig. 5.19.
A progression of color corrections.

Fig. 5.19a.
Original scan.

Fig. 5.19b.
Red correction.

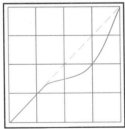

Fig. 5.19d.
Green correction.

Fig. 5.19c.
Blue (final) correction.

HSV Color Corrections

There are methods for correcting in a hue, saturation, value color space, but HSV color corrections are useful mostly for creative visual purposes because no reproduction methods use HSV. The examples in figure 5.20 show some effects of using HSV color space. Solid familiarity with RGB and CMY provide a precision that matches the requirements of your eventual output.

Fig. 5.20.
Examples of HSV corrections.

Fig. 5.20a. *Original.*

Fig. 5.20b.

Fig. 5.20c.

Fig. 5.20d.

Color tinting is a color correction that involves adding a color bias into an image. Although in most reproduction cases you want to remove an unnatural cast, tinting can provide a needed cast of color to create a more real effect or to create a mood or design effect. HSV color correction methods are a direct way of color tinting an image.

Special Areas

Color-correcting an area of an image is done by isolating that part of the image and applying any desired correction based on the methods mentioned previously. This often is called a localized correction. (See figure 5.21.) After an isolated area is color corrected, artifacts may remain which indicate that an image correction was made. The artifacts are usually sharp jumps from one color value or tone to another tone. Ragged pixelized edges are a common result of color-correcting a specific area. Too much adjustment and little consideration about how the correction matches the entire image gives you an unnatural look. Always consider how the entire image will look if you correct only one area. If the correction is needed, any ragged pixels can be smoothed and blended with the rest of the image to achieve a better overall look. The next chapter discusses tools for smoothing.

Fig. 5.21.
An example of a localized color correction.

Color Palettes

In every program, you choose colors by picking from a color palette. Most palettes have a mixing area in which to mix colors. In many programs, this palette enables you to paste images or parts of images directly into the palette. You can save and retrieve multiple versions of different palettes. Saving your palettes means you can access a myriad of color combinations without having to re-create them. (See figure 5.22.)

The color palettes also are used to indicate the specific values of color. The palette uses color values of 0 to 255 or percentages of 0 to 100. (See figure 5.23.) When working with CMYK values, you use only percentages because they directly relate to the halftone dot percentages you receive during output. This concept is discussed in Chapter 14.

The palette indicator is always an excellent reference point to check how you have changed the value of color in a specific area. The palette indicators are a good second check to make sure you have done what you intended during the color correction. You always should double- and triple-check and never should assume that what you see onscreen is what you want, especially if you desire specific color values. (See figure 5.24.)

Fig. 5.22.
Samples of different mixing palettes.

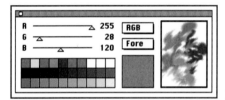

Fig. 5.22a.

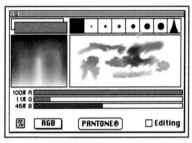

Fig. 5.22b.

Fig. 5.22c.

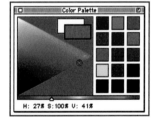

Fig. 5.22d.

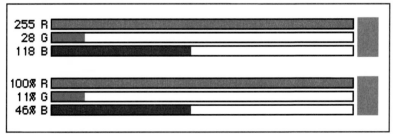

Fig. 5.23.
Levels and percentages can be used to choose color.

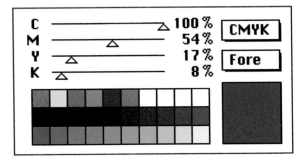

Fig. 5.24.

A palette shows the value change after a color correction.

Conclusion

Most digital imaging programs available today do not give the power that a traditional film separator had before digital technology. Surprisingly, as far as the technology has come, it still does not offer controls that many professionals require and have used for decades. Programmers are advised to understand that the process of image retouching does not stop with a software program. Further detailed research into the end uses beyond digital retouching is necessary. As people learn more about color and digital imaging, they will require more precise controls. It is encouraging that many software programs now are moving in this direction.

The next chapter discusses the basic tools available on most Macintosh painting programs and the tools' uses.

6

Basic Tools and Functions

Introduction to Tools

tool as used in digital retouching and painting is a device within a program that performs a specific function on an image. Blur tools blur an image; paint tools paint on an image. A tool may have various options and may perform many tasks, but in general, tools have specific functions. In image programs on the Macintosh, each tool has a unique icon. (See figure 6.1.) Typically, the tools are placed in a toolbox similar to your toolbox containing wrenches and screwdrivers, but more organized (if your toolbox at home is anything like ours). Each tool usually has several variations from its basic function that make the tool more adaptable and customized. We will not discuss individual tools in every program; that would take an enormous amount of time. But many common tools are available in nearly every program. It is important to recognize the similarity each tool has from program to program, especially because you may need to work with a variety of programs to perform certain tasks. Regardless of how the programs implement their specific tools, the tools have a universal commonality of purpose.

In this chapter you will find basic guidelines on some of the more effective ways of using particular tools that will lead to your own experimentation. Keep in mind that you are the user of the tools, not the other way around. By no means are the techniques described here the only ones that are effective. Not only are you encouraged to experiment, but you will find that experimentation is necessary to become accustomed to the tools you are using. The methods discussed are simply ones that work for many retouching projects. You will discover many variations of these methods that are effective for your purposes. Such is our intention.

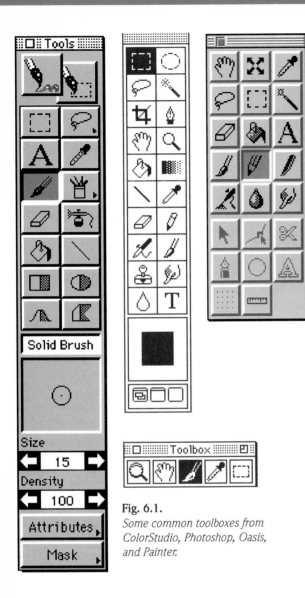

Fig. 6.1.
Some common toolboxes from ColorStudio, Photoshop, Oasis, and Painter.

The tools are broken into three categories: paint or draw tools, selection tools, and viewing tools. (See figure 6.2.) One tip you will find useful is that when navigating different programs, you must access many tools and additional options differently. The following six suggestions may help in finding the tool options:

- Double-clicking always has been the perfect Mac standard for bringing up many different options, most of them good.

- You're looking for options; the option key may give them to you, right?

- The command key is a favorite for toggling choices on tools.

- The control key is a seldom-used but fast-growing toggling choice for many programmers.

- Combining any of the previous keys with the Shift key as well as with one another is always a fun and fruitful exercise.

- The sixth and most boring suggestion is to actually read the manual. Hey, why not? It's there for a reason, and you may find some very interesting information.

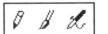 

Fig. 6.2.
Paint tools, selection tools, viewing tools.

Figure 6.3 shows some of the options different tools offer.

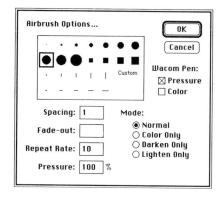

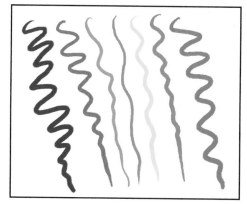

environment, you are reassigning the color values of the existing pixels, even though you may feel as though you are placing new pixels on the page. Michelangelo once said that his sculptures existed in the blocks of stone before he began working. All he needed to do was take away the bits of stone that didn't belong. In a blank digital image file, your images already exist; you simply must turn on or off pixels to reveal those images. (See figure 6.4.)

Fig. 6.4.
The effects of paint tools.

Fig. 6.3.
Tool options.

Paint Tools

Tools you use to create or alter color values of pixels into lines, curves, and shapes are considered paint tools. When you start with a white blank page from an image program, you may think there are no pixels, but in fact all the pixels are present. The pixels are simply white. When you draw in a digital

The Color Palette

Dipping your brush into a pan of digital paint is an accurate way of describing how you choose colors for a drawing tool from a color palette. The color palette on most programs enables you to choose colors in two ways: by using sliders to adjust the values of red, green, and blue (RGB), or by picking color from an area that has a range of color premixed for you. Most programs also enable you to mix your own color like with a real painter's palette. This flexibility in a program gives you a freer sense of determining the colors you want to use in your image.

Paint tools simulate the action of real painting brushes without the smell and mess. Imagine 16.7 million tubes of colored paint and a cat who likes to wander. Paw prints would be an understatement. Any discussion regarding draw tools and how draw tools make marks must start with an understanding of the concepts of alias and anti-alias drawing.

Alias and Anti-Alias Drawing

The biggest drawback in bitmap images results from how a bitmap actually works with individual pixels to create continuous lines and curves. A vector or postscript object can be drawn as continuous smooth lines and curves, whereas the bitmap can only approximate curves such as circles with pixels on a grid. The result of the bitmap commonly is called stairstepping or jaggies, as mentioned in Chapter 1, "What Are Pixels?" Referring to everyday experiences is always an excellent reference point from which you can begin to understand the implications of anti-aliasing.

When you see people and objects, you perceive a physical depth to them. The reason you see depth and not simply a flat surface is twofold. First, by virtue of having two eyes you can see stereoscopically, adding to the perception of depth. The second reason is that light bends around objects. No matter how three-dimensional objects are lit, a shadow is cast along the edges of the objects. This edge shadow is not a solid dark shadow. In fact, from the lit area of an object through the edge to the darkest shadow of an object there is a transition or blend of light to dark. Simple and immediate white-to-black transitions do not exist in nature. There is always a gray area that introduces the lightest area to the darkest area. This phenomenon is studied in geometric or optical physics and is

based on defraction principles. These principles are applied to the concept of anti-aliasing.

Edges, which are borders separating one color area from another color area, are considered places of clearly identifiable transition. By averaging the pixels along an edge, you can create a smooth transition from one color to another. This transition mimics what you see in nature, the bend of light around an edge. Your way of seeing is the reason anti-aliasing is necessary. Blurring an edge simply is not enough. If you average the pixels on an edge too much, the edge becomes unnaturally blurred. If you do not blur the edge enough, you do not gain the pleasing visual advantage of a natural look. Figure 6.5 gives a good example of how aliasing and anti-alias appear.

The definition of alias is something against something else. If you look at the color edge of aliasing, you see that the color is directly against what it is laid on. Anti-aliasing opposes the "againstness." Being opposed to aliasing (anti-aliasing) means creating a transition, a merging, or a blurring of borders. The colors may have their own location or space, but they are linked by a common blurred border that they both share. You often hear anti-aliasing spoken of as blurring an edge, softening an edge, or blending an edge. Depending on how you use anti-aliasing, these all are part of the description but not the complete picture.

Anti-aliasing uses an algorithm to produce the averaging. Most paint tools have anti-aliasing built into them. In the brush or draw tools, anti-aliasing usually is uniformly distributed. When vector objects, such as type, are introduced into the bitmap, the anti-aliasing is more specific. Anti-aliasing is necessary for creating pleasing type in a bitmap image. You can see in the example that along the curved edges of color the averaging is more than it is along straight portions. Anti-aliasing directly considers the shape and direction of the edges in the image. When you are merging postscript objects such as type into a bitmap, sophisticated algorithms determine the amount of anti-aliasing the edges need. (See figure 6.6.) Chapter 13, "Reproducing Vectors as CT Bitmaps," presents specific production techniques regarding merging objects into bitmaps.

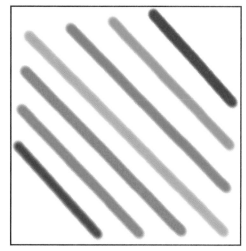

Fig. 6.5.
Alias strokes and anti-alias strokes.

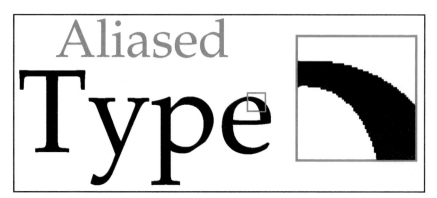

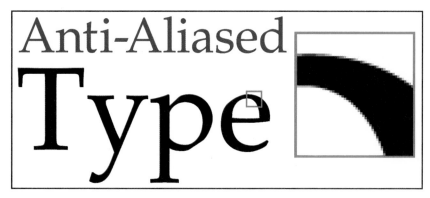

Fig. 6.6.
Aliased versus anti-aliased type.

As mentioned, many draw tools in Macintosh image programs have anti-alias edges that are distributed uniformly. The section on painting tools describes this in greater detail. The processing time required to perform the calculations can slow the use of drawing tools using anti-aliased edges. As you discovered previously, the cost of higher quality is slower processing. Anti-aliasing usually is worth the cost in speed. Increasing the processing power of your Macintosh with special accelerators is suggested if you plan extensive use of anti-alias drawing tools. Examples of aliasing and anti-aliasing follow. (See figure 6.7.)

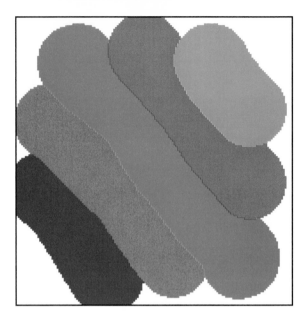

Drawing Tools

Pencils

Drawing tools called pencils give you a flat, *aliased*, jagged-edged mark. Using pencils is an excellent way to draw large amounts of flat color into one area. Because pencils do not use anti-aliasing algorithms, the speed of drawing on the screen is extremely quick. (See figure 6.8.)

Pencil tools are one of the few drawing tools that draw in near *real time.* The standard of real time is how you draw with a real lead pencil.

Real time on a computer means that the motion you make with your mouse or pen immediately transfers to the screen with little or no waiting time. The amount of processing speed and RAM on your computer has a direct impact on how close you come to real-time drawing. The speed at which you move your mouse also contributes to how close you come to

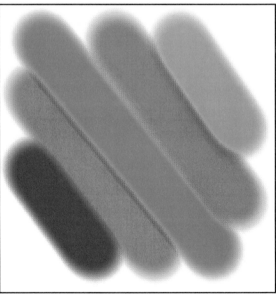

Fig. 6.7.
Aliased edges are hard and jagged, whereas anti-aliased edges are smooth.

real-time drawing. When you hear someone speak of drawing *near* real time, that means the amount of time between making your stroke and seeing the mark on the screen is small. Any waiting is annoying; depending on your system and the image size, you will need to slow your drawing pace.

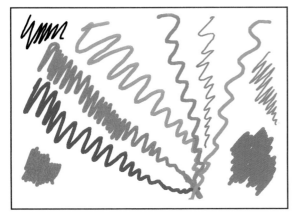

Fig. 6.8.
Pencil marks.

Scribbling is the benchmark by which all computer drawing is measured. Scribbling is not a quantifiable figure, but when you can scribble as fast as you do with a lead pencil without any waiting for the marks to appear on the screen, you have reached real-time digital drawing. Pencil tools come closer to scribbling than any other draw tool. (See figure 6.9.) Achieving real-time drawing for all drawing tools is an ongoing goal for many developers. Real time is a buzzword you always should temper with the actual experience of using the tools and measuring the performance by your own standards.

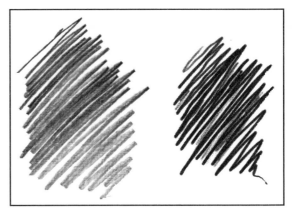

Fig. 6.9.
Real pencil scribbling and digital pencil scribbling.

The pencil, despite the aliased edge, makes marks quickly and often produces the effect of a real lead pencil. You can make your marks with a pencil and later apply a blurring effect to soften the hard edges. You can achieve the softening using either a blur tool or a filter, which is discussed later. As mentioned, the pencil tool is used for flat fills of color. It acts like a very big paintbrush you use to cover a wall when you are not concerned about intricate areas such as molding, which are left for other brushes. If you need to get rid of the background of an image, you can use a pencil tool to quickly scratch out the main areas while leaving the more detailed areas for finer drawing tools. Most programs provide for drawing straight lines. Using the pencil tool to draw perfect horizontal or vertical lines avoids the problem of anti-aliasing. In fact, for horizontal and vertical lines, using an aliased tool such as a pencil tool is preferable because the lines are crisp and clean. The horizontal and vertical lines of anti-aliased tools leave an averaged soft edge that gives a undesirable out-of-focus effect. You also can use the pencil tools to trim ragged edges of an image horizontally and vertically for the same reason, to give crisp, clean cuts to an edge. The pencil tools are simple but effective drawing tools. Figure 6.10 illustrates some of the pencil tool's uses.

Fig. 6.10.

Drawing horizontal and vertical lines and cropping away parts of an image work well with a pencil.

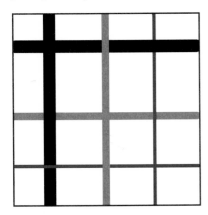

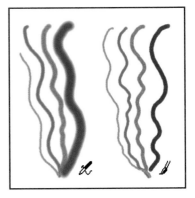

Fig. 6.11.

Paintbrush and airbrush tools.

Fig. 6.10a.

Horizontal lines.

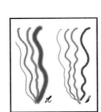

Both a paintbrush and an airbrush tool should have the option to adjust the opacity of the color being painted. Opacity usually is indicated from 0 to 100 percent. The value of 0 percent is completely clear; 100 percent is completely opaque. Opacity is a very useful option that helps the airbrush mimic the action of a real airbrush. In most programs you have the option of keeping the opacity of the chosen color constant or allowing the opacity to build with repeated passes over the same area. A traditional airbrush artist sprays paint on a page gradually and with each stroke adds color until the desired opacity is reached. By gradually laying down color, the artist has control over the shading and depth of the strokes. You can achieve the same effect by setting the opacity control of a brush tool 50 percent or lower. (See figure 6.12.) Even if a program does not allow the building of opacity, straight opacity is a useful way of achieving subtle color effects where harsh, flat color otherwise would be a distraction.

Fig. 6.10b.

Vertical lines.

Because the brush tools have anti-aliased edges, the brushes are excellent for cropping an image with a soft edge around an image. The anti-aliased nature of brush tools also is extremely useful when you are creating soft-edged masks. We discuss masks in

Brush Tools

Paint tools generally come in two types: paintbrushes and airbrushes. (See figure 6.11.) Usually the two tools act very similar, with two exceptions. Both tools have soft anti-aliased edges, but the airbrush typically is much softer. And because the airbrush has more of an anti-aliased edge to compute, the airbrush is slower than a paintbrush tool.

Chapter 8, "Merging and Collaging Images." Because the brush tool marks are complex, the speed and real-time drawing of the brushes is not very good. You may need to adjust your drawing style away from a scribbling motion to keep on an even pace with the speed of the computer. Even with the lack of speed, the brush tools are at the core of all image creation on Macintosh image programs, and they are extremely flexible and useful. As the processing speed of the Macintosh increases, the real-time speed of the brush also increases. Each image program on the Macintosh system has variations on how it implements brush tools. How versatile an anti-aliased brush is in a program is one indication of the overall versatility of the program.

Fig. 6.12.
A digital airbrush, like a real airbrush, can regulate opacity by layering color.

Color Palettes

You use a color palette to choose the color of each drawing tool. The color palette also gives you information about the values of a pixel. Although not a tool itself, the color palette is an important link to the drawing tools. Chapter 5, "Color," has more on color palettes.

Eyedropper

The eyedropper or syringe enables you to pick up color from your image without having to go to the color palette. In this way you can be assured of having an exact color match because you choose the color directly from the image. Most programs enable you to access the eyedropper while using a drawing tool by holding down either the Option key or the Command key. This method of choosing a color is extremely convenient because you do not need to stop drawing to change your color.

The eyedropper usually has the option of picking up either the value of the individual pixel it touches or the average value of a group of pixels. This sampling method is a convenient way of getting the overall color value in an area of an image. But for precise pixel-by-pixel retouching, you often need to sample the value of the pixels individually. (See figure 6.13.)

Fig. 6.13.
Three methods of picking color with an eyedropper.

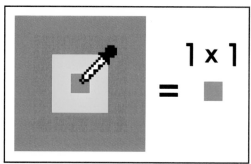

Fig. 6.13a.
Point sample.

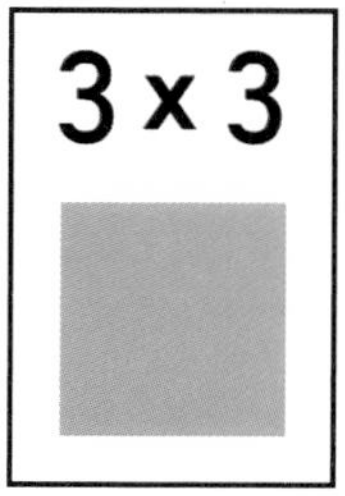

Fig. 6.13b.
3x3 sample.

Fig. 6.13c.
5x5 sample.

Softening and Blurring Tools

Usually, the icon for blur is in the shape of a raindrop. The blur tool averages pixels it touches to create a softening effect. This effect is extremely useful when you are trying to get rid of unwanted jagged edges when compositing different images together. Softening an edge sometimes is called feathering an edge. (See figure 6.14.) Blurring should be used sparingly because too much blurring along even a jagged edge may create an undesirable soft halo effect, defeating the purpose of hiding jagged edges in the first place.

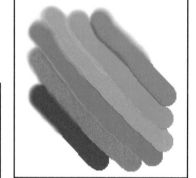

Fig. 6.14.
Blurring an edge creates a softening effect.

A great way to understand how the blur tools work is to pass over the same area repeatedly and see what blurring does to a single group of pixels. Figure 6.15 illustrates that with enough blurring all the pixels eventually become the same value, devoid of any texture or depth. In areas such as flesh tones, variable tone is a critical part of the image, and texture is needed for a more realistic look. A good method to try when using a blur tool is not to follow a specific pattern. Instead of placing even strokes on the same area over and over, use an irregular, spotty method. Use the unevenness of an image to hide the

retouching. Patterns in digital images are easy to identify; it is useful to stay away from predictability as much as possible to lend a more realistic flavor to an image.

Fig. 6.15.
A straight line blur on an edge is easier to detect (left) than a blur applied irregularly (right).

Sharpening Tools

Sharpening tools, usually combined with the blurring tool, increase the contrast of the pixels you touch, effectively increasing the difference between those pixels. (See figure 6.16.) Most useful near edges of color, the sharpening tool is of little production use in flat areas of color tone or blends of color. In fact, in these areas of tone, you should avoid the sharpening tool. As with the blur tool, making repeated passes over the same area gives you an excellent indication of how the sharpening tool works. Again, as with the blur and, in fact, as with all tools, avoiding predictable drawing patterns adds to a realistic look of an image. If you need an area sharpened, use a slightly irregular method rather than simple back-and-forth strokes.

Remember, you always can use a tool more if needed. Resist the temptation to simply jump to the effect you need; start slow and then build up to the point where you achieve the desired effect. With time and experience you may be able simply to make the stroke you need and move on, but you never will go wrong by taking it easy. A slower method may take more time, but the final result will be more appealing overall.

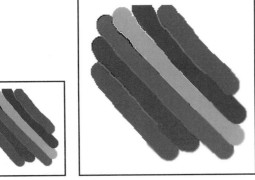

Fig. 6.16.
Sharpening an edge increases the contrast between colors.

Cloning Tools

Clone tools enable you to take the values of actual pixel groups from one area of the same image (or from a different image) and paint those pixels in another location on the bitmap. Remember, even though it may look as if you are moving the pixels, you simply are reassigning the pixels you paint with the values of pixels from another area. Programs such as ColorStudio incorporate the clone feature with existing drawing tools. Some of these programs, such

as Photoshop, have separate tools specifically for the clone feature called rubber stamp tools. The clone tools take a sample of the entire image. You choose the origin or source point for a clone tool. When you begin drawing the first stroke, you begin literally to redraw starting with the source point you have chosen. Clone is the most significant tool to use when retouching images because you can repair, alter, or create images based on existing textures and color. You can measure the power of Macintosh retouching programs by the versatility of the clone feature contained in the program.

There are three important variations of clone tools: clone align, clone non-align, and clone revert. Clone align enables you to choose a source point, and then no matter how many times you stop drawing to judge how the image looks, clone align picks up where you left off without leaving any seams or interruptions in the image you are cloning. Clone align is extremely useful in copying a large part of an image when you must pause frequently to judge the progress of the image creation. Figure 6.17 shows examples of clones.

Unlike clone align, clone non-align returns to the original source point each time you stop drawing. This enables you to create multiple copies of the same area if you desire. The example in figure 6.18 shows one way for the clone non-align feature to work.

Clone revert enables you to revert or paint back to the saved version of an image. Clone revert truly acts like an eraser because you can paint back to whatever you started from without having to reopen the image and start over. Clone revert is an excellent and important creative and production tool. The example in figure 6.19 shows how revert can be used.

Fig. 6.17.
The source of the clone is indicated by a cross.

Fig. 6.17a.

Fig. 6.17b.

Fig. 6.17c.

Fig. 6.18.
Clone non-align returns to the source point each time you stop painting.

Fig. 6.19a.
Clone revert acts like a true eraser and reveals the original image. Shown are two examples of clone revert.

Fig. 6.19b.

Erasers

Erasers simply paint back to the background color of the image. Most eraser tools have an aliased edge. (See figure 6.20.) The eraser in Photoshop has an option of painting back or erasing any changes back to the originally saved image. Most programs, including Photoshop and ColorStudio, use clone revert tools to perform this paint-back erasing function *with* soft anti-aliased edges. Any of the drawing tools can perform the job of an eraser by simply choosing the background color and painting with that color value.

Fig. 6.20.
Erasers usually have jagged edges.

Line and Shape Tools

In some programs you can create anti-aliased shapes directly on the bitmap. Circle, polygon, and line tools sometimes are useful ways of creating bitmap objects. If the edges of shapes are not anti-aliased, their use is limited. (See figure 6.21.) Bitmap shapes and lines are not easily enlarged or scaled without losing a degree of quality. Creating lines and shapes with vector-based object programs such as Freehand, Illustrator, and Shapes (ColorStudio) is much more effective and flexible. You then can convert the object into a pixel bitmap for further manipulation using ColorStudio or Photoshop. We discuss this further in Chapter 13.

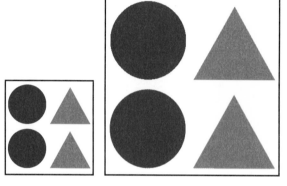

Fig. 6.21.
Alias shapes and anti-aliased shapes.

Smear, Smudge, Stretch

Various drawing tools in Macintosh programs allow for unique creative effects. Smear, smudge, and stretch are close variations of one another, and each program can intermix the terms to describe the same effect. Smearing is an option in most programs that spreads the color of one area into another. The effect is like dragging your finger through a charcoal drawing or wet paint. If you ever have drawn with a lead pencil or charcoal, you know how useful taking your finger to blend and soften harsh areas can be. In fact, the icon most often used for this effect is a finger. A smudge tool acts in the same way as a smear tool but usually with a greater amount of color mixing. Stretch tools, sometimes called pull, take a portion of an image and pull that portion, creating an elastic stretch effect not unlike Silly Putty. Stretch tools usually do not mix colors like the smear or smudge tools but keep the colors and texture intact. Stretching part of an image into another also is an excellent way of touching up areas of an image because you closely match textures. Figure 6.22 shows how smear, smudge, and stretch appear.

Fig. 6.22a.
The effects of smear, smudge and stretch.

Drawing Tool Sizes

All draw tools have variable drawing or pen tip sizes. Pen or drawing tips are measured in pixels and are

defined from very fine tips (one pixel) to very fat tips (20 or more pixels). (See figure 6.23.) The size of your pen tip directly relates to the speed at which you can draw. The larger the tip, the more computation is required and the less quickly you can draw.

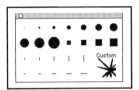

Fig. 6.23.
Various pen tips.

With larger tips, you can use a spacing feature that enables you to determine how far apart each deposit of color lands. If you make a single 20-pixel mark, you need only another 20-pixel mark spaced 10 to 20 pixels apart from the first to achieve a continuous line. Spacing helps relieve the amount of computation necessary for a drawing to work and results in faster drawing times. The spacing, by placing spots of color at regular intervals, also works well for design effects. (See figure 6.24.)

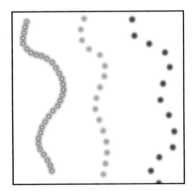

Fig. 6.24.
Spacing a 20-pixel brush by 10 pixels, by 20 pixels, and by 30 pixels.

You can create and define your own custom drawing tips in most programs. The ability to custom create the tip of your drawing tool is useful for design and production techniques. A custom tip also can mimic traditional paintbrushes in determining how the color is dispersed. (See figure 6.25.)

Fig. 6.25.
A few of the custom tips created in Photoshop.

Many specific variations on the previously discussed tools are available in many different programs on the Mac. These variations include the capability to define a particular pattern and then use a tool to paint that pattern repeatedly. Some variations also enable you to paint with graduated shades, and paint on only specific ranges of color. We address many of these features and techniques in Chapter 7, "Digital Painting."

Fill Tools

Fill tools, also called paint bucket tools, enable you to fill designated areas with flat or graduated color blends. Instead of using a drawing tool, you can use a fill tool as a quick way to pour and place color. Most Macintosh programs enable you to control the specific areas in which the fill tool pours the color by protecting selected areas. See the discussion of selection tools in the next section. Besides providing flat color, the fill tools allow graduated blends of color. You normally create graduated color by choosing two colors and creating linear, circular, radial, or (with three colors) triangular blends. These blends can be extremely useful for creating new backgrounds. Besides some of the fantastic rainbow-type colors, blends in nature also can be simulated. Sunsets and blue sky are typical examples. Except for the sky and some unique tropical flowers and shadows, uniform blends or vignetting tones do not exist in nature. That is why many uniform digitally created blends seem a little unrealistic. When using blends, you should be aware that the more colors you use, the more the blend may appear unnatural.

The most common exception to blends in nature is blue sky. The blue color in a sky becomes less saturated (more washed out) near the horizon. To create a realistic blue sky in the background of an image, be sure to use a fill tool to create a blend from a saturated blue in the upper sky to a less saturated blue near the horizon.

Figure 6.26 illustrates how fill tools work.

Fig. 6.26.
Linear blends, circular blends, and triangular blends.

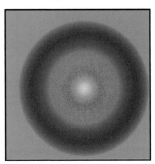
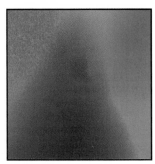

Selection Tools

Selection tools are a critical part of any image program. By isolating chosen pixels, the selection tool enables you to modify or protect areas of an image without affecting other elements of the image. Selected areas of an image can be cut and copied from and then pasted into a different image or into the same image for placement in a different location. When a selected part of an image is cut or copied, the cut or copied piece is placed into the Macintosh clipboard. The clipboard is a buffer area used by Macintosh programs to hold pixel information. You can apply or paste any pixel information in the clipboard into any chosen image. The clipboard acts like a holding area for pixels chosen by selection tools while you decide where those pixels should be placed. When you paste pixel information of an image in a clipboard into another image, that pasted group of pixels is called a floating selection. A pasted image is called floating because you can move that group of pixels without affecting the image beneath the selection. Dropping a floating selection literally bonds the floating pixel information directly to the position on the bitmap that the floating selection was above. (See figure 6.27.)

There are four variations of the selection tool: rectangular, oval, lasso, and automatic selections. Rectangular selection creates square or rectangular selection regions. Oval selection creates circular or oval selections. Lasso selection enables you to freely select areas and pixel groups. Automatic or magic wand selections select pixel groups based on a chosen value range of color. You can mix these selection methods to create irregular selected regions by adding or subtracting from a selection. You also can alter the paths of a selection to expand or contract or create borders by designated pixel amounts. (See figure 6.28.)

Fig. 6.28.
Selections created by rectangle, oval, lasso, automatic, and combinations of all four.

A selection area can act as a mask. A mask is used to either protect or modify a specific area. We further discuss masks in Chapter 8. Figure 6.29 shows how a selected area is used to limit where a drawing tool can paint.

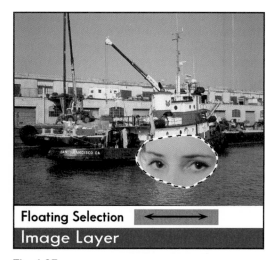

Fig. 6.27.
Floating selection top view and side view.

Fig. 6.29.
The selected area is the only area in which painting is allowed.

Selections also are used to crop unwanted portions of an image. Some programs, such as Photoshop, have a separate cropping tool that crops or clips away unwanted portions of your image.

You can save the paths of selections for use later. Some selections may take a great deal of time to create, and saving these selections at intervals while creating a selection ensures that your work is not lost.

Viewing Tools (Zoom and Pan)

Zoom tools as viewing tools enable you to see an image at different levels. Like a magnifying glass, this tool enables you to zoom into an area of fine detail, fix something, and then zoom back to see the overall image. Traditional artists are familiar with the process of working with their noses inches from their drawing board to make sure the finest detail is captured and then holding the page an arm's length away to see whether they achieved the desired effect. The zoom tool does just that but on a much bigger scale. The capability to see and adjust individual pixels in an image is vital to the detailed effects you may need to create. Changing the eye color of a person is a typical fine-detail job which requires individual pixel work that only a zoom tool can provide. It is useful to work in a magnified area and at the same time see an overall view of an image, as figure 6.30 shows.

Pan tools enable you to quickly move to a different part of an image without having to use the zoom tool. A hand is usually the icon used to indicate a pan tool. Panning is useful when you are working with an image magnified to the individual pixels. By using the pan tool you need not stop working at that magnification; you only move the image to the area you need. (See figure 6.31.)

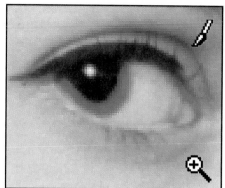

Fig. 6.30.
Retouching an eye is easier with the image magnified.

Fig. 6.31.
Panning moves the image like moving paper on a table.

Many types of video boards include both the zoom tools and the panning tools. Hardware-implemented zoom and pan tools are much faster than software-controlled zoom and pan. Using a video board with this capability adds speed to retouching digital images.

Conclusion

With any craft, the better you know your tools, the better you will become at that craft. You will find your own preferences and effective combinations of tools. Always be aware of the available tools because you never know when a tool you seldom use may meet your needs for a special effect.

The next chapter addresses specific drawing techniques and the uses of pressure-sensitive tablets.

Digital Painting

The roots of design and art are not being ripped out by digital imaging. Rather, digital imagery simply has brought forward new branches of art and design that have yet to be explored fully. The concepts of digital art and design still are forming, and the techniques involved in creating digital effects for art and design are developing rapidly. As the digital image programs become faster and more sophisticated, the options for digital art and design will expand. Although discussing the design and aesthetic implications of digital painting is tempting, these topics have been handled better by texts dealing specifically with those issues.

In this book we discuss the basic techniques that digital image programs provide to create the image effects you desire. You constantly should remind yourself that the computer is a *tool* that facilitates your ability to create. *Tools* do not create. *You* do. The art, design, aesthetics, and creation of images always are where they have been and where they should be: within *you.*

Paint Programs and Image Programs

Paint programs differ from image programs. Paint programs concentrate primarily on the creation of images, whereas *image programs* concentrate primarily on processing images that come from paint programs or scanned originals. In a pure sense, paint programs and image programs are the same, because scanned originals are digital information, and this digital information also is incorporated into paint programs. But most paint programs do not have the facilities to process images for color separations. As features from both types of programs are incorporated into each other, the distinction between paint programs and image programs will blur. Appendix E, "Hardware and Software Companies," lists paint programs and image programs available on the Macintosh.

The Color Palette

The *color palette* in all digital programs is the source of your color options. Like a traditional paint palette, this electronic palette enables you to mix colors. The mixing palette introduces the first part of improvisation available to the digital artist. The color that is in use, or active, is indicated visually as well as by number values. Sliding indicators show the value of the color chosen. You can alter the color by moving the sliding indicators.

You choose color from any number of different color spaces, such as red, green, blue (RGB); cyan, magenta, yellow (CMY); hue, saturation, value (HSV); or hue, saturation, brightness (HSB). In each case the color is formed and has a basis in the red, green, and blue color space. Figure 7.1 shows the components of a mixing palette. (Review Chapter 2, "Color and Tones," regarding color.)

Changing the display controls on your monitor does not change the real values of the actual digital file. The color palette is your link to the reality of the values of color you use. Regardless of how the image is displayed on your screen, you always can check and base your choices on the values indicated on your palette. If you rely solely on what you see on the monitor, you risk not reproducing your image in the way you need.

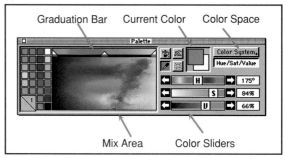

Fig. 7.1.
The parts of a mixing palette.

A perfect example of monitor dependency was a job brought in by a client who needed slide output. After we took his file and produced the slide, the client remarked that the colors were wrong. "That is not supposed to be red; it's supposed to be green," he said. Displaying the image on our Macintosh revealed that the slide produced exactly what was in the digital file. The client suggested that we had altered the file somehow. We showed how this was not possible, but we could not come up with an alternative solution to the radical color shift.

We suggested that the client return to his system and display the file he had given us. When the person called back, he said the file was displaying exactly as he thought it should. When we looked closer at the color shift, we realized that the colors red and green were being exchanged. We asked the person to check the cable link from the video board to the monitor. That turned out to be the problem. The red cable was plugged into the green port and the green cable into the red port. Swapping cables had exchanged the red and green channels of the monitor, and the colors of the image that the client thought he was creating were not actually there. We repaired the image by reswapping the red and green channels during output processing to produce an accurate slide.

Although this example is extreme, it does illustrate the difference between the digital information and the monitor display. From that day on, this person always made sure to check the values of his displayed colors with the values indicated on his palette.

Drawing and Painting Tools

As mentioned in Chapter 6, "Basic Tools and Functions," drawing and painting tools come in four major types: pencil, paintbrush, airbrush, and clone-brush. We discuss and show examples of these types of tools in this section.

In every case of digital painting, experimentation is the key to understanding the many uses of the tools. As you use digital image programs more, the drawing and painting tools' creative possibilities will become more familiar to you. References to traditional tools such as paintbrush and airbrush are used only as convenient slang to communicate the concept of the draw tool. But digital drawing and painting tools do not act exactly like traditional paintbrushes or pens and pencils. Linking the description of digital tools to traditional tools ultimately limits the ability to describe digital drawing tools accurately and effectively.

Drawing tools are better described as aliased or anti-aliased with the anti-aliased drawing tools described by the amount of anti-aliasing produced. Clone drawing tools also are described as having either aliased or anti-aliased edges. (See figures 7.2 through 7.5.)

Fig. 7.2.
Pencils (aliased edges).

Fig. 7.3.
Paintbrush (anti-aliased).

Fig. 7.4.
Airbrush (anti-aliased).

Fig. 7.5.
Clone (aliased and anti-aliased).

Pressure Sensitivity

Drawing with a bar of soap is not considered natural. Drawing with a mouse is similar to using soap. A mouse is not a good drawing tool because the actual movement and holding of the mouse are unnatural for drawing. Also, there are limited resources for changing the thickness of the marks you make while drawing on the fly. Pressure-sensitive pens offer a more familiar and realistic way to draw. When you use a special pen and a table, the physical action of creating pressure enables you to vary your marks in many ways. Pressure-sensitive pens are the most significant tool for digital artists and retouchers to arrive on the scene in many years. Wacom was the first to introduce these pens; three companies now offer pressure-sensitive styluses for use in many programs. All the tablets use a Wacom emulator to achieve the action of pressure. In short, the tablet sends and receives digital signals, which translate into variable strokes and marks. Pressure pen functions are divided into four types: pressure radius, pressure opacity, pressure blends, and combinations of all three.

Pressure Radius

The amount of pressure a pen applies to the tablet can alter the radius of the marks made on the digital image. The harder you press, the fatter the line becomes. This effect corresponds with what you expect with a real paintbrush. Because the pen information is digital, you also can reverse your usual thinking, by making the harder you press result in a thinner line and the lighter you press give a thicker line radius. (See figure 7.6.) This variation opens many avenues not available in a traditional drawing

environment. Also, it is impossible to match the simple mark made by a pressure pen with a mouse.

Fig. 7.6.
Changing the radius of your marks with a pressure-sensitive pen stylus.

Pressure Opacity

The amount of pressure you apply with a pressure pen regulates how dark or light a mark appears. You regulate the opacity of a pen in the same manner as the radius. The harder you press, the darker the mark appears. (See figure 7.7.) As mentioned before, you can reverse this process and make the harder pressure result in a lighter, less opaque line.

Fig. 7.7.
Changing the opacity of your marks with pressure.

Pressure Blend

Many programs enable you to describe a blend of color and have the pressure of the pen regulate the position of the marks on the blend. In figure 7.8, the blend has been defined from red to blue. As the pressure increases, the mark becomes more blue, and as the pressure decreases, the mark color changes to red.

Fig. 7.8.
Changing the color blend of your marks with pressure.

Combinations

Mixing the techniques from all three pressure effects creates many interesting marks. By combining radius, opacity, and blends in different ways, you can create marks that simulate many traditional methods. Figures 7.9 through 7.13 show examples of effects you can get with pressure sensitivity.

These effects are by no means the only types of marks you can create. But there is no way to create any of these marks without a pressure-sensitive stylus using digital media. At first, you may find working with a tablet unusual. But just as you learned to use a mouse, you can learn to use a tablet; in fact, using a tablet becomes more natural and often preferable. The

features of this tool are especially attractive, but not limited, to artists.

Fig. 7.9.
Simulating charcoal marks.

Fig. 7.10.
Simulating pastel marks.

Fig. 7.11.
Simulating watercolor marks.

Fig. 7.12.
Simulating oil marks.

Fig. 7.13.
Simulating pencil marks.

are doing to the mark you are making. As pressure becomes more a part of the digital image environment, more variables are added. The new variables include adjusting marks by the speed at which you move the pen and adjusting marks by the angle at which you hold the pen. (See figure 7.14.)

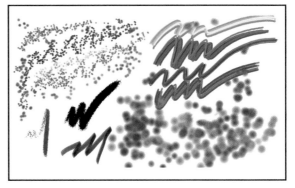

Fig. 7.14.
Some of the marks available in a paint program.

Establishing Techniques

Many programs give you the opportunity to save versions of a particular technique. But you also may want to keep a list of your favorites. As though conducting a science experiment, try to change one variable at a time to discover the result instead of changing many variables simultaneously. A step-by-step method helps you understand what the variables

The Undo Catch-22

The undo function is a wonderful and useful option that enables you to revert and undo marks or strokes you just made. In a strict production environment, undo is necessary for seeing the before and after of image processing. But in a creative setting, undo causes many users to get bogged down. People may get bogged down because they tend to think about a mark as though that mark will make or break the entire image. People make a mark and then undo to try the mark again, then repeat this process in a catch-22. As time passes, if they eventually become satisfied with a mark, they already have broken whatever rhythm they need to be creative. Unfortunately, the wonder of the computer, in cases like this, has undermined the fluid expressive nature of creating images.

If you are not sure you like the mark, save a version of the file before the mark was made and move on. You may surprise yourself and realize that the fluid nature of image creating is more important than trying to make everything perfect on the first pass. Don't get caught up in a loop of undo, undo, and undo because you never will reach completion—or if you do you never will be satisfied.

Most programs give you the option of turning off undo. This may sound a little scary at first, but try it. You'll save disk space while undo is off, and you always can go back to the original. Working straight through is a good way to examine how you are drawing and is much better than lamenting over each stroke, which interferes with your creative flow.

With advances in Macintosh technology, digital painting will change constantly, as will your techniques for using the Mac for creating marks. Don't be afraid to venture into unknown territory. The Macintosh is a tool that is under your guidance and control, not the other way around. The next chapter discusses the power of image programs to merge and collage images.

Merging and Collaging Images

A t the core of all image manipulation exists the merging and collaging of images into one cohesive image. Everyone is familiar with cutting pictures from a magazine and pasting them together to create a new scene. Mac programs use so many different techniques to produce collaged images that it is impossible to mention all these variations.

Masks

In traditional layout, the simplest process involves cutting an image and then pasting it directly onto the layout board. For more elaborate collaging areas, where specific areas of the image are to be protected, a material called Rubylith is used. The Rubylith material acts as a protector or mask for a chosen area. A mask indicates where spot color is to be laid into an image or protects an area that is not supposed to be altered.

Digital masks work in the same way as Rubylith. By designating an area, you can protect or leave unprotected specific areas for alterations of color or collaging of images.

Selection Masks

The simplest mask involves using the selection tools (see Chapter 6, "Basic Tools and Functions") to define a pixel area of the bitmap image. Having an area selected indicates that any alteration such as painting or color correction is performed only in the selected area. The selected area protects or masks any other area. (See figure 8.1.) Different Mac programs may implement this action in different ways, but the result remains the same.

Fig. 8.1.
Only the selected pixels can be affected. The pixels not chosen are protected from alterations.

The four most common types of selecting tools are the Rectangular, Oval, Lasso, and Automatic selections. Rectangular selection creates square or rectangular selection regions. Oval selection creates circular or oval selections. Lasso selection enables you to freely select areas and pixel groups. Automatic or magic wand selections select pixel groups based on a chosen value range of color. All of these various selection methods can be mixed to create irregular selected regions by adding or subtracting from a selection.

When you are working with complex image areas, making a selection mask is usually time consuming. Rather than trying to make a selection perfect in one pass, you should select the general area you want, then pick away or add what you need selected. Usually a combination of selection tools is critical to producing an accurate selection mask. Some people think the automatic selection tool is the only tool they require. The automatic selection tool is an excellent method of selecting a range of color values, but this method is not perfect. Unless you have an area of color values that is vastly different from other adjacent values, a selection that is automatically chosen usually requires some kind of refinement. The automatic selection tool provides an excellent starting point from which you can make further adjustments. (See figure 8.2.)

Fig. 8.2a.

Fig. 8.2b.

Fig. 8.2.
A typical process to achieving a desired selection.

Fig. 8.2c.

Saving Selections

During the course of creating a selection, you should save your selection periodically because a simple click of the mouse outside the selected area deselects that area and you lose the selection. Also, by saving a selection you can retrieve the selection for use at any time during your retouching work.

Saving a selection basically involves saving a mask. Most programs have separate areas called alpha channels for saving mask information. Many selection masks are fairly difficult to reproduce, so saving the information in a separate layer or channel ensures that you need not repeat your effort of defining an area or areas to protect. A channel containing a selection mask often is referred to as a mask layer. This layer does not affect the RGB composite color of an image. Instead, this channel layer holds the selection information for later use. The mask layer is an 8-bit channel and contains up to 256 levels of gray-scale information. Each time you add a mask layer to an image, you effectively increase the size of the file by one-third the size of the color image. A mask channel's gray-scale information is fully editable with any of the tools used on the color image. (See figure 8.3.)

Many programs also enable you simply to save a selection as a path. Saving a selection to a path and not to a mask channel eliminates the problem of increased file size because saving a path requires very little memory. Still, as you read further, you will see that the mask channels are a useful part of merging images together.

Fig. 8.3.
A selection saved to a mask layer.

Cut, Copy, Paste

If you are familiar with word processing programs, you are familiar with the options of cut, copy, and paste. Image programs use these same options in much the same manner as word processing programs.

Cut and copy options take a selected area of pixels and place that pixel image information into a buffer called the clipboard. A *buffer* is an area where you place and store pixel information while working with an image or a group of images. The Macintosh's single buffer area is called the *clipboard*. As the name implies, the clipboard is like the traditional hand layout area where you keep an image until you decide where you want to place that image. The cut option removes the selected pixels and leaves behind

115

a blank space. The copy option simply duplicates the pixel information of the selected area but leaves the original area untouched.

After you place pixel information into the clipboard, you can paste the pixel information into a different location on the same image or paste the clipboard information in an entirely different image. Pasting the image from the clipboard onto the image puts that pixel information above the image, literally floating above the image area. This floating action enables you to move the pasted pixel information freely without altering the image underneath. Like taking a clipping from a magazine and experimenting with different positions, you easily can move a *floating selection* . (See figure 8.4.) When you decide the proper position for the selection, you drop the selection into the image. Dropping or deselecting a floating selection into an image locks the floating pixels directly onto the pixels underneath. You cannot move that group of pixels after you have dropped the floating selection. Many programs offer several variations of pasting that allow adjustment of the transparency of floating images to create subtle collaging effects.

Transparency of the floating image is controlled while the pixels still are floating and not after the selection has been dropped or placed into the image. (See figure 8.5.)

Fig. 8.5.
Transparency is adjusted while the selection is floating.

Fig. 8.4.
You can move the floating selection without affecting any part of the image underneath.

Because the clipboard actually is holding image information, the operating speed of your program may diminish slightly. To help alleviate this problem, after you are finished using large images in the clipboard, simply make a small selection of pixels and copy that information into the clipboard. The clipboard can hold only one image at a time, so the smaller copy resides in the clipboard and eliminates any potential speed compromises.

How a Mask Works

In most programs when you are implementing masks, the black area indicates full protection and the white area indicates no protection. When you paste an image from the clipboard as a floating selection, the areas that have white in the mask layer allow the floating image to show through completely; the areas of black protect the base image from the floating selection. (See figure 8.6.)

When the mask contains areas of gray, depending on how close the gray value is to white or black, that percentage of the image shows through. For example, a mask with 50 percent gray shows 50 percent of the floating image. (See figure 8.7a.) A 30 percent gray shows 70 percent of the image, and so on. (See figure 8.7b.) Gray in the mask creates a transparent effect in the floating image.

Fig. 8.6a.

Fig. 8.7a.
A mask with 50 percent gray.

Fig. 8.6b.

Fig. 8.6.
A mask and the effect of a mask on a floating selection.

Fig. 8.7b.
A mask with 30 percent gray.

117

Anti-aliased Masks

The capability to have gray values in the mask is an important advantage of a digital mask. The soft edges that create a sense of optical and visual realism are important for mask layers. Accurate, soft-edged masks are nearly impossible to make using the traditional Rubylith or photographic methods of mask creation. The benefits of anti-aliasing are clear, and masks using anti-aliasing on the edges are far more effective than masks that do not use the anti-aliasing the 256 levels of gray provide. The examples in figure 8.8 indicate the striking differences involving images merged with and without anti-aliased masks.

Fig. 8.8.
Images merged with and without anti-aliased masks.

Fig. 8.8a.
An aliased edge mask.

Fig. 8.8b.
An anti-aliased edge mask.

Fig. 8.8c.
The result of an aliased edge mask.

Fig. 8.8d.
The result of an anti-aliased edge mask.

Why Use Masks?

Why do you need a mask? Why not just place exactly the image you need exactly on top of the image you are creating? The key word is *exactly.* It is difficult to merge exactly what you want onto another image. Although some masks take time and are intricate, you can be assured the results are going to be accurate and are not going to need large amounts of touching up. Plus, the advantage that anti-aliased edges provides is not obtainable by any other method. The examples in figures 8.9a through 8.9d show the relative ease of merging two elements using masks.

Fig. 8.9a.
Blue sky.

Fig. 8.9b.
Sky to be replaced.

Fig. 8.9c.
Masking out old sky.

Fig. 8.9d.
New image with new sky.

The quality of your collaging is directly proportional to the masks you create. If you are careful and spend time with the edges of a mask, the result shows this time in the form of the seamless merging of image elements. If you do not take care during this mask making, the realism of the final image suffers. As always, the best masking and collaging examples are the ones you do not notice.

Simple Guidelines

Most programs that use masks enable you to "see" through the mask so you can base the creation of the mask on the original image. The capability to create a mask based on the original image is vital. Without this opportunity, you lack any of the subtle control necessary to use masks effectively. A perfect example of where masking must be based on the image involves masking out hair.

Masking out frizzy hair is always a very difficult process because the light thin lines of hair typically are not solid colors but are a mixture of the background and hair colors. Careful examination of the edge of the hair usually shows that any mask created there must be a soft gray and never have solid white or black areas for these individual hairs. If you disregard the frizzy hair altogether, the result often is an unnatural "cut out" look. (See figures 8.10a and 8.10b.) Making intricate masks is a painstaking operation, and shortcuts usually are regretted. Although creating some of these masks requires a lot of time, you must decide how much time the image requires to reach the desired quality.

Obviously, the more masking you perform, the better you become. The best way to attack masking of any kind is to make a quick general selection and then work on specific areas, getting closer to your goal by refining each area of the mask. (See figure 8.11.)

Fig. 8.10a.
Poor masking around hair.

Fig. 8.10b.
Good masking around hair.

Fig. 8.11.
The progression of general mask to finished mask.

Fig. 8.11a.

Fig. 8.11b.

Fig. 8.11c.

Fig. 8.11d.

Fig. 8.11e.

Depth of Field

The tendency in digital imagery is to keep everything in sharp focus, which is rarely the case with photographic images. Creating a more realistic depth of field effect lends a better quality and believability to your overall image. The *depth of field* is how far a scene stays in focus in front of and behind the spot you focus on. As you look at objects in nature, you scan back and forth so quickly that everything appears in focus. But when you examine a photographic image, objects in the distance often are out of focus. When you take photographs, images out of focus are the objects outside the depth of field. We understand how photos with images out of focus are at different distances. Our perceptions have been trained to understand that in a two-dimensional system, focus and lack of focus help create a sense of depth. (See figure 8.12.)

Fig. 8.12.
Creating the illusion of depth with focus.

Perspective

Perspective also helps create depth. Perspective is the perception of the spatial relationship of objects relative to one another. Perspective can be achieved by simple awareness of the relationship between objects. For example, in a group of people, the persons in the back of the picture should not be the same size as those in the front. If you are trying to create a realistic crowd scene with different persons, take into account their positions and what their sizes should be in relation to one another.

When collaging images, you should remember the basics of focusing and perspective. As in a photograph, you have a depth of field. When trying to create a sense of depth with images, remember that objects at different depths are not always perfectly in focus. Even a light bit of fuzziness for an image that is supposed to be a different depth leans toward a more realistic image. Figures 8.13a and 8.13b illustrate the effect of creating an image with a realistic depth of field using perspective.

Fig. 8.13a.
Poor perspective.

Fig. 8.13b.
Improved perspective.

One of the hardest accomplishments to make in a two-dimensional space is to create a sense of three dimensions. Some programs, called 3-D programs, concentrate on creating realistic three-dimensional objects. These elements can be imported into an image retouching program. But even these programs still display images in a two-dimensional space.

When creating realistic collaging, always keep in mind anti-aliased edges, depth of field, and perspective.

The next chapter discusses how dynamic effects can be used to create distortion effects or a better sense of realism.

Dynamic Effects

Image scaling, skewing, stretching, rotating, and flipping are called *dynamic effects.* You can perform all dynamic effects on the entire image or on selected areas within the image. With nearly all dynamic effects, sampling up or down must occur because dynamic effects need to create new pixels to achieve their distortion effects. Sampling is the creation or deletion of pixels. Sampling uses either interpolation or replication. Interpolation averages existing pixels to create new pixels; replication simply duplicates existing pixels. Review the effects of interpolation and replication in Chapter 1, "What Are Pixels?"

Rotation

Rotation seems like a natural process. Taking a piece of paper and turning it is quick and easy. Rotating bitmap digital images is a far more complex and lengthy process because of the sampling needed to produce the effect of turning an image. The pixels used on the Macintosh are square and are displayed square. Displaying square pixels at any angle is impossible. So if you rotate an image even by a small amount, the program must achieve this rotation by sampling and creating new pixel information. (See figure 9.1.) This sampling takes processing time. Programs and computer processors often are judged by the speed at which they rotate an image. For most dynamic effects including rotation, you should use interpolation for sampling, although sampling by replication accelerates the process. Review the difference between replication and interpolation in Chapter 1 if you are unsure about which method you should use.

Fig. 9.1.
A horizontal and vertical line when rotated 45 degrees must sample pixels to create the effect of rotation.

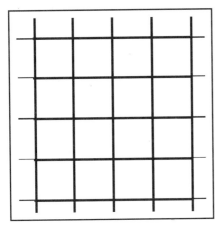

Fig. 9.1a.
Horizontal line rotated 45 degrees.

Fig. 9.1c.
An image normal.

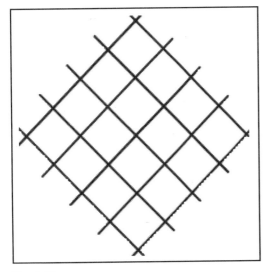

Fig. 9.1b.
Vertical line rotated 45 degrees.

Fig. 9.1d.
An image rotated 30 degrees.

No sampling need occur if you are rotating an image by 90-degree increments or flipping an image. Because you are rotating the square pixels from the edge of one side of a pixel to the next edge, there is no reason for any type of sampling. If a sampling is performed for 90-degree rotations or for flipping, the image is adding pixels. Softening occurs, and you are waiting for processing that is not necessary.

Fig. 9.2a.
Landscape orientation.

Rotating for Output

There are two types of image orientation: landscape (head left or right) and portrait (head up). Landscape is when the longer edge is the horizontal edge. Portrait is when the vertical edge is the longer edge and the top of the image is up. (See figures 9.2a and 9.2b.) Most output devices are set for portrait printing. If a printer receives information from a landscape-oriented image, the printer must turn the image to match the method of output. You will find that rotating an image page into a portrait layout before printing decreases the amount of time needed to process and output the image. The reason for the speed increase is that the Macintosh has more processing speed than most output devices. Rather than making the printer perform the work of rotating, you should rotate the image while it is still on the Mac. In general, you always should prepare the image to meet the method in which the output device prints before sending this image to the output device. Typically, a print output device outputs in the portrait layout, and film recorders output in the landscape layout.

Fig. 9.2b.
Portrait orientation.

Flipping

Flipping an image creates a mirror of the image or
selected area. Programs have the option to flip either
horizontally or vertically. (See figure 9.3a through
9.3c.) As mentioned, flipping an image should not
introduce any type of sampling. But if your program
must sample, choose replication over interpolation
because of the time-saving factor.

Fig. 9.3b.
Horizontal flip.

Fig. 9.3a.
Original image.

Fig. 9.3c.
Vertical flip.

Scaling

Scaling an image or a selected area means you are resizing the area. Usually, you have two options when you scale something. You can scale proportionally or nonproportionally. Proportionally means that you maintain the ratio between the height and width during resizing. The symmetry between the horizontal and the vertical measurements stays the same when you scale proportionally. (See figures 9.4a and 9.4b.)

Nonproportional scaling means that any resizing you perform can stretch either the width or the height without any relationship to each other. You can stretch an image solely in the vertical or solely in the horizontal direction or a combination of the two. The effect of this nonproportional scaling is usually distortion in either the horizontal or the vertical direction. Distortion can be seen easily in objects that should be perfectly round but are stretched flat or tall. (See figure 9.4c.)

Fig. 9.4b.
Scaled proportionally.

Fig. 9.4c.
Scaled but stretched horizontally.

Fig. 9.4a.
Original image.

Scaling is useful if you need to create the effect of elements that are supposed to be in relative sizes compared to one another. A person standing next to a building is a perfect example. The person does not lend to the realism of the image if the person is three or four stories tall compared to the building. Scaling either the building up or the person down keeps the proper balance between the two elements in an image. (See figures 9.5a and 9.5b.)

Fig. 9.5a.
Original image with no scaling.

Skewing

Slanting an image only on the horizontal or only on the vertical lines is skewing. You can think of skewing as italicizing an image. Skew tilts the image to an angle. You can use skewing to create a sense of perspective or to better fit an image into a scene. Skewing often is used to simulate shadows. (See figures 9.6a through 9.6c.)

Fig. 9.6a.
Original image.

Fig. 9.6b.
Horizontal skew.

Fig. 9.6c.
Vertical skew.

Fig. 9.5b.
Scaling helps produce the feeling of realism.

Perspective

Although programs enable you to distort a selection to simulate a sense of perspective, the effect is limited because there is no information in the image to actually create the real perspective of an object. Still, using perspective can be an extremely effective way of helping the parts of an image display an impression of depth. Perspective pinches pixels inward along an edge and distorts the image to create a perspective effect. (See figures 9.7a and 9.7b.)

Fig. 9.7a.
Original image.

Fig. 9.7b.
Perspective distortion applied to the image.

Production Tips

Because dynamic effects usually take an enormous amount of processing time, we recommend that you work with a low resolution version of your image and experiment with the effects you want to perform before applying them to a high-res file. Although you will not be able to use the low-resolution information, the time you save waiting for processing to occur enables you to experiment with many options. If you work only with the high-res file, you will find that the processing time limits the number of variations with which you can experiment. One program, ColorStudio, offers a unique approach to implementing dynamic effects. The dynamic effects are applied to a screen version of the image areas selected. This process enables you to experiment quickly with many different options. Then, after all your decisions on scaling, rotation, and skewing are made, you start the processing and the program performs all the complicated computation to achieve the desired effects. Although you still need to wait for processing, you greatly reduce the time spent on experimenting with different effects because you do not have to wait for every individual rotation or scaling to process. Even with ColorStudio, you first should experiment with low-resolution files to decide the best effects for your image and then apply those effects later on your high-resolution file. (See figure 9.8.)

Fig. 9.8.
In one hour you can try several versions of an effect on a lo-res file but only one or two versions on a high-res file. (Each clock face represents one image version.)

Conclusion

Producing a quick sketch or rough draft always has been necessary to help formulate ideas. More traditional methods of hand layout and retouching always have required well-thought-out plans and experimentation to find the best possible solution to producing a particular job.

Working on the Macintosh should not change this important process of creating a plan of action. If you have established a blueprint of how to assemble your concept, you will waste less time waiting for an image to be processed.

You very well could spend hours waiting for an effect to be completed, only to find that the result is less than desired. Usually this disappointment occurs when you do not have the luxury of additional time to try something different. A low-resolution version of your image provides the quick-sketch environment you need to plan your project.

The concept of working with lo-res files for experimenting is even more evident in the next chapter, which discusses special effects created by filters.

Filtering Effects

ilters alter the wave form of a raster line of pixels with a numeric matrix (algorithm) and change those pixel values into a new wave form and new pixel values, resulting in a new image. More simply, filters adjust the values of a pixel or group of pixels based on a mathematical formula that can result in visually fantastic effects. When you begin to understand how a filter works, you can apply that knowledge to an effective use of filtering.

Introduction to Filters

The term *filtering* refers to the action of removing unwanted substances by passing them through a porous substance. Passing pixels through a digital filter is similar to using a real filter because the digital filter removes unwanted pixel values. The digital filter adjusts pixel values in much the same way sound filters remove unwanted frequencies. If you are familiar with sound, you realize that filters often are used to remove undesirable noise from a sound wave. Filters used with digital images work in a similar way.

The distribution of pixel values in an image is described by a histogram. As the name implies, a histogram shows the current history of an image. (See figures 10.1a and 10.1b.) A histogram is the number of pixels that fall within a certain value range. An entire image can be described as a histogram, which is a graphic representation of the distribution of like-valued pixels within a given image. A histogram shows the distribution of the RGB values or the distribution of a specific color. No matter on what values the histogram is based, the corresponding pixel values in the digital image are represented graphically.

Fig. 10.1a.
An image.

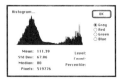

Fig. 10.1b.
The histogram of the image's values.

The values of pixels easily are adjusted by color correction methods and painting. Filters simply represent another way of altering pixel values with those value changes based on formulas. Figures 10.2a through 10.2c show a blur filter used several times on the same image. The histogram of the image, in figure 10.3, shows how the values of the pixels are

bunching into one range of values. The histogram shows that the image's pixel values are becoming more alike as the effect of blurring increases. (See figures 10.2 through 10.5.) The math can be complex, but it is not necessary to discuss the specific algorithms to understand how a filter works. If you become more interested, there are avenues that enable you to create your own filters.

Fig. 10.2a.
The original image.

Fig. 10.2b.
The image blurred.

Fig. 10.2c.
The image over-blurred.

Fig. 10.4a.
The original image.

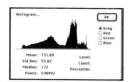

Fig. 10.3a.

Fig. 10.3.
The histogram shows how the values of the image change when blurred.

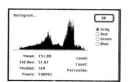

Fig. 10.3b.

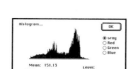

Fig. 10.3c.

Fig. 10.4b.
The image sharpened.

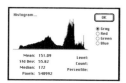

Fig. 10.5a.

Fig. 10.5.
The histogram shows how the values of the image change when sharpened.

Fig. 10.5b.

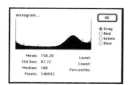

Fig. 10.5c.

Fig. 10.4c.
The image over-sharpened.

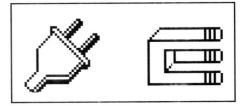

Catch a Wave

The pattern of waves is predictable, but each wave has its own identity. Filters similarly are very predictable, but each filter with a new image produces unique results. Like the surfer who learns the nature of waves and how tides and the time of day affect surf conditions, those of you who ride the pixel waves have more success when you understand the mathematical tides that create the waves of filters. Understanding what a filter does to your images is important. This understanding helps make your rides more intense.

Many filters are static, meaning the filter has only one setting. Other filters have adjustable variables that determine the intensity of the filter. Each filter with variables prompts you if variables need to be input. We discuss some of the most widely used filters and their uses later in this chapter.

Plug-In Filters

Many programs on the Macintosh accept plug-in filters. A plug-in filter is a separate module written separately from the main program, but it is literally plugged into the program, usually by placing the plug-in module in a specific folder. The plug-in feature of Photoshop filters, which has been adopted by many other programs, is a useful way of incorporating custom filters. Many third-party developers create specialty filters for use with programs that accept plug-in filters. A third-party developer is a company that creates additions to existing programs to enhance the performance of the main program. Aldus, which markets Gallery Effects plug-in filters, is one such company.

Both Photoshop and ColorStudio provide methods of creating custom filters within their programs. Being

able to create your own filters using a matrix of numbers called a convol enables you to create unique filtering systems. Understanding how the filters work could make it extremely useful for you to have someone write a filter for you or to write one yourself. (See figure 10.6.)

Fig. 10.6.
Icons of plug-in filters.

Production and Creative Filters

Filters are classified into two major types: production filters and creative filters. *Production filters* are used to specifically improve the reproduction quality of the image. *Creative filters* are used to create effects that do not necessarily contribute to improving the reproduction quality of the image. A production filter obviously can be used for creative effects, but many filters have specific production uses you should be aware of.

Filter "More" Options

There are "more" filters that basically take a simple filter—for example, blur—and apply it a fixed number of times. For example, using a "blur more" filter might be equal to using the regular blur three times. When you know that one pass of a filter is not enough, the "more" option works well.

Gaussian Distribution

Many filters offer the option of using a Gaussian distribution curve. A Gaussian curve resembles a bell curve. This mathematical distribution produces an overall higher quality effect for the filter used because the distribution of the effect is based on the distribution of the pixel values. A simple linear distribution is faster, but in many cases, the quality of a complex Gaussian distribution of data is worth the additional processing time.

Experiment

With all filters, testing with extremes gives you an idea of how the filter actually is manipulating your image. In the case of blur filters, if you use the blur filter on the same image over and over, the filter eventually produces a flat blob of one color. Without a doubt, the most useful exercise is to repeatedly apply the same filter to an image until you have a firm grasp of the filter (not to mention that it actually can be fun to see the resulting effects of filter excess!).

Production Filters

Blur Filters

Blur filters average values of a selected area of pixels. The blur filters, which soften an image, are extremely useful when you are trying to create continuity between different images or elements. If you use the blur filter too much, you risk losing texture and depth in an image. (See figures 10.7a through 10.7d.)

Fig. 10.7a.
The original image.

Fig. 10.7b.
The image with regular blur.

Fig. 10.7c.
The image with Gaussian blur.

Fig. 10.7d.
The image with motion blur.

The Gaussian blur filter uses the bell-shaped distribution mentioned earlier. This distribution regards the values that exist in the image and decides which pixels to blur by what amount. For example, a pixel near the lower part of the Gaussian bell curve would not be averaged as much as one at the peak of the bell curve.

Motion blur filters create a sense of movement, producing effects much like photographs of racing cars in which the car seems in motion because of blurring in one direction. Motion blur filters ask for the direction of movement to produce a sense of motion.

Fig. 10.8a.
Sharpen.

Sharpen Filters

Sharpen filters increase the contrast between the values of neighboring pixels. In general, sharpen filters should be used only when you want to accentuate the differences between one color area and another. (See figures 10.8a through 10.8c.) Typically, for high-contrast applications, these areas involve edges. But you may want to use a sharpen filter to accentuate the grain in wood or the texture in stucco. The amount of sharpness is determined by the subject you sharpen. Subjects with flesh tones or blends of color should be kept smooth and not sharpened, whereas subjects with defined edges such as product shots or buildings can benefit from sharpening. If a sharpen filter is used on a flat tonal area of color, you usually produce an undesirable patterned effect.

Fig. 10.8b.
Sharpen more.

Some of the most useful sharpen filters include the filters that detect edges and apply the contrast sharpening only to those edges. A sharpen edges filter does this adequately, but the most useful sharpen filter by far is the unsharp masking filter.

Fig. 10.8c.
Sharpen too much.

Unsharp Masking

Unsharp masking is an unusual name for a filter. The name is borrowed from the traditional process of photographic film separations. When color separations are made photographically, masks are created to enhance high-contrast edge sharpness. These masks exaggerate the contrast at the edge, which makes the edge look sharper. The photographic masks then are made intentionally "unsharp" along the edges. This unsharpness creates more visually pleasing edges but retains the high-contrast edge. The method was incorporated into the first high-end electronic scanners with its name, unsharp masking, following along.

With modern retouching programs on the Macintosh, you can produce the same unsharp mask effect. (See figures 10.9a through 10.9d.) The unsharp filter seeks out edges and sharpens only those areas of high contrast. For example, a subject with both products and flesh tones should be adjusted so there is plenty of sharpness in the product without adversely affecting the flesh tone. Too much sharpening destroys the realism of the reproduction. Food looks plastic and eyelashes look razor sharp. Extreme sharpening also creates strange halos of color around the edges of an image. A *halo* is an area of contrast surrounded by an area of opposite contrast, such as white around a black edge. If sharpness is applied correctly, you do not notice it.

Fig. 10.9a.
The original image.

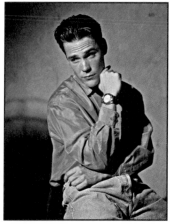

Fig. 10.9b.
The image with perfect unsharpness.

Fig. 10.9c.
Too much unsharpness with halos appearing.

Fig. 10.9d.
Far too much unsharpness.

Noise Filters

Filters that randomly mix pixel values are called noise filters. Like blur filters, noise filters have normal and Gaussian distribution methods. And like blur filters, the Gaussian takes longer to process. Noise filters create some very interesting texture effects, but the most productive and useful way of using the noise filter is with blends of color.

Digital blends are so perfect that when they are reproduced you notice bands of color where the tones change from one to another. This occurrence is called "banding." Your eyes are tuned to finding patterns; they easily can pick up the patterns of digital blends. To create smoother, more realistic blends of color, you need to interrupt the predictable patterns of a blend. A noise filter breaks apart the pattern very effectively. By simply mixing up the values of the pixels, the noise filter helps create a more realistic and believable blend. (See figures 10.10a through 10.10d.) A noise filter gives you the option of producing noise at a certain percentage. For most blends of color, 5 to 10 percent is adequate. More than 10 percent noise starts to create a graininess that distracts from the blend itself. As with most production filters, if you have used the filter correctly you do not notice that a filter was used.

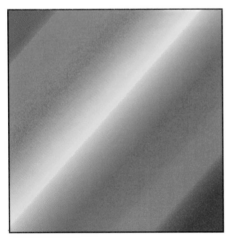

Fig. 10.10a.
A digital blend.

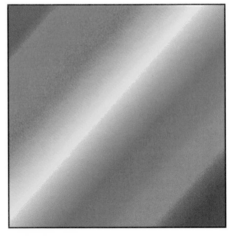

Fig. 10.10b.
Noise added 5 percent.

Fig. 10.10c.
Noise added 10 percent.

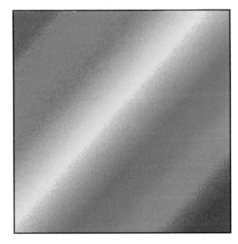

Fig. 10.10d.
Noise added 15 percent.

Recommendations

Before applying any filter to a high-resolution file, experiment with the particular filter using a lower-resolution version of the file. When you get the overall effect you desire, apply the same filter to the larger high-res file. The time you save waiting for processing is substantial, and you can try many more variations before deciding on the one that works best.

Most production filter effects are most effective after you have experimented with them all the way through to final output. Eventually, you reach a level of comfort where you easily can predict what the filters will do to your image.

Creative Filters

The skill in using filters comes from experimentation. With that in mind, we will stop talking and let the following examples show the typical effects created by creative filters. To slightly alter a quote from Steve Martin, "Talking about *filters* is like dancing about architecture."

Conclusion

With any digital effect, the more you know about the program's function and its effect on the image, the more you can control the effect for your own purposes. Remember to experiment with the filters on lo-res files before applying the filters to large files, which take longer to process. To better understand filters, apply the same filter several times to the same area to see what actually is going on.

A useful method for viewing a filter effect is to apply the filter and then immediately use the undo command several times to flip back and forth to view the filter effect before and after. This method is extremely useful when you are using very subtle effects you may not immediately see. Another powerful method of viewing how a filter works is to zoom in to see the individual pixels and observe how each pixel reacts to the filter.

The next chapter displays examples of digital artwork on the Macintosh, and it comments on future implications of digital art.

CHARCOAL

TWIRL

DARKEN STROKE

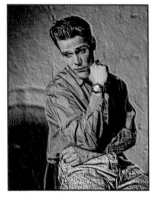

EMBOSS

ORIGINAL

PHOTO: AHMET SIBDIALSAU

MOSAIC

POINTILLIST

GRAIN

WATERCOLOR

RADIAL ZOOM

TRACE EDGES

PIXELATE

TURBULENCE

RIPPLE

FRACTAL TURBULENCE

GRAPHIC PEN

TEXTURE RIPPLE

POND RIPPLE

RECT TO POLAR

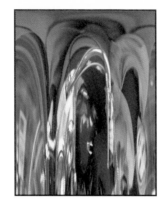

POLAR TO RECT

TURBULENCE

SPATTER

ORIGINAL

PHOTO: AHMET SIBDIALSAU

FIND EDGES

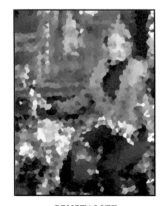

CRYSTALIZE

SPHERIZE

DARK STROKE

RADIAL ZOOM

GRAPHIC PEN

CHARCOAL

EMBOSS

FRACTAL TURBULENCE

GRAIN

WATERCOLOR

TILE

POINTILLIST

147

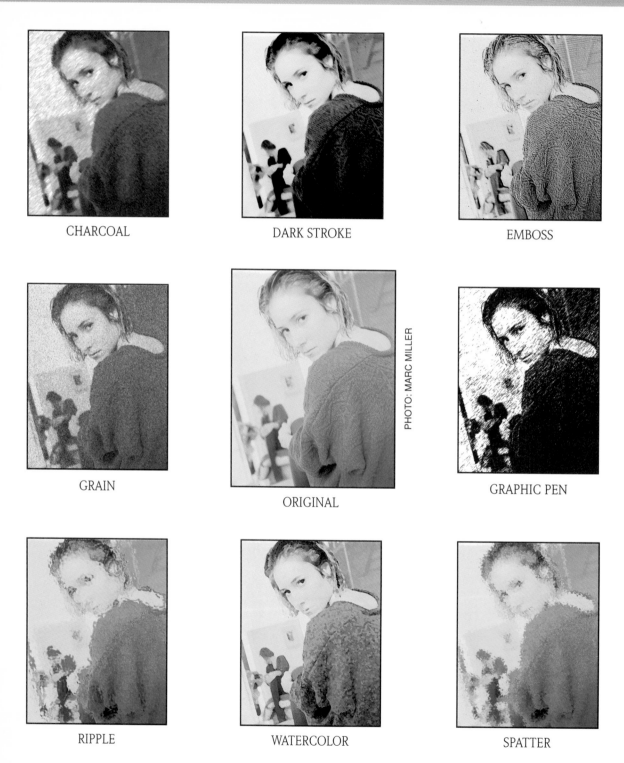

CHARCOAL

DARK STROKE

EMBOSS

GRAIN

ORIGINAL

PHOTO: MARC MILLER

GRAPHIC PEN

RIPPLE

WATERCOLOR

SPATTER

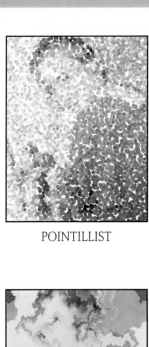

POINTILLIST

PIXELATE

TURBULENCE

FRACTAL TURBULENCE

FIND EDGES

RADIAL ZOOM

TILES

TEXTURE RIPPLE

POOL RIPPLE

11

Gallery of Images

The images presented on the following pages are from a number of artists working with the digital medium. The artists all have different styles and methods but the one common thread is their use of the digital medium provided by the Macintosh computer.

Artists have always used technology to expand the boundaries of art. From a historical perspective the meeting of technology and art is nothing new. Technology has always played a natural part in the practice of art, in many cases, more easily than it does today. The sheer volume and rapid change of technology can be overwhelming at times, but the thought of a new renaissance so blinding we can not fully recognize the future implications is thrilling. Artists are only now beginning to tap into the present zeitgeist and discovering the styles, feelings and emotions digital expressionism provides to the experience of art.

The processes each artist goes through to produce a work are as varied as the works themselves. To mention each particular piece of software would run counter to the belief that the images should stand on their own and not be unintentionally influenced by the software of choice. Different software programs provide different tools, and often it is necessary for an artist to use several software programs to produce a work. Seldom does a writer need to mention the word processor used to write a story. The story stands ultimately separate from the tools used to produce it.

The methods used by the artists are as varied as the styles—many incorporate scanned photos, objects, or sketches; many are completely drawn on the Mac; other images are unique mixtures of both.

Each artist relies not only on knowledge and experience but on a sense of discovery. It is proper to say that each artist possesses his or her own vision, and desire to leap ahead and explore the meanings of digital art. We hope you enjoy the explorations of these artists and hope that you also will participate in the discovery of art, either through digital artists or through your own exploration.

Kate
© *Chelsea*
Sammel 1991,
San Leandro, CA

Assimilation
Hagit Cohen
San Francisco, CA
© *Hands On Media 1991*

Raging Pencil
© *John Derry 1991*
San Francisco, CA

Abbey Road1, © *John Derry 1991*

Tulips in Window
© *Chelsea Sammel 1991*

America
Hagit Cohen
© *Hands On Media 1991*

Chesty
© *John Derry 1991*

Facade1, © *John Derry 1991*

stevie1
© *Larry Cohn 1991*
Los Angeles, CA

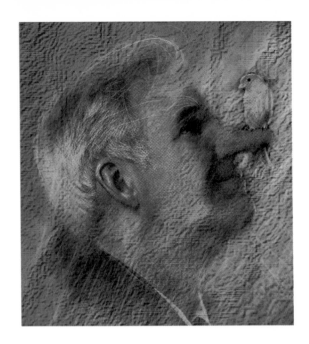

Anne's Friend
© *Chelsea Sammel 1991*

156

The First Time I Saw My Father
Hagit Cohen
© *Hands On Media 1991*

Venice1, © *John Derry 1991*

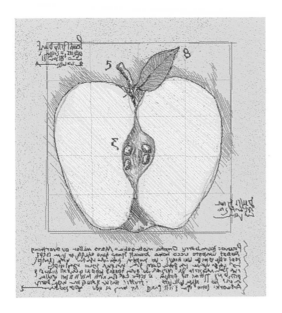

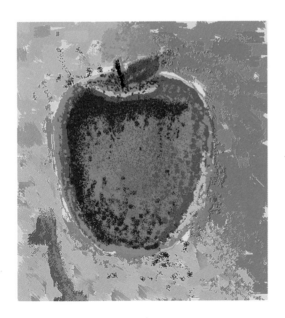
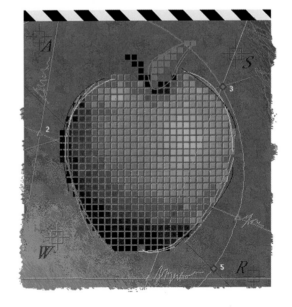

Apples © *John Derry* 1988

Spider-women
Hagit Cohen
© *Warner New Media 1991*

Spider-sun rise
Hagit Cohen
© *Warner New Media 1991*

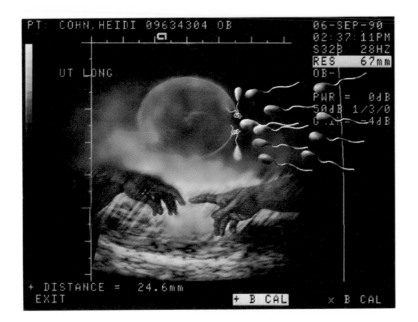

On the Way
© *Larry Cohn 1991*

Wave
© *Larry Cohn 1991*

Dreams, *©John Derry/Marc Miller1992*

Maori-men die
Hagit Cohen
© *Warner New Media*

Family Wave, *© Marc D. Miller 1992*

Eurynome, *Hagit Cohen ©Warner New Media 1991*

Bridgeman
© *John Derry/Marc Miller 1991*

Second Front
© *Marc D. Miller 1992*

Compass, © *John Derry 1991*

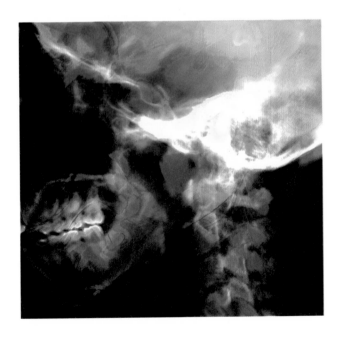

Skull Exp12
© *Larry Cohn 1991*

Paint Flow, © *Marc D. Miller 1992*

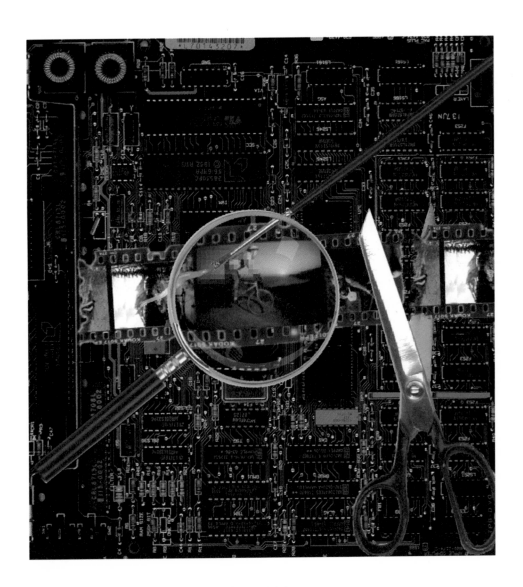

Artisan Tools, © *Marc D. Miller 1992*

Preparing Digital Images for Output

No greater emphasis can be placed on preparing a course of action before you embark on any journey of color reproduction. You must lay out your travel plans to get to your destination. Plan ahead the roads you want to take, and keep a road map with you at all times to ensure that you do not lose your way. You may find you can reach your destination without a map or plan, but your journey may end somewhere you had not intended. Travelers who plan a trip by having enough fuel and a knowledge of which roads to take succeed in reaching their intended destinations.

Plan Your Trip, Fuel Up, and Take a Map

The first and most important part of preparing for image output is deciding what type of output you want. You can consider the type of output your destination. During the course of a trip you may want to visit several destinations, which is like producing different types of output at different sizes. Making these stops is not a problem *if* you decide on all your possible destinations *before* you start your trip. If you do not, you may run out of fuel during your trip.

Having enough fuel to complete a journey is of paramount importance. The amount of pixel information you have in your images is the fuel to take you wherever you want to go. Obviously, the more fuel or pixels you have, the further you can go. But if your destination is close and your trip is short, the additional fuel does nothing but weigh you down. Having the perfect amount of fuel to reach your destination ensures that you run at top speed and peak efficiency.

Take your map and follow it. Guessing often leads to wrong turns and longer trips. You may be tempted to go exploring; that is fine if no one is waiting for you at the destination. Deadlines mean that following your map is imperative. Go exploring when you have time and no one is expecting your arrival. The following sections discuss some of your possible destinations, the fuel you need, and the maps you should follow.

Where Do You Want to Go?

The type of output to produce is the first decision you must make. There is no limit to the kind, size, or amount. Print, film transparency, and video display are the three most common types of output. There also are variations of printing, transparency, and video output. Each of these types has special associated concerns.

Every output choice has three primary considerations: final output size, the number of pixels (resolution), and the color information. We will follow the path of each type of output and address each of the three concerns.

Video Display (Monitors)

A monitor has a fixed number of display elements. These elements match one to one, pixel for pixel, during display. When you are transferring images for display on monitors or video, the only pixel resolution consideration is the total number of pixels the monitor can display. You simply match that number to create a continuous tone image.

Standard NTSC television monitors have 525 lines or pixels by 480. PAL, the European standard, has 625 lines by 480. Apple 13-inch monitors have 640 by 480 pixels. An image file you want to display on an Apple 13-inch monitor simply needs to be 640 pixels across by 480 pixels down. This number of pixels results in the best quality full-screen continuous tone image. More than the required pixel information is not displayed and therefore is not necessary. Less than the required pixel information for full-screen display results in pixelization. (See figure 12.1.) Because monitors display color with RGB, there is no need for any color conversion to the file.

Fig. 12.1.
Continuous appearance when pixels match one to one. Pixelization occurs when the number of pixels is less than the monitor's full capability.

Film Transparency

Files that eventually will be reproduced to transparency film require very high resolutions because of the fine grain used in photographic film. Like video displays, film recording devices have a fixed number of imaging elements. Film recorders produce their output by direct pixel imaging. *Direct pixel imaging* means that every imaging element on the output device matches to a pixel in the image file one to one. High-quality film recording devices have up to 50 imaging elements per millimeter (epmm), which is 1,270 imaging elements per inch (epi). To determine the number of pixels your image file would need for output to a transparency, you simply would match the number of imaging elements per inch to the physical size you require.

Typically, transparencies are created no more than 4x5 inches physical size. A 4x5 transparency requires an image that is 5,080 pixels by 6,350 pixels (50 ppmm; or1,270 ppi). An image this size is more than 96 megabytes. To help work with smaller files, film recorders accept digital images with a resolution of 25 ppmm or 635 ppi (2,540 pixels by 3,175 pixels for a 4x5) and interpolate the file 200 percent during imaging to reach the required resolution of 50 ppmm. This file is nearly 25 megabytes and is much smaller. Doubling a image file's resolution is a perfectly acceptable and common practice for transparency output, for which higher resolutions result in very large files. The nature of film transparencies accommodates the interpolation just fine without any loss of detail.

Just as in the monitor output, if you do not meet the required number of pixels per inch or millimeter, you risk pixelizing and not producing a continuous tone image. The images are exposed to film as RGB files so there is no need for any color conversion. The film recorder makes three passes for each color of RGB to expose the image to the transparency film.

Continuous Tone Printing

Prints that have a photographic continuous quality are called CT prints. These continuous tone prints are direct digital output, and they use the same method of imaging as transparency output does. Continuous tone output devices that create photo-realistic output do not use halftone dots. Each imaging element on the output device matches with each pixel in the image file to produce a printed picture element. (See figure 12.2.)

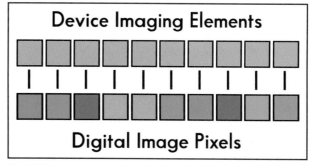

Fig. 12.2.
With direct pixel imaging, 10 digital image pixels will match with 10 imaging elements of the output device.

These prints are created using a dye sublimation process. Thermal dyes of CMY are transferred to paper by the heat generated by the imaging element. The amount of heat generated is dependent on the amount of electrical energy sent to the heating elements. The electrical energy varies based on the color values in the digital file. The amount of dye transferred to the paper is proportional to the amount of heat generated by the heating element. In color printing the paper makes three passes, receiving the dye of each color of CMY. The dyes are transparent, allowing a mixing of color to occur to produce the various colors in an image.

Typically, CT printers have between 200 and 300 elements per inch (epi). So for every physical inch of output, you require 200 to 300 pixels. For a CT printer with 300 epi and a maximum printing size of 8 inches by 10 inches, an image file 2,400 pixels by 3,000 pixels is required to produce a continuous tone image at 8 inches by 10 inches. Because the prints are created using the CMY color, the complements of RGB, there is no need for a four-color conversion to CMYK.

Halftone Printing

Halftone printing output involves special considerations not present in the previous three types of output. Halftone printing is the most economical and efficient method of reproducing large quantities of hard-copy color images. The per-unit cost on a printing press is pennies compared to the cost on previous types of output. The low cost helps make halftone printing the most common and widely used method of reproduction in the world. Knowing how to produce high-quality film output is critical to color reproduction success. Even if you are not involved directly in the film preparation but only are providing digital files to someone who is preparing the halftone film output, understanding the needs of halftone reproduction will help you avoid potential quality problems. (See Chapter 14, "The Basics of Four-Color Process Separations.")

The halftone printing process uses a series of various-sized halftone dots to create the illusion of varying tone. These halftone dots are created by a matrix of the imaging elements present in the output device. The number of imaging elements per inch determines the potential quality of the halftone dot. The higher the quality of the halftone dot, the higher the quality of the output.

Line Screen Frequency

When deciding to create halftone dots, you first must consider the line screen frequency. The *line screen* is the number of halftone dots per square inch (dpi). Line screen also is referred to as lines per inch (lpi). The number of halftone dots per inch determines a matrix of how many of the imaging elements in the entire output device are available to create a single dot. Figure 12.3 illustrates how the elements of an imagesetter or a plotter create a halftone dot.

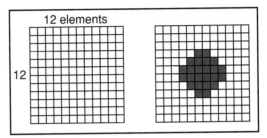

Fig. 12.3.
A matrix of imaging elements is the basic grid for creating a halftone dot.

You can determine the potential matrix for a halftone dot by dividing the total number of imaging elements per inch (epi) by the planned line screen ruling. The more elements in a matrix, the more continuous the halftone dot. A matrix of 16x16 image elements or more is considered a good-quality halftone dot. For example, a 300-dpi printer creating halftone dots with 100 line screen (100 lpi or dpi) has a matrix of three by three image elements per halftone dot.

A 2,400 epi printer creating halftone dots for 150 line screen (150 lpi or dpi) has a matrix of 16 by 16 image elements per halftone dot.

Figure 12.4 shows how the matrix that creates a halftone dot can be determined based on the epi of the output device you use.

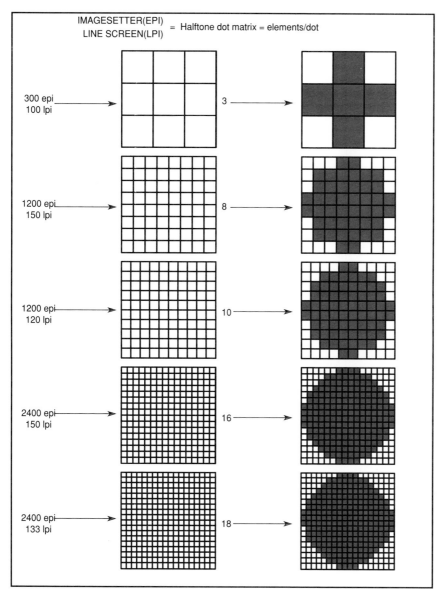

Fig 12.4.
The quality of the halftone dot is determined based on the number of dots per inch (line screen) and the number of imaging elements per inch (epi) on the output device.

Understanding that a number of exposing elements make up a single halftone dot and that the number of elements per inch determines potential image quality gives you the ability to produce high-quality continuous-looking halftone images.

Pixels

As discussed in Chapter 1, "What Are Pixels?" digital images are composed of pixel information. The three previous types of direct pixel output required only a one-to-one match of pixels to available image elements. For good quality, halftone dots require more than a one-to-one relationship with pixel information. With halftone printing, the number of pixels required is determined by the line screen used. The most common and simple method is to double the number of the line screen to get the number of pixels per inch (ppi) you to need to produce a continuous tone image without any apparent pixelization.

So if you print with a line screen of 150 halftone dots per square inch, you need to double that number to determine the number of image pixels you need—in this case, 300 pixels per square inch (ppi). This then means that an image file containing 300 pixels across and 300 pixels down can be reproduced accurately with a 150-line screen one inch across and one inch down.

Using less than double the line screen does not necessarily mean the quality will be diminished, only that doubling is near optimum. (See figure 12.5.) Many images will not suffer greatly with slightly less pixel information, but the quality of the image will not increase if you have substantially more than double the pixel information. Using more than double the line screen for print output is usually a waste of file space and does not contribute to making the image quality any higher. However, in some critically high-quality cases, the sampling rate for halftone output used is 2.25 to 2.5:1. This often is done when the epi of the output device is not known or when a cushion to ensure a high-quality level is required.

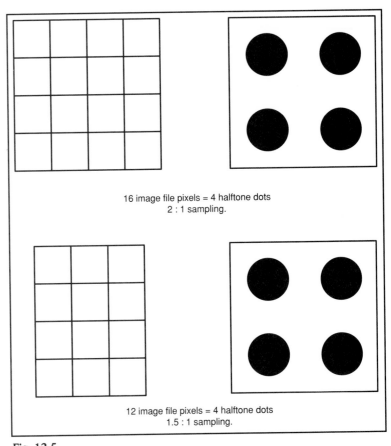

16 image file pixels = 4 halftone dots
2 : 1 sampling.

12 image file pixels = 4 halftone dots
1.5 : 1 sampling.

Fig. 12.5.
The sampling rate of 2:1 pixels to halftone dots is a standard, but for lower quality requirements a sampling rate of 1.5:1 often is used.

The very common number 300 ppi did not drop out of the sky. Rather, as digital images were expanded in the late '70s, metric units were the standard measure used. Twelve pixels per millimeter was established as a standard for creating a continuous tone with 150 line screen. Better known as "Res 12," this number works out to exactly 304.8 pixels per inch, which has been rounded off to 300 pixels per inch for 150 line screen. (When working with separators using metric units, be aware of the conversion factor: 25.4 millimeters equal one inch.)

Physical Size

When you choose the number of pixels necessary for an image, the number is predicated on the size at which you ultimately will reproduce this image. The size at which you output an image is the next determination for the amount of information necessary to complete the job properly. As previously mentioned, the need to match the necessary pixel information to the output pixel requirements is important for retaining a high-quality image reproduction. To determine the total number of pixels required, you need the final physical output size of your reproduction.

If you do not know what size your final output will be or if you plan on a number of different sizes, always choose the largest possible size you will output and work from there. For example, if you want to print an image 5 by 6 inches at a line screen of 150 (lpi or dpi), you need 300 pixels per inch (ppi) and therefore 1,500 pixels across and 1,800 pixels down. If you plan on smaller output or output at different line screens, simply resample the 1,500-by-1,800-pixel file to the desired number of pixels. The following calculations show how the physical size of your output determines the total number of pixels you will need:

Physical size of output x Sampling rate (pixels to halftone dots normally 1.5 or 2.0) x Line screen frequency = total # of pixels required

Or:

(5 inches) x (2.0 x 150 lpi) = 1,500 pixels wide

(6 inches) x (2.0 x 150 lpi) = 1,800 pixels high

Remember to keep a copy of the original file whenever you perform any type of resampling. This ensures that the best possible source material always is available for you to work with in case resampling is required again. You never should resample an image more than once if you can avoid doing so.

Separation Film

The last requirement for halftone printing is the type of film you need. Because the color space for halftone printing is cyan, magenta, yellow, and black (CMYK), you need a set of film for each color. Chapter 14 discusses the special requirements of four-color printing.

Checklist

Each of the three types of output has different requirements for resolution.

Before addressing any of the production concerns, you must have the proper source material. If you do not start with enough pixel information, the likelihood of quality output is diminished.

If you require your image to be used for more than one type of output—for example, print and video—always prepare the file for the output that requires more pixel information first and then resample the file to the output that needs less pixel information. In this case you would meet the requirement of print first, then video.

Check each of the following steps before starting work on an image:

1. Decide on your output device and reproduction process.

2. Determine the final size or sizes at which you will reproduce the image.

3. Based on the output device's requirements, determine the number of pixels per inch you need.

4. If the number of pixels of your source file is less than required, resample the file by no more than 200 percent to retain the highest quality of the image.

When in doubt, use more than enough pixels. A good barber always can cut away more hair if you want your hair shorter, but it's extremely hard to put the hair back after it has been cut. Likewise, you always can take away pixels, but the quality decreases when you try to put them back.

Appendix F, "Image Pixel Resolution Requirements," gives you exactly the amount of pixel information you need for highest quality output for different devices. The next chapter discusses preparing object-based images such as Postscript for conversion to a bitmap and eventually output.

Converting Images to Bitmaps

he advent of PostScript brought the world of objects to the Macintosh. The differences between objects and bitmaps always seemed to have been difficult to understand and more difficult to explain. Objects and their relationship to bitmaps are important because both environments offer unique advantages.

Vector-Based Objects

As mentioned in Chapter 1, "What Are Pixels?" *objects* are vector-based drawings and shapes. *Vectors* are lines defined by points and connected by formulas. Whereas a pixel represents a fixed location-area, a point describes only a location. Points on an object have a location but no area until output. Without a specific area to describe, objects easily are resized without any resolution considerations. Because of the lack of resolution considerations, objects are considered resolution independent. *Resolution independent* means that regardless of output size, the continuous quality of objects remains the same.

PostScript type is a common object-based element often scaled to many different sizes while retaining its quality, whether the type is small, such as 10 point, or large, such as 72 point. (See figure 13.1.) You can resize and change any object freely without loss of relative quality. With this flexibility in mind, why would you use anything but objects to create images? The primary reason surfaces when you are dealing with color.

PostScript Type

a b c d e f g h i

A B C D E F G H

Fig. 13.1.
PostScript type is the most common use for objects.

Using objects to define more elaborate color such as continuous tones or blends has disadvantages. The complexity of the formulas to create color are so great that the file sizes become large and often completely unmanageable. The size also increases the processing time required to output. Color used in objects typically is limited to spot colors and simple blends, although blends created solely with objects often result in steps or bands of color.

The complexity of color makes objects a poor choice for dealing with photographic images. The bitmap is better equipped to handle and produce vignettes and blends of colors. A bitmap simulates how you see the world and images. Every image you see is made of particles. You can go as far as the atom to understand that everything is composed of groups of individual elements. Because you instinctively can understand this concept, working with picture elements is more natural than you first may believe.

The difference between object points and pixels is like the difference between line copy and halftone dots. Type, logos, graphs, and diagrams are objects with sharp edges and no continuous tones. These objects are reproduced best as lines.

Photos, color paintings, color wash, and shaded areas are pixel-based images with continuous tones. These images are reproduced best using continuous tone methods such as direct pixel imaging and halftones.

Objects deal best with outlines and shapes; bitmaps, with color and blends. An ideal solution would be to bring the two together. This combination first was introduced to the Macintosh by ColorStudio. Both ColorStudio and Photoshop now incorporate PostScript objects into digital image pixel bitmaps.

Raster Image Processing (RIP)

Contrary to the feelings of many persons who have waited long hours for their printed output, RIP does not stand for "rest in peace." The term *RIP* or *RIPing* is used to indicate the process of converting digital information into physical output. Each horizontal line of a bitmap's pixel information can be referred to as a scan line or raster line. Raster images are therefore images with lines of pixels. The simplest output devices accept only one raster line at a time, then image that line to film or paper. A more complete method is to have an entire image sampled and have a processor convert all the necessary information into printable output. The method of converting digital information into output is called raster image processing (RIP). The processing of an image is independent of the specific type of output.

All types of output, as noted in Chapter 1, are some form of bitmap imagery. No matter how smooth an image is, it still is composed of individual parts. The digital information of PostScript objects does not have these individual bits of information, only points. Whenever you output PostScript-based information, the objects or vector lines must be converted into raster bits or elements of printed data. RIPing is the action of converting the objects into printed material and, in many cases, into halftone dots for printing. A RIP also is used to convert objects into digital bitmap pixels and bitmap pixels into printed output. (See figures 13.2a through 13.2c.)

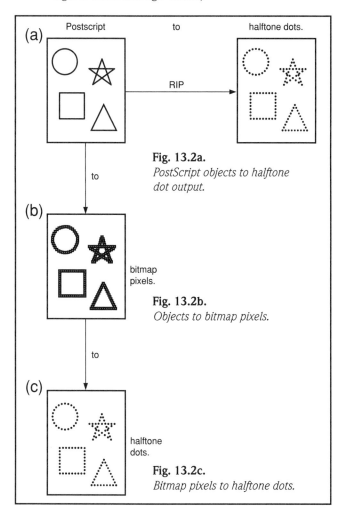

(a) Postscript to halftone dots.

RIP

Fig. 13.2a.
PostScript objects to halftone dot output.

to

(b)

bitmap pixels.

Fig. 13.2b.
Objects to bitmap pixels.

to

(c)

halftone dots.

Fig. 13.2c.
Bitmap pixels to halftone dots.

The RIPing process is complex, and much of an output device's rating is based on the image processing speed. The speed of the PostScript interpreter or RIP is a big factor in the efficiency of the entire reproduction process.

Because the PostScript objects need to be converted first to raster information and then to halftone dots, in general, the RIP process of converting pixel-based, bitmap color images to halftone dots is faster than the process of converting PostScript-based color images into halftone dots. Also, there are output devices such as film recorders that image pixels directly and do not have any PostScript RIPing capabilities. For non-PostScript printing devices, you can output only bitmap images.

Object Rendering

Objects created using PostScript information can be imported and rendered into a pixel bitmap. Rendering or rastering is similar to the term RIPing. *Render* describes the process of interpreting vector image information into bitmap pixel image information. (See figures 13.3a and 13.3b.) The RIP process of converting PostScript objects into a bitmap has two requirements: the image resolution and alias or anti-alias edges. First you must determine at what pixel resolution the objects should be rendered. Because objects are resolution independent, there is no restriction on the amount of resolution you can decide to have. Base your decision on the guidelines outlined in Chapter 12, "Preparing Images for Output." Remember, the higher the resolution, the larger the file size is and the longer the rendering process from object to bitmap takes.

Fig. 13.3a.
PostScript to lo-res bitmap.

Fig. 13.3b.
PostScript to high-res bitmap.

The next choice involves whether you want alias or anti-alias rendering. As you recall from Chapter 6, "Basic Tools and Functions," alias edges are hard edges, and anti-alias edges are softer averaged edges. (See figures 13.4a and 13.4b.) Alias rendering processes much more quickly than anti-alias rendering, which is more complex. In most cases, especially with blends of color and curved edges, you will want anti-alias rendering, but there are some notable exceptions. When you are working with images that are a very high resolution (above 500 ppi), PostScript outlines used for type look better with a sharper aliased edge. Without high resolution, though, the edges may look pixelized and ragged, and anti-aliased edges should be used. Straight horizontal and vertical lines do not benefit from anti-aliasing; they look better with aliased rendering. (See figures 13.5a and 13.5b.) Flat-colored objects with few

curved edges are also candidates for the quicker processing speed of alias rendering. Anti-alias rendering always is used for type in video displays, because type and edges on video always are more visually pleasing with soft edges. (See figures 13.6a and 13.6b.) For more information on the difference between aliasing and anti-aliasing, see Chapter 6.

Fig. 13.4a.
Alias rendered edges.

Fig. 13.4b.
Anti-alias rendered edges.

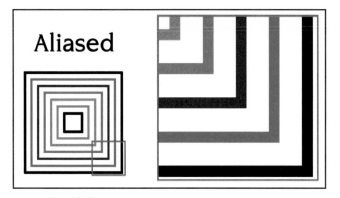

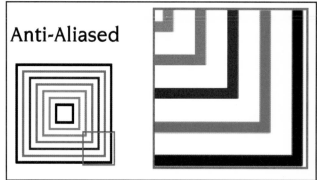

Fig. 13.5a.
Horizontal and vertical lines, rendered alias.

Fig. 13.5b.
Horizontal and vertical lines, rendered anti-alias.

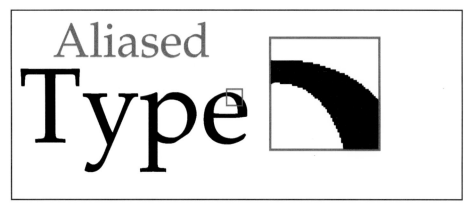

Fig. 13.6a.
Type with alias rendered edges.

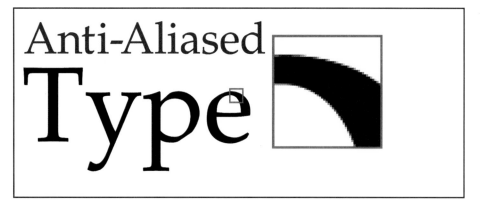

Fig. 13.6b.
Type with anti-alias rendered edges.

Objects As Masks

Because you can render objects with soft anti-aliased edges, objects are excellent for creating masks. Rendering an object or objects into a mask channel rather than into the image channel creates a mask based on that object. (See figure 13.7.) As seen in Chapter 8, "Merging and Collaging Images," soft-edge masks provide a much higher quality than masks with hard aliased edges.

Object Blends

Objects are extremely useful for creating transitional steps between two objects. In this process, often called in-betweening or "tweening," two or more objects can metamorphose into a sequence of intermediate steps from one object to another. Blends of color often are created using a tweening process. (See figures 13.8a and 13.8b.)

Blends or vignettes of color created by objects are the best candidates for rendering into a bitmap layer. Because of the complexity of color, rendering blends into a bitmap improves quality and increases the speed of eventual output. Object blends usually have a

Fig. 13.7.
Objects used as a mask.

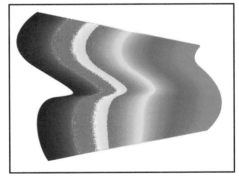

Fig. 13.8b.
Color objects can create a blend of color with tweening.

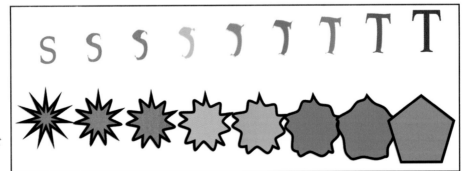

Fig. 13.8a.
Two objects that have been tweened.

problem with banding or sharp tonal steps in the color. Always render object blends using anti-aliasing. And after a blend has been rendered, use a noise filter from your image software program (5-10 percent) to break up any color bands, which are typical by-products of digital blends. Bitmap blends of color are of higher quality because you can apply filters to a bitmap image but not to objects. (See figures 13.9a and 13.9b.)

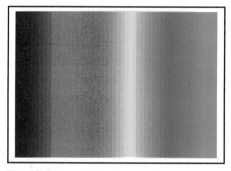

Fig. 13.9a.
An object-only blend.

Fig. 13.9b.
A bitmap-processed blend.

Conclusion

Object-based drawing programs such as Aldus Freehand, Adobe Illustrator, and ColorStudio Shapes are important elements in a creative environment. By linking objects created in a PostScript outline environment into a pixel bitmap environment, you expand your creative and production capabilities. Even if you work solely in a bitmap environment, you should understand the many capabilities object-based graphics give you. Object-based graphics are flexible and easily resizable. Curves and lines are quickly created and adjusted. Object-based drawing enables you to create intermediate steps between two or more groups of objects.

Whether or not you use vector-based objects such as PostScript in your drawing environment, you still should know the best ways to reproduce these objects. Using the rendering capabilities of Photoshop and ColorStudio is an excellent method of incorporating objects into bitmaps.

Most high-end systems such as Crosfield and Scitex systems prefer to receive CT bitmap files rather than objects. Understanding the methods of rendering objects into a bitmap is important on every level of image processing.

Preparing images for eventual output is critical before the actual color reproduction is performed. The next four chapters discuss the methods of preparing images for color reproduction. The first two chapters discuss the process of color separations for processing printing, and the remaining chapters discuss film recorder output and video output.

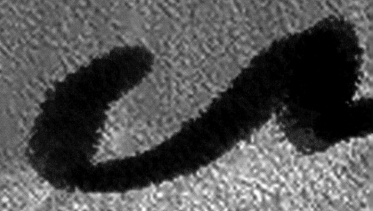

The Basics of Four-Color Process Separations

reating a CMYK output for an RGB file requires many important considerations: highlight and shadow density points, memory colors, sharpness, and gray balance. You must convert the RGB file to the proper CMYK values for the densities of the original image to get a reproduction with matching tonal steps, good gray balance, memory colors, and sharpness. This chapter addresses the CMYK halftone printing process, goals of color reproduction, and the color calibration process.

The Color Separation

When a digital file is output for use on a printing press, you must use software to create a separate film record of each printing ink color used. Typically, this 32-bit CMYK file must contain data for each of the subtractive colors: cyan, magenta, yellow, and black. These four colors are called process inks.

The process of converting a color image into the printing ink colors is called color separation. Hardware or software takes apart (separates) an original image into three color files, each representing a third of the visible spectrum of light. (See Chapter 3, "Scanning: Obtaining Color Pixels.") An additional file for the black ink printer is computed from the original 24-bit RGB data. Color data for each of the four color files is exposed to a high-contrast color separation film by an output device called a plotter or an imagesetter designed for imaging color separation film.

After the separation films are output, a prepress proof is made, which is a preliminary version of what the color images will look like on the press. Color craftspeople analyze this proof for reproduction quality and send it to the customer for approval. The alternative to a prepress proof is to press proof the job: print a small quantity of color from the separation films on the press before printing the entire number of copies the customer requires. Prepress proofs take less than an hour to make and cost much less than setting up a printing press for a short run of press proofs. Prepress proofs are used extensively in the printing industry and are available from many manufacturers. They are quick and easy to make, and they come close to matching the final appearance of the press sheet.

The next step in the reproduction process is to get the separations to the printing press. After the color separations are made, the films are exposed photographically to printing plates. The plates are mounted on a printing press, and they transfer the separated image to a printable substrate such as paper. When the subtractive CMYK plates are printed in exact position (register) on top of each other, they produce a full-color reproduction of the original image on the press. (See figure 14.1.)

The CMYK process inks combine to reproduce a wide range of colors, or color gamut, that represents all or most of the colors in the original image. The printing press house has books called color charts. Color chart books contain series of two-, three-, and four-color ink combination patches that show the color gamut of the ink set being used to print the specific job.

If the customer has a critical product color that cannot be matched by the ink set, the printer may have to run a specially formulated ink made to match that critical color (also called a spot color). In this case, an additional separation film of the color print areas must be made. Some printed products may have as many as seven inks and a varnish coating (for extra gloss), requiring eight film records to print the piece.

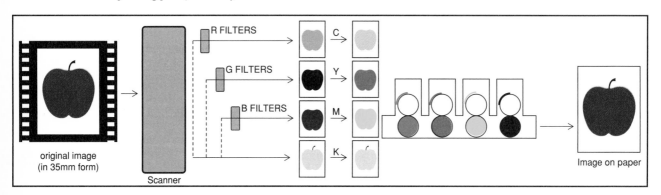

Fig. 14.1.
The color printing process.

Film Characteristics

Each color separation film represents the amount of ink that is printing in the reproduction. The color separation film image is either opaque black, metallic silver, or clear transparent acetate. If the type of film is negative, the ink prints in the clear areas. The opposite is true of positive type films: the ink prints on the black, metallic silver areas of the film.

The type of film is determined by the kind of printing plate the printer uses: negative acting or positive acting. Printing plates are selected according to the printing process and the number of prints. Also, printing plate types vary from country to country. Film type information should be supplied to the separator prior to output of the color files.

All separation film consists of two parts: a photo-sensitive layer called the *emulsion* coated on a supporting acetate layer known as the *base*. The film

emulsion direction, or image orientation, is needed before output. Emulsion direction is expressed as either image right reading emulsion down (designated as RRED) or image right reading emulsion up (designated as RREU). Right reading means the image is normal, not reversed from right to left. RRED means the image is right reading as you look at it and the emulsion is down, on the bottom side of the film.

Contacting is a procedure in which the halftone dots of one film are copied photographically to another film, usually with sections from various films to make a complete ad of text and graphic elements. The dots are copied by pressing the master film in contact with an unexposed film in a vacuum chamber and passing light through them. It is important in contacting to copy each halftone dot exactly, with no distortion of size or shape.

The emulsion-to-emulsion contacting process reverses the emulsion direction of the intermediates, making RRED final films (see figure 14.2). The best dot-to-dot reproduction is achieved by emulsion-to-emulsion (E to E) contacting. Contacting through the film's base material (E to B) spreads the exposing light and changes the size of the dots, which causes a change in the dot percentage in the new film.

Fig. 14.2.
The contacting process.

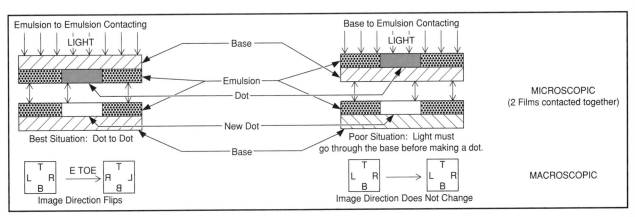

Fig. 14.2a.
Emulsion-to-emulsion contacting reverses the image direction.

Fig. 14.2b.
Emulsion-to-base contacting does not flip the image.

The required emulsion direction is determined according to the films' end use. Separation films that are directly exposed to a printing plate are called final films and must be RRED. Films that are composited with other films such as linework and text must be RREU. RREU films are reversed, presenting a mirror image of the final reproduction. Emulsion up films also are called intermediates because they are not used for platemaking and must be converted photographically (contacted) to become RRED final films.

Each separation film is a black or white (ink or no ink) record of each printing ink color. But when they are combined on the printing press, you must achieve a full-color reproduction from black to white and all shades in between. To produce a reproduction of a continuous tone image using a black and clear only set of film, you must screen the separations into dots of various sizes that represent all tonal densities from the lightest white to the darkest black. Seen with the naked eye, the screened image appears to be made of a continuous tone of ink, in the same way color images composed of pixels appear to be made of continuous tone images on the color monitor. The screened image on the separation film is called a *halftone*.

In the reproduction, the smallest halftone dots are called highlights. Highlight dots print typically from 3 to 6 percent in size and create tone and detail in the bright areas of the image. When no dots are printing, there is no detail or tone because only the pure white paper is showing. An area with no dots is called a *specular highlight.* The specular highlight is the brightest possible tone if the printing is done on paper. Reflections on water, metal, and glass are examples of specular highlights.

Dot sizes are referred to by the amount of ink they print. The quartertone dot prints 25 percent ink, the middletone dot prints 50 percent ink, and the three-quartertone dot prints 75 percent ink. Ink levels beyond 99 percent are called solids. (See figure14.3)

In addition to the type of separation film and desired emulsion direction, you must specify the number of dots per square inch before outputting a separated file. This measurement, called the *line screen ruling*, the *line screen frequency*, or the *line screen requirement*, is given in *lpi* (lines of dots per inch). Fine, intermediate, and coarse line screens are available on most output devices. A fine line screen ruling of 175 lpi can produce 30,625 dots per square inch (175 squared) and effectively reproduces fine detail and rendition smooth tones. A much lesser ruling, such as an 85 lpi, can produce only up to 7,225 dots per square inch and gives a coarser visual appearance when compared to finer screens. (See figure 14.4.)

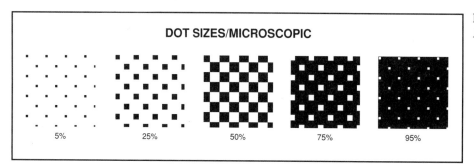

DOT SIZES/MICROSCOPIC

| 5% | 25% | 50% | 75% | 95% |

Fig. 14.3.
Magnified dot sizes.

Fig. 14.4.
The same image screened at 85 lpi, 133 lpi, and 175 lpi.

The printing method and substrate (material) on which the print is being applied determine the line screen requirement. High-quality offset printing handles finer screens such as 175 and 200, whereas silkscreen and high-speed web presses print only coarser screen rulings from 65 to 133. Coated paper stock works best with fine screens, and noncoated stock such as newsprint demands coarse screens because of its ink absorbency characteristics. (Having fewer dots per square inch compensates for the dot spreading that the ink absorption causes.)

Most separation output devices also produce dots of various shapes and configurations, such as square, round, elliptical, and chain. Square dots are the industry norm, but the other shapes produce smoother effects on *vignetting tones* (areas that gradually go from light to dark) and flesh tones.

The printer supplies line screen requirements and special dot shape information to the separator for every image separated. If this information is not given, the result may be an unprintable set of separations.

Dot quality is determined by the accuracy of the exposing light source; the quality of the optics and hardware used; the number of scan lines, or line pitch, used to image each dot; and the number of exposing elements that make each dot. The microscopic edge quality of the halftone dots has a macroscopic visual effect on the reproduction. An image made with perfectly shaped dots holds sharp detail and smoothness in delicate tones. A dot matrix that is poorly shaped or distorted causes tone breaks and looks choppy when compared to an image of good dot quality. Dot quality always should be a criteria when you are purchasing an output device.

Rosette and Moiré Problems

The CMYK dots are printed next to each other at a critical distance. You achieve this by placing each color's dots on an angle. Putting the four color dots down on different angles forms a *rosette pattern.* If you use the correct angles, the rosette dot pattern is invisible to the naked eye. Cyan 105 degrees, magenta 45 degrees, yellow 90 degrees, and black 75 degrees are commonly used angles because they create an invisible rosette for most printing applications. These angles *can* change to match a particular output device's characteristics; what is important is using a combination of screen angles that remain invisible to the naked eye and maintain a continuous tone appearance.

If the rosette pattern becomes visible, you start to see the dot pattern and a rainbow effect because the different color dots do not become visible equally. Called a *moiré pattern* (pronounced more-ray), this effect is one of a color separator's biggest headaches. (See figure 14.5.) Moiré patterns are caused when the photographic original introduces another pattern that does not mesh well with the rosette pattern angles. Fabrics in clothes, burlap, heavy textures, and dot and line patterns from grills on computers or machinery are examples of these extra patterns. (You actually can see "live" moiré patterns when a television program's camera moves on a line pattern of miniblinds over a window.)

Fig. 14.5.
A moiré pattern.

You can subdue moiré patterns by swapping the angles of the CMYK printers, scanning the original at a different angle or out of focus, or locally blurring the problem area. If the dot pattern becomes visible in most normal work, you should consult the manufacturer of the output device about the best screen angles to use for CMYK.

The Goals of Color Reproduction

To make a good-looking, sellable reproduction, you must satisfy four main criteria. If the final reproduction is weak in any of these areas, the chances are good the customer will reject it. The four areas are

- Tone reproduction
- Gray balance
- Memory and special colors
- Sharpness

Tone Reproduction

To determine whether a prepress proof is good, the first characteristic to look for (even before seeing the original) is a three-dimensional appearance. For example, if you are looking at a reproduction of a fruit basket on a table, it should look as though you could reach into the scene and pull out a piece of fruit. This appearance demonstrates good tone reproduction.

Proper tone reproduction means that for each part of the conversion process, the resulting reproduction looks realistic from a dimensional standpoint. This realism is accomplished by maintaining all the tonal steps from light to dark. *Steps* is the key word here. All the tonal steps in the original must be represented in the reproduction.

The term *contrast* often is used in association with tone reproduction. *Contrast* is the relationship of all tone steps from light to dark. The length of the tonal range, from where the smallest dot starts printing to where the largest dot prints, sets the contrast of the reproduction. The contrast of the reproduction must match the contrast of the original or the appearances differ. The customer undoubtedly will gripe, "Hey, they don't match!"

Figures 14.6a, 14.6b, and 14.6c demonstrate contrast effects on neighboring tone steps.

Fig. 14.6a.
Minus 10 percent contrast.

Fig. 14.6b.
Normal contrast.

Fig. 14.6c.
Plus 10 percent contrast.

Figure 14.6b shows a step between two neighboring tones. Figure 14.6a represents a low-contrast reproduction, which causes the difference between the tones to diminish. Figure 14.6c's contrast is high, so the difference between the two tones is exaggerated because the dot percent differences have increased.

The squares at the top of figure 14.6 represent a photograph of a light gray card on a white table. The eye distinguishes a tonal step between the card and the table.

A flat reproduction does not have enough dot percentage difference between the tonal steps when compared to the original. If the halftone reproduction is too flat (tonal range is too long), the card starts to disappear into the table. If the tonal step is diminished enough, the eye is not able to differentiate between the two tones. Most people cannot see between two tones if the difference is less than 3 percent dot value.

Additionally, in flat reproductions colors appear weak and undersaturated, and detail disappears (see figure 14.6c). Typical customer comments include "not enough pop," "no sparkle," "washed out," "weak," "dull," and "too flat."

If the halftone reproduction has too much contrast, the step between the card and the table is exaggerated: The card looks darker and the table appears lighter. A reproduction with too much contrast goes to solid in the shadow areas and appears too heavy when compared to the original. Smooth tones like vignettes and flesh tones start to break up into steps that are not in the original. Customers' comments usually are "too much weight," "too much color," "too jumpy," "oversaturated," and "what are those bands in the vignette?" (See figure 14.6a.)

A deep red rose provides an example of tonal steps in a color image. Proper tone reproduction shows each petal. Flat tone reproduction makes the image appear dull and causes the steps between the petals to disappear. A reproduction with too much contrast oversaturates the color, and the rose appears too dark and heavy.

Tone reproduction is controlled on the scanner hardware or software by the highlight and shadow density point selections. These selections set the range of tones that are represented by dots. All tones of the original outside this range are either paper white or solid ink. Control of the interior part of the tonal curve exists with adjustments like the middletone. Selection techniques for these tones, or densities, are discussed in the next chapter on highlight, shadow, and interior curve movement.

If the tonal steps of the original are not represented properly in the reproduction, no amount of adjustment with any other available controls helps. Bad tone reproduction almost surely results in a rejected proof.

Gray Balance

Color craftspeople often refer to gray or neutral when they analyze color. Neutrality represents an important factor of a reproduction. *Neutral* means that something has no bias, does not take sides on an issue; in this case, the issue is color. So a color that is neutral has no unnatural color bias such as warm or cool. The neutral color is a pure hue, such as sky blue or apple red. Neutral colors look normal, as you expect to see them. Gray, as explained in Chapter 2, "Color and Tones," is a tone between white and black that has no color. A neutral gray has no color bias: it doesn't look pink, greenish, warm, or cold—just gray.

A gray scale is a tonal scale that runs from light white to dark black with intermediate shades of gray in between. The scale is used as a guide for color systems to ensure proper calibration and unbiased color balance settings.

The color separation process is in between the photography stage and the ink-on-paper stage of the entire reproduction conversion process. This in-between position dictates that the color separator must be concerned with the neutrality of the photographic original and the neutral balance the ink set on the printing press needs. For example, if the original image to be scanned appears neutral, the separations should be made with a neutral ink balance. If the image to be reproduced has an undesirable color cast, the balance of the printing inks must be adjusted to defeat, or neutralize, the cast.

The original photography's lighting and processing conditions influence the neutrality of the image. If you use proper viewing conditions when analyzing images with the customer, the customer can recognize obvious casts and request that you remove them before scanning.

A good reproduction contains no obvious color casts. Whites appear as whites, gray tones are gray, and no colors have a bias toward a certain color direction.

Each photographic emulsion type's dyes has its own color balance and gamut, which the scanner does not always recognize as neutral. Also, the scanner does not see color like the human eye because the eye is an organic system of vision and the scanner uses a mechanical photoelectric system (see Chapter 3).

Because of this difference in vision and color sensitivity, the scanner usually detects color casts that are too subtle for the eye to see. The transparency may look neutral in the viewing booth, but the readouts on the scanner indicate that the original has a color cast.

But how do you know when the reproduction is going to be neutral by looking at a four-color dot percent readout on the scanner? Novice operators must learn to read and determine neutrality along with additive and subtractive color relationships. Knowing what is neutral on the press and being able to determine the neutrality of the original you scan is a necessary skill for anyone who wants to produce quality color separations.

Table 14.1 lists the gray balance values needed to reproduce a neutral gray scale as neutral on a prepress proof made by a specific manufacturer. The dot percent difference between the cyan printer and yellow/magenta printer is important to notice. The cyan printer must print heavier than yellow and magenta printers to achieve a neutral gray with ink on press. This cyan, magenta, and yellow imbalance is necessary because inks are not pure and do not subtract one-third of the visible spectrum as they theoretically should. (Pure inks are too expensive for most printing jobs.) Notice that the gray balance difference changes as you go from highlight to shadow. The difference between the three subtractive color printers to make a printed neutral is called *gray balance*. Proper gray balance reproduces a neutral gray scale as a neutral gray.

Table 14.1. Gray balance differences.

Density	Cyan Percent	Y/M Percent	Black Percent	Difference
.20	4	2	-	2-3 percent highlight
.30	10	6	-	
.43	20	13	-	
.60	30	21	-	7-10 percent quartertone
.78	40	29	1	
.98	50	37	5	12-15 percent middletone
1.25	60	46	14	
1.58	70	57	25	
2.10	80	71	42	8-12 percent three-quartertone
2.68	90	82	62	
2.80	95	87	75	7-10 percent shadow

Note: The magenta and yellow values are equal for the type of proofing to which this chart is calibrated. This is not necessarily true of all proof or press conditions.

Starting at the beginning of the tonal curve, notice the highlight step where the halftone dots start to print. The highlight step is the brightest area of the tonal scale because it is closest to paper white. The highlight also is the easiest area for the eye to detect a color cast in because it is so bright. The recommended dot percent difference here involves the cyan printing 2-3 percent more than the magenta and yellow. This dot percent difference yields a neutral tone in which the dots are of highlight values. Because the dots are small, the percentages appear to be white. Again, the highlight is the easiest area for the eye to detect a cast in, so you must use the gray balance difference of 2-3 percent.

Printing the cyan, magenta, and yellow ink at equal values does not print neutral. (See figure 14.7.) Equal values of CMY in the highlight appear warm, not white. Shadows print brown. This undesirable result becomes evident immediately.

Ascending the tonal scale, you notice that at the 25 percent area, called quartertone, the gray balance difference increases to 7-10 percent. This area produces a neutral tone a couple steps darker than the highlight white. The next important tonal area for gray balance is middletone, the 50 percent dot area in the center of the tonal curve. Gray balance difference is greatest at 12-15 percent. Now the tonal scale moves toward the dark side, the three-quartertone's 75 percent dot area. The gray balance difference decreases to 8-12 percent to make a neutral tone in the 75 percent area. This area on the tonal scale carries the last of the shadow detail. Tonal areas with dots larger than three-quartertone percentages cannot rendition shapes and detail visible to the eye. At the top of the scale is the shadow point, the area of the largest printing dots. Here, the gray balance difference is 7-10 percent.

Fig. 14.7.
Equal dot percentages of 6 percent, 50 percent, and 90 percent do not print as neutrals.

Using the Gray Balance Chart

The scanner detects color casts in photographic originals by comparing to neutral, which is the neutral condition of the press inks or of the prepress proof. By comparing to neutral, the scanner has no bias in its readouts. For example, a green-casted subject reads green casted rather than neutral or to the pink (opposite cast) side.

You will find that almost all transparencies are not completely neutral. (See figure 14.8.) The color casts can be different at different areas of the tonal scale too. It is not unusual to find that a highlight has a green cast and the shadow reads a blue cast.

Fig. 14.8.
A neutral and casted (green) subject.

The gray balance chart should become a permanent part of any scanner operator's memory. By using additive/subtractive color relationships, discover which inks should be added or subtracted to neutralize a cast. Using a gray balance chart helps you determine color casts. When used with the four-color readout from the scanner, the chart shows how much to move each printer to eliminate a cast.

For example, assume you are to scan a scene of a model with dark hair in a white shirt standing in front of a gray wall. The transparency looks neutral on the viewer, the shirt is a cast-free white, and the wall is a noncolor cast gray. The scanner readout in the shirt averages around 7 percent cyan, 4 percent magenta, and 8 percent yellow. The gray balance chart in the highlight area shows that the gray balance difference from cyan to magenta/yellow is 2-3 percent, and the yellow and magenta values should be equal. This means the shirt prints light green, even though it looks white in the viewer. To correct this hidden cast, the yellow dot percent must be made equal to the magenta, which is 3 percent less than the cyan. The neutralized highlight is 7 percent C, 4 percent M, 4 percent Y.

When you check the gray wall, the readout is 57 percent cyan with 47 percent magenta and 47 percent yellow. The middletone area of the gray chart shows that you need a gray balance spread of 12-15 percent before the wall reproduces as gray. The correction here is to add 2-5 percent cyan to achieve the proper gray balance difference.

Finally, you should check the dark hair for any color imbalances. For dark, neutral black hair, the gray balance difference is 7-10 percent on the chart.

Figures 14.9a and 14.9b show an attempt to neutralize a very bad transparency. Unfortunately, some originals can be improved but not perfectly neutralized. You sometimes need local masking techniques to perfectly normalize images like figure

14.9 because of the color cast's unevenness throughout the tonal scale. The saying "garbage in, garbage out" applies here.

Fig. 14.9a.
A match of an original transparency brought in for scanning.

Fig. 14.9b.
Cast correction applied to original separation.

An original that is all color with no whites or neutrals can have a color cast, even though the eye cannot detect one easily without a neutral tone present as an indicator. All the scene's colors, in this example, are biased toward one direction, which can be corrected by shifting the scanner's gray balance. A journeyman's knowledge of color and tone curve adjustment is necessary to make this type of correction. The CC filter method previously described is recommended for the novice operator in this situation.

Gray balance is the second most important factor in producing a sellable reproduction. The customer never accepts a proof or print with an obvious cast even if the scanner is just reproducing what is in the original. The reproduction must appear real, and a color cast is not what the eye sees in the real world.

To begin learning cast detection and neutralizing, the novice color separator needs to memorize gray balance differences at the five most important areas of the tonal scale: highlight, shadow, quartertone, middletone, and three-quartertone. Knowing how to make a neutral balance at all areas of the tonal scale gives you the ability to handle all possible cast correction situations an image presents.

Memory Colors

Memory colors, or psychological reference colors, are colors in a reproduction that everyone knows without having to compare to an original. You do not need to compare a proof of a hand holding an apple to the original subject to know whether the colors look real: everyone remembers in his mind what an apple and the color of flesh looks like. Food, blue sky, flesh tones, and white are typical examples of memory colors. (This information comes from Miles F. Southworth's book *Color Separation Techniques.*)

If a reproduction has a memory color that does not look real, the customer is certain to reject it. The automatic response to poor memory colors is that something looks "fake." The tone reproduction and gray balance can be excellent, but customers do not buy orange flesh tones and pink skies!

White is one of the most often-seen memory colors. A reproduction of a person in a white shirt that is reproducing as pink never will sell. Using the gray balance rules shows how to determine optimum dot percent readouts for a satisfactory white.

Special colors are colors the customer wants to match in the reproduction, regardless of their appearance in the photographic copy. Special colors are specifically requested and carefully examined when the prepress proof is delivered for approval, so they are just as important as memory colors. Special colors are usually product colors. The customer gives the scanner operator a PMS (Pantone Matching System) color number, paint chip, or color swatch, or brings in the actual product. Then the scanner operator must convert the colors of the product into CMYK values to match the appearance in the reproduction.

Reproducing special colors involves changing the color in the photographic original to a color not in the original. This color should be in the ink-on-paper color gamut. You must consider whether changing this color would have an effect on other colors in the scene. Because the color correction controls affect color globally (overall), you may need to use an electronic retouching station or dot etcher to correct the special color area locally.

Handling Some Commonly Used Memory Colors

Following are some four-color formulas to help you to reproduce the commonly seen colors of blue sky, flesh tones, orange, and red.

Blue Sky

Violet, or blue, consists mostly of cyan and magenta ink. A bright blue sky may be composed of only cyan. The sky starts to gain depth and the tone starts to get darker when you add the magenta ink. The increase in magenta ink, as well as the cyan, causes the sky to darken away from the horizon area.

The ratio of cyan ink to magenta tells what kind of blue you have. If the magenta ink is less than a 40 percent ratio to the amount of cyan—for example, cyan 30 percent, magenta 8 percent—the blue appears cool. When the ratio of magenta to cyan is around 50 percent, the sky appears neutral blue. If the magenta-to-cyan ratio is 60-75 percent of the cyan value, the blue appears warm. When the magenta-to-cyan ratio exceeds 75 percent, such as cyan 98 percent and magenta 88 percent, the blue shifts to an undesirable purple color. (See figures 14.10a through 14.10c.)

Pink skies result when the magenta-to-cyan ratio exceeds 60 percent in the lighter parts of the sky.

Sky blue's complementary color, yellow, contaminates, or "dirties," the sky's appearance. Yellow also tends to make a blue color look greenish instead of darkening the color toward black. (We recommend examining a color chart to see this phenomenon. Compare the 100 percent C, 50 percent M, 20 percent Y patch to the 100 percent C, 50 percent M, 20 percent K patch in the chart.) If depth of color is necessary in sky, use black ink to give a deeper, richer blue. Try to keep yellow out of your skies as much as possible.

A good ratio to make a deep violet color on most proofing systems is 100 percent C, 75 percent M, 25 percent K, and a minimum amount of yellow.

Fig. 14.10a.
Cool blue/cyan 60 percent, magenta 15 percent.

Fig. 14.10b.
Neutral blue/cyan 60 percent, magenta 30 percent.

Fig. 14.10c.
Warm blue/cyan 60 percent, magenta 45 percent.

Flesh Tones

Flesh tones are very important memory colors, especially if you are scanning a lot of work using human models. (See figures 14.11a and 14.11b.)

Customers do not buy scans of people who look orange, sunburned, or jaundiced. Examine figure 14.11a. The flesh of the original transparency looks warm from the effect of the morning sun's lighting. The transparency also has a slight overall green cast that is subdued by adding magenta and subtracting yellow. The combination of these two effects contributes to the hot flesh seen in figure 14.11a.

Use the color correction control in the orange/red channel to adjust the flesh to the result of figure 14.11b. Notice that all reds in the scene also adjusted because of the color correction's global effect. (See Chapter 15, "The Process of Four-Color Process Separations.")

Fig. 14.11a.
Normal scan produces warm flesh.

Fig. 14.11b.
Flesh color corrected, minus 20 percent magenta and yellow.

Every time a scan is done with a flesh tone, the operator should take several readings to determine the flesh's appearance. Take readings in normally lighted areas. Avoid taking dot percent readings in shadowed areas or hot spots that are overlighted. Find a spot that is a good average of the overall flesh color.

It is a good rule of thumb to make sure the yellow dot percentage is equal to, or does not exceed by 10 percent, the value of the magenta dot percent to avoid yellowish Caucasian flesh. For example, if the magenta is 55 percent, the yellow should not exceed 65 percent. This is a very typical correction that yields an acceptable flesh tone most of the time.

The cyan dot value should be between one-third and one-half of the magenta value, depending on the warmth and depth of the flesh tone. And because the cyan is flesh's complement, it should just contour a normally lighted flesh tone. Values of over 30 percent cyan should be only in the darker, heavier areas of the flesh. Sunlit, bright areas of flesh should carry a minimum of cyan or no cyan.

The flesh in figure 14.11b is adjusted from 20 percent C, 60 percent M, 62 percent Y to 20 percent C, 40 percent M, 42 percent Y. The subject's forehead was the reading point. The level of cyan seemed correct, so the magenta and yellow each were brought down 20 percent so the cyan was half of the value of the magenta. This minus magenta and yellow move was a minus red correction. The flesh "cooled off" accordingly.

Novices first should check the yellow-to-magenta relationship and then should wait to see a proof before making further adjustments. Write down the four-color readouts of the flesh tones you take and notice how they look on the proof. Comparing four-color readouts to corresponding areas on a proof is the best way to learn important memory colors.

It is vital for scanner operators to be expert at reproducing flesh tones. Remember, flesh colors may look great in the transparency but can end up looking completely different on the proof. Always take a few quick readings to check.

Oranges and Reds

Orange colors are made mainly of yellow ink, with magenta ink determining how warm, neutral, or cool the colors look. If the magenta-to-yellow ratio is between 30 and 40 percent, the orange is cool, or to the green side. A magenta-to-yellow ratio around 50 percent yields a neutral-looking orange, or an "orange-orange." A 60-75 percent magenta-to-yellow ratio gives a warm-looking orange. When the magenta-to-yellow ratio exceeds 75 percent, the orange becomes an orangish red. (See figures 14.12a through 14.12c.)

Fig. 14.12a.
Cool orange: 80 percent Y and 27 percent M.

Fig. 14.12b.
Neutral orange: 80 percent Y and 40 percent M.

Fig. 14.12c.
Warm orange: 80 percent Y and 60 percent M.

Creating a rich, deep red is always a special challenge for scanner operators. The type of prepress proofing system you use is important because each seems to produce different reds with various color gamuts. Scanner operators should try different combinations of CMYK to create red on their proofing systems. Many operators prefer to make red with cyan as the only contaminant. Others prefer to use black, and still others swear by a ratio of cyan and black.

The first thing you need in order to create a deep red is lots of magenta, 95 percent to solid. Then add yellow in the 80-90 percent range. When the yellow nears the magenta value, the red becomes orange-red. So to make a deep red, you need to keep the yellow at least a 10 to 20 percent dot value away from the magenta percent.

Next, add the cyan and black values. Once again, you should view the resulting color on your proofing system to find the best ratios. Create red tints with various values of cyan and black. You may need to adjust the yellow further to get a cooler red. Keep these proofs and color ratios by the scanner. Reds are strong colors, and many customers have special preferences about how they should look. Operators also should research gold, foliage (green), and wood (brown) memory colors.

The novice operator should develop a CMYK color memory for the most reproduced colors. Knowing CMYK values of commonly seen colors reduces rescans that are rejected for poor memory and special colors. Too many novices get caught up in the button punching or gray-scale routine of setup and forget they are *color* separators.

Sharpness

After you reproduce the tonal steps, solve cast problems, and check memory colors, the last hurdle to creating a sellable reproduction is sharpness. Sharpness added during the reproduction sequence ensures that the scene appears in focus. If the sharpness in a reproduction has been selected properly on the scanner, it should not be noticeable.

Sharpness control on the scanner has a wide range of control and applications. The novice operator easily can get in trouble by overdoing the sharpness settings. Having too much sharpness creates a fake appearance on the reproduction. Not enough sharpness enhancement produces a soft or out-of-focus result. (See figures 14.13a, 14.13b, and 14.13c.)

Contrast has an effect on sharpness too. Good tone reproduction goes hand-in-hand with sharpness to create a natural, three-dimensional look. Unsharp controls operate at their best when contrast is good.

Poor tone reproduction has an effect on the perceived sharpness of the reproduction. A flat contrast range hinders sharpness because the tonal steps are not as distinct. A reproduction with excessive contrast exaggerates the tonal steps, and the sharpness circuitry puts abnormally higher sharpness in the reproduction. This exaggeration comes about because the scanner's sharpness circuitry has its strongest effect on the highest contrast areas. Figures 14.6a, 14.6b, and 14.6c offer good examples of contrast versus sharpness. Notice how the low-contrast reproduction, 14.6c, appears softer than 14.6a, even though all three figures are reproduced with the same sharpness settings.

The sharpness settings are the most delicate controls on the scanner. Holding sharp details and keeping flesh and vignetting tones smooth in the same reproduction takes experience and careful adjustment. You should remember that good sharpness is not always noticed, but it certainly is missed if absent.

Fig. 14.13a.
Soft, sharpness too low.

Fig. 14.13b.
Normal sharpness.

Fig. 14.13c.
Overly sharp.

The Importance of Calibration

During the color separation procedure, CMYK readings of the dye densities in the photographic originals are compared to neutral standards to determine what kind of color balance the originals contain. The calibration to neutral standards that is used for comparison must be calculated carefully to achieve the best possible standard program.

A well-calibrated standard program means that setting a proper highlight and shadow point produces a reproduction that is a very close match to most normally exposed originals. Complicated adjustments are not necessary to get good color if the scanner is calibrated for normal subjects of that particular type of original. Originals with exposure and cast problems always take more work, but normally exposed subjects should come off with a minimum of adjustment.

The importance of calibration is demonstrated by figures 14.14a and 14.14b. Figure 14.14a is an E-6 transparency separated with an E-6 calibration. Original and separated reproductions are a close match. Figure 14.14b is a Kodachrome emulsion type original taken of the same scene at the same time, also separated with an E-6 setup. *Both transparencies look similar on a viewer* but do not reproduce similarly using the same separation calibration program. The reproduction of the Kodachrome using an E-6 calibration does not match the Kodachrome transparency. A separate calibration for the Kodachrome emulsion's gray balance and color gamut produces a closer match to the original transparency 's appearance. Figure 14.15 compares Ektachrome and Kodachrome spectral response.

Fig. 14.14a.
E-6 original.

Fig. 14.14b.
Kodachrome original scanned with E-6 program.

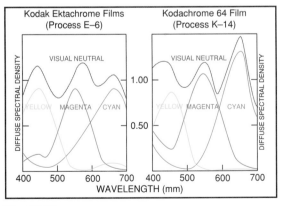

Fig. 14.15.
Ektachrome versus Kodachrome spectral response.

Table 14.2. Calibration table.

Input Originals	Output Conditions
Transparency emulsion types (E-6, Kodachrome, etc.)	Prepress proofs (color key, matchprint, cromalin, naps, etc.)
Transparency formats (35mm, 4 inches x 5 inches, etc.)	Coated stock
Color prints	Noncoated stock
Cibachrome prints	Newsprint/web press
Art/drawings	Gravure press

Table 14.2 lists calibration possibilities the scanner should have in storage to handle almost any kind of reproductive situation.

Customers who have quantities of art with special pigments should supply the separator with a color gamut and gray chart that use their pigments so the separator can calibrate to those pigments' color conditions. You can get a closer match to the customer's originals with this new calibration.

For scanners located in press houses, each press in the pressroom can have a calibration program made for its particular printing conditions.

Getting Calibrated

Newly installed scanners and color separation software are set up to factory default values. You must feed these color separation devices the proper data for the color conditions of the proofing material or press for which the scans are made. The manufacturer's supplied settings are just starting points for producing color, so calibrating to your color system is your responsibility.

The first step of scanner calibration is to ensure predictability. If the scanner or software says it makes a 10 percent dot, is there a 10 percent dot on film? To determine this, you must lock in two variables: the

film processing conditions and the output unit that exposes the film. Be sure the film processor is operating properly with fresh chemistry. Run several control strips, record their values, and write down the development time and developer temperature. Keep these parameters constant! Next, follow the manufacturer's instructions for linearizing the scanner or software and output device to the film processor. When you complete this procedure, run 5 percent, 25 percent, 50 percent, 75 percent, and 95 percent tints; check them with your eye and the densitometer; and record the resulting dot percentages. If your calibration is off by more than 3 percent, start again. You must be confident that the readouts on the scanner or computer screen densitometer are giving you the same dot on film.

The next step in calibrating is to set the gray balance by reproducing a neutral subject tone-for-tone that is completely cast free on your proofing system. The resulting dot percentages are the base gray balance settings off of which all other calibrations are set.

The best neutral test subject to use for calibrating is a gray scale made of dyes. The available silver scales are cheaper, but these scales have a light-scattering side effect called Callier's Q factor, which reduces the accuracy of the scanner's readouts. Check the scale's neutrality on the scanner or a densitometer by looking for equal densities of yellow, magenta, and cyan in each step. On a monitor densitometer, look for equal values of RGB in the gray-scale steps, which indicate neutral. Ask your film supplier about obtaining one of these scales. Desktop scanner users can cut the gray scale into two halves and mount them on acetate so they can be scanned flat.

To determine gray balance, make a scan of the gray scale, then separate and proof. Compare the proofs to the original gray scale for neutrality and weight throughout the tonal area. Make adjustments as necessary and rescan. When you achieve a match, record the values of CMYK and enter them in the separation device's software.

After the base gray balance settings for the scanner are established, color charts and originals of the Ekta-chrome and Fujichrome families should be scanned. These two emulsions separate alike and also account for a large majority of the transparencies brought in for scanning. Carefully analyze these scans and adjust their color gamut characteristics into the scanner using the yellow, magenta, cyan, orange/red, violet, and green color correction controls for each of the four printers. Knowledge of color combinations and correction is necessary to perform this operation correctly.

After you record a program for the Ektachrome and Fujichrome emulsions, start a new calibration procedure for Kodachrome emulsions.

Try to see as many proofs as possible during the calibration procedure. Work closely with the proofer and be certain that the proofing conditions are to manufacturer's specifications. A bad proof invalidates your settings.

After the transmissive subjects are calibrated, switch to the reflection mode and run a reflective gray scale. Proof the results and compare. Because both mediums are reflective, the comparison should be easier. You will find that the reflective gray program is different from the transmissive gray program; reflective copy has a shorter density range, so the gray settings are lower than the transmissive values.

When you have completed these steps, record all settings and keep a log book to track any correction trends you notice during the daily work. If you constantly make a certain correction over a period of time, make it a permanent part of the calibration program. Calibration is an ongoing process that takes many scans to perfect. You should repeat the entire calibration process every time you install a new proofing system.

At the minimum, you should store a calibration for each proofing system that can be used, with a separate calibration for three types of originals: C prints, E-6 transparencies, and Kodachrome transparencies (see table 14.2).

Always have at least one backup copy of your calibration standards. Accidents can happen, and recalibrating from scratch takes a long time.

Checking Software Calibration

If you are not scanning your originals personally, check the gray balance of the software you use to ensure it reproduces gray on the proofing medium being used. To accomplish this verification, produce a series of gray patches from light to dark with equal RGB values from 0 to 100 percent in 10 percent increments. (Note: Turn all GCR and UCR functions off. See "The Black Printer" and the "UCR/GCR" sections in Chapter 15.) Have the resulting 11 patches proofed, and examine them for color casts.

If any areas of the tonal curve are casted, you should compensate to neutralize the casted areas. Consult a color specialist or your software manufacturer on the proper procedure if you are unsure.

Monitor Calibration

Monitor manufacturers have given a lot of attention to screen calibrators. These devices optimize and standardize the color and contrast of the viewing monitor. Unfortunately, some people believe that because their screen is calibrated by one of these units, the color on the screen matches the color on the press sheet.

An exact match of the monitor image and press sheet image is not possible. The two mediums do not match because of their distinct visual differences. The monitor screen's image is created by illuminating phosphors on a glass screen dot matrix, and the press sheet's image is created by light reflecting through an ink film made of pigments and reflecting back a

substrate (usually paper) through the ink to the eye. Additionally, the range of colors, or gamut, of these two color systems is extremely different, so it is unrealistic to expect a monitor screen image to match a press sheet's contrast and color. (See figure 14.16.)

Comparing a press sheet (or prepress proof) of a gray scale and color chart to the digital file on the monitor shows the many discrepancies between the two color systems' visual appearances. (This is how further calibration can be achieved—adjusting the monitor to get as close as possible to an actual press sheet.)

How does an operator know whether the image on the monitor matches the original copy on the press sheet? The answer is the software's onscreen densitometer. A densitometer gives the percentage of printing dot for each of the four color printing inks. It is the color separator's link to the realities of the printing press.

A monitor alone cannot show the size and position of the highlight dots needed or fine detail and tone on a printing press. Also, the monitor's contrast is not necessarily the same as the press sheet's. For example, an image of an apple on the monitor may look ripe and perfectly red. The densitometer readout is cyan 2 percent, magenta 90 percent, yellow 90 percent, and black 5 percent. An experienced color separator knows by these readings that the apple does not print as a deep red. An apple must have at least 20 percent cyan and 20 percent black, as well as a near solid magenta, to reproduce a

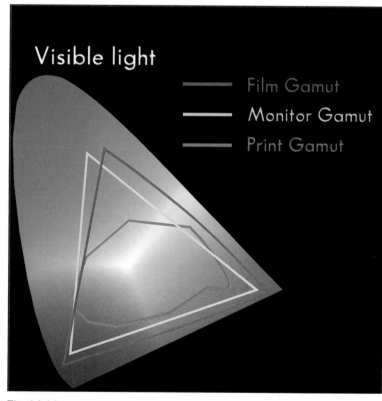

Fig. 14.16.
Spectral sensitivity curves of monitor phosphors versus printing inks.

deep red. It is obvious, because of the improper dot percentages making up the apple, that the pretty picture on the monitor will not be so pretty when printed.

The monitor screen cannot replace the color separation knowledge needed to produce printable reproductions of good fidelity to the original subject.

Monitor calibration devices *are* useful. A calibrated screen does promote a consistent appearance of the images on the monitor. Consistent tones and colors give you a visual feel for the image's appearance on the monitor versus the printed result.

Colors may not match too well from monitors to proofs because of the gamut difference, but you should be able to develop an eye for the contrast of the image on the screen. If an image comes up looking too flat or too heavy, you should recognize this problem and make the appropriate corrections. (See Chapter 15.)

Spending the time to have the scanner properly calibrated benefits both the operator and the management. Anyone buying his first scanner should have it programmed by a professional to guarantee maximum efficiency from the machine.

The next chapter continues with the principles of working in CMYK color space. Specific aimpoints to produce good printable color are given, and the resulting visual effects are described and demonstrated.

Who Should Calibrate

An experienced, qualified color specialist should be on hand to perform the basic calibration procedure. Some journeymen scanner operators are familiar with this process and would prefer to calibrate their own scanners.

If nobody in the shop is experienced with calibration, contract a manufacturer's representative or a color consultant. First-time scanner owners should not let a novice operator attempt this procedure by himself.

An uncalibrated scanner is an inefficient tool. Setup times increase, and rejected color may happen too often. All rescans are expensive and can be the difference between profit and loss on every color job.

15

The Production of Four-Color Process Separations

Introduction

hether done on a $200,000 or a $2,000 scanner, an RGB scan must have proper tone reproduction, gray balance, memory colors, and sharpness. If any of these reproduction parameters is lacking on a high-end scanner's CMYK separations, the same image properly scanned and separated on a less-expensive scanner looks better.

If four-color process separations are the final destination, it is critical to have knowledge of CMYK parameter values for a good reproduction, even though the Macintosh works primarily with RGB files. This chapter takes the goals of color reproduction discussed in the previous chapter and explains how to set the proper CMYK values in an image to produce great color no matter what kind of scanner was used to digitize the original.

The tool relied on most to achieve good color is the densitometer. A densitometer reads out the CMYK dot values of any particular area the cursor is placed in on the Mac screen. The CMYK readouts represent the halftone dot sizes that appear on the final separation film at the cursor point.

Special note: When setting color separation parameters, be sure to turn off any UCR or GCR effects. These controls seriously interfere with the CMYK theories discussed in this chapter. The UCR and GCR functions should be turned on prior to separating, if they are required. See the UCR/GCR section of this chapter if you do not know how to accomplish this.

The highlight point and shadow point determine where detail and tone print in the tonal range of the original copy. The tonal range of an original runs from the lightest density to the darkest density. Therefore, all the original's tones between the highlight and shadow point densities print a halftone dot. All other densities are either paper white (no ink) or solid ink. The following sections show you how to set the proper highlight and shadow points in original copy that will be separated for four-color printing.

To get started producing color separations in CMYK color space, begin with the brightest part of the reproduction where the smallest printing dots reside: the highlight zone.

The Highlight Point

In all color separation procedures, highlight density selection (highlight point) is the first parameter to select because it affects all other steps that follow it.

The highlight point of a separation is the density where the smallest (3-4 percent) printing dot of the yellow, magenta, or cyan printer starts to print. This highlight density is found in whites or colors. Highlight selection is crucial for a good reproduction because it controls the appearance of the brightest part of the scene and any detail in these bright areas. After you find the correct highlight density point, you must place the appropriate dot percentage of CMY there using the controls available on your software.

Fig. 15.1a.
Heavy highlight (density too low); HL density .15.

Fig. 15.1b.
Correct highlight; HL density .30.

Fig. 15.1c.
Highlight too clean (density too high); HL density .45.

Selecting a highlight that is too "clean" (density selection is too high) results in a printed reproduction that is missing in detail and brighter than the original. This problem occurs because the smallest dots required for fine detail and light tones are too small or not present at all. Figure 15.1c has a highlight density of .45; the detail and tones below that density do not carry a dot. Compare figure 15.1c to 15.1b to see which tone and detail are below the .45 density. Figure 15.1b has the correct highlight density for a good reproduction of that image: .30. The missing detail and tones of the two separations reside between .30 and .45 density.

If the highlight is too heavy (density selection is too low), it reduces the brightness of the reproduction and gives everything in the image a dull, low-contrast appearance. Some colors are dirtier (less pure) than usual because a heavy highlight setting increases the size of the complementary colors. (See the "Drawing or Unwanted Color" section in this chapter for more information on complementary colors.)

Figure 15.1a has a highlight density of .15, which is too low for a good reproduction of this image. Notice that selecting too low a highlight density causes the highlight dots to print too big in the bright areas. The result is a reproduction that is dark in areas that should be bright.

The key to selecting the best highlight point is knowing where the smallest dots of cyan, magenta, or yellow will start to print. If you can locate this starting density, the resulting reproduction has the necessary pop and sparkle in the brightest areas of the image. We now look at how to find where *not* to put a highlight dot.

Specular Highlights

Before we get into techniques of finding the exact highlight density, you need to understand specular highlight. Specular highlights are areas that should carry no color or dots. They are so bright in nature they must be reproduced at maximum brightness as paper white to look correct in the reproduction. Examples of speculars are reflections in metal, glass, and water.

Specular highlights are not highlight setting points. Their density is normally well below the image's true highlight density. Placing a dot in a specular density results in abnormally heavy highlight to middletone dot values.

Figures 15.2a and 15.2b illustrate the pitfall of setting a highlight in a specular. Figure 15.2a is scanned with a highlight density point of .15, the density of the specular on the metal tray that contains cheese. This is the lowest density found in the transparency. Figure 15.2b is scanned using the highlight point where the detail in the noodles is drawn by the magenta dots with a .40 density. Obviously, the figure 15.2b scan looks more natural; it matches the original transparency.

An area of paper white in a scene such as this adds to the sparkle of the bright areas. Putting a dot in the speculars reduces the scene's visual contrast, sometimes dramatically. Dots in speculars can be especially harmful in images with water and jewelry. These dots diminish the brightest reference for the eye, which makes all bright areas less bright. The dark areas also are less dark in appearance, because the eye compares the two areas to sense contrast.

When inspecting an original image for a highlight point, locate all the obvious specular highlights and ensure that these highlights do not carry a dot when the image file goes to CMYK color space.

Fig. 15.2.
The consequences of putting dots in specular highlights.

Fig. 15.2a.
Highlight in specular.

Fig. 15.2b.
Proper highlight.

The following section contains alternative ways to find the highlight point. Journeymen scanner operators and dot etchers use these methods, which can find the highlight point in any kind of subject.

An alarming number of novice operators are being trained to locate the lowest density in an original and make it the highlight point. This technique ignores the importance of the specular highlight and can end in disaster, as in figure 15.2a.

Locating the Highlight Point

The simplest and most widely practiced method of setting a highlight involves finding the brightest white that looks as though it has tone and putting a dot in it. This method is successful because if the white is not a specular, it is usually at or near the optimum highlight density. Remember, the smallest dots make the brightest tones.

Folds or seams in a white shirt are great aimpoints for highlight dots. Without dots, there is no detail; to reproduce folds and seams in the shirt, a printing dot must be present.

Minimum printing dot values should be 3 percent to 4 percent for coated paper, 5 percent for uncoated paper, and 7 percent for newsprint. Dots under this size do not hold consistently in the printing process and revert to speculars.

Problems arise when a specular is mistaken for a detail white and the reproduction comes up heavy in the highlights. One way to recognize speculars is to understand that almost all specular highlights are less than .20 density; many are generally .05 to .09 density. (The cheese tray in figure 15.2 averaged .15 density.) If you see a density this low on the densitometer's readouts, carefully check the area you are reading to see whether it is indeed a highlight point.

For those whose hardware or software does not give density readouts, carefully inspect the image before scanning to identify any specular highlight areas. Make a practice of recognizing speculars.

How White Is White?

The next logical question after locating a bright white with tone is "How white do you make it?"

There are three ways to create a true white in a color halftone reproduction. The first method is to use the specular white, as already mentioned. A second method is to use a small cyan dot. The eye assimilates this light, cool tone into the white paper, and the area appears white. The cyan dot should be less than 8 percent or the white shifts to a blue tone. Magenta alone does not work (it appears pink), and yellow alone also creates a cast. The third way to achieve a white is to print all CMY in gray balance: 7 percent C, 4 percent Y, and 4 percent M, or 6 percent C, 4 percent Y, and 4 percent M. Both white balances carry the full detail of an image with all three colors printing. These dots are minimums, so the resulting tone is bright because the tone is mostly paper white with a minimum of ink.

Making White Appear White

Because most transparencies have some casting in the highlights, you must make a decision when whites are involved. Remember, white is a memory color, so it must be neutral or nearly neutral. The operator must reproduce any color casts as the scanner sees them, reduce any color cast, or neutralize any casts completely. (See figure 15.3.)

A Set White option corrects near-whites to white in the RGB color space very easily. (See Chapter 5, "Color.") The result in CMYK is a specular white, cyan dot white, or three-color white, depending on the amount of tone and detail in the area.

Fig. 15.3a.
Casted white.

Fig. 15.3b.
Half-cast removed.

Fig. 15.3c.
Neutralized white.

If there is a color cast in the white, the half-cast method works very well. (See Table 15.1.) When you remove half of the color cast, the resulting reproduction's appearance is not drastically different from the color-casted original and is usually an improvement. Also, not trying to perfectly neutralize all whites reduces the risk of overcorrecting a highlight cast, which reverses the cast and is not visually pleasing.

The half-cast method is highly recommended for novice operators. Be sure to include the 2-3 percent cyan highlight gray balance difference in your calculations.

If there is one main white in a scene, such as a close-up of a man in a white shirt, it is best to neutralize any cast present. Remember, white is a memory color, and no customer likes pink or green whites. Select the brightest area of the white that carries all three printer's dots, and adjust the area to a neutral balance.

When there are several whites in the same scene, analyze each white for its color balance to see whether it reproduces as a white. If each white is of a similar balance, it is best to neutralize the white with the least amount of cast. This step makes the lightest casts white and the heavier casts closer to neutral.

Neutralizing the heaviest white overcorrects the lighter color cast whites, causing them to go beyond white balance and reverse their cast. Having two opposite casts in the same scene is called a cross curve. Cross curves are undesirable and customers reject them.

You should scan a scene with several whites of different casts as is, because helping one cast increases another white's cast. Therefore, be sure to read the balance of all whites in a scene.

Because of the variety of software available to perform color manipulations on the Macintosh, you should familiarize yourself with all the controls to adjust highlight density and cast balancing available with your software package.

Brightening with Highlight

Often, a customer submits a dark, low-key original to scan, saying, "It's all I have—can you help it?"

Highlight density selection helps normalize dark originals. A good way to normalize dark originals is to make any apparent whites in the scene bright whites. For example, a dark shot of a white car in a showroom looks muddy and reads a heavy .55 density. If you were actually in the showroom, you would know the car appears bright. A properly exposed original of this white car should read out at around a .30 density. Find the lowest density spot on the white car, and enter a bright white dot percentage of 7 percent C, 5 percent M, and 5 percent Y. This makes the dull white appear as a bright white. Figure 15.1c demonstrates this lightening effect. If the original image is too dark from the start, select a very high highlight density to help normalize the image toward a lighter appearance.

Special note: Brightening with highlight improves the reproduction, but depending on the severity of the exposure problem, it may not completely normalize the reproduction.

Table 15.1. Examples of half-cast and neutral correction.

Densitometer Readout	Neutral	Half-Cast
12% C, 5% M, 5% Y	8% C, 5% M, 5% Y	10% C, 5% M, 5% Y
9% C, 2% M, 9% Y	9% C, 6% M, 6% Y	9% C, 4% M, 7% Y
3% C, 3% M, 10% Y	5% C, 3% M, 3% Y	5% C, 3% M, 6% Y

The Surrounding Color Effect

Viewing conditions can influence the eye to perceive a casted white as a neutral, as discussed in Chapter 14, "The Basics of Four-Color Process Separations." In addition to viewing conditions, the colors that surround a white in a scene also can influence its appearance. For example, a white golf ball photographed in a red room looks warm, whereas the same ball photographed in a blue room looks cool (see Chapter 2, "The Psychology of Color").

The scanner operator should take this effect into account when deciding whether to neutralize or make a half-cast correction on a white. A surround color of similar balance to any cast in a white hides the cast, whereas a surround color of opposite cast accentuates the color cast of the white.

Figures 15.3a, 15.3b, and 15.3c show the three methods of highlight cast adjustment and the effect of surround colors on a white. Unless a white looks extremely color casted, using the half-cast removal method shown in 15.3b is the safest way to maintain a neutral look and get a good reproduction. Whenever you are in doubt regarding a cast removal, try half-cast first.

No White Highlights

Many novice operators get off to a great start with the white highlight method only to run into problems when encountering a subject with no whites in it. Figure 15.4, the pistachio nuts, is a good example.

Fig. 15.4.
An image with no whites.

During the prescan analysis, you should put originals into exposure categories of high key, low key, or normally exposed. This procedure is handy for highlight selection whether or not the transparency has a white.

The viewing booth enables the operator to make the best possible decision because of its controlled lighting. This consistency is especially important for desktop operators who must make their highlight selection on a video screen. The screen cannot show the original as accurately as the chrome under controlled lighting because it is physically unlike a chrome or proof.

Table 15.2 supplies approximate highlight densities for the three exposure categories. If the original copy to be scanned has no white highlight or light tones to assign a highlight density to, use table 15.2 to approximate a highlight density value. As the table shows, the majority of transparencies have a highlight density between .20 and .40.

Table 15.2. Highlight density table.

Density	Classification
.01 to .20	Specular highlight, high key or overexposed transparency
.20 to .40	Standard highlight range for most normally exposed transparencies
.40 to .55	Low key, underexposed transparency

Figure 15.4's original transparency was normally exposed and a little to the low-key side. According to table 15.2, you want to select a highlight density of .40. Then set the scanner's highlight density to .40 at the standard neutral calibration for transparencies, and scan the original. The result is very close to the appearance of the original transparency.

Be sure to have the scanner in a standard setting when no obvious casts or whites are present. Just use the highlight density controls to set in the normal highlight density selected from the chart. The resulting scan should be acceptable.

For scanners and software programs without density readouts, the highlight density table is of no help unless you scan a step or continuous tone gray scale with the original. (Ask your graphic arts film supplier for a gray scale.) Then you can set the highlight dots (4 percent or so) at the density determined from the chart on the part of the gray scale that reads the desired highlight density. (Before separating, simply crop out the gray scale.) In the pistachio nut example, you would find the .40 density position on the gray scale and place a 4 percent cyan dot there. How you place the 4 percent dot at the highlight point depends on your software. Be sure you are affecting the correct area of the tonal curve for the effect you want.

If it is not possible to incorporate a gray scale with your scan, we recommend the unwanted color technique discussed later in this chapter.

Vignetting Tone Method

A vignette, also known as a gradated tone, is a smooth tone that goes from light to dark. When these tones start from specular white, they can be used as a guide to set the highlight density point.

Because the highlight point tells the scanner at what density to start putting down dots, and dots mean tone, just look for a vignetting color that goes down to a specular. Take a reading in the spot where the color is just starting to become visible from specular white. Choose the proper C, M, or Y printer that has a 3 or 4 percent dot in this spot to make the color or tone, and adjust the highlight dot percent until the printer's readout is 3 or 4 percent. That is the exact highlight density point—where the color just starts to come in from the specular area.

For an example of this technique, examine figure 15.5. The mirrors on the motorcycle are .08 density, specular highlights. Where should the highlight dots start printing?

Fig. 15.5.
Vignetting tone method.

Many operators find the lowest density in the white license plates and place a 5 percent cyan dot there. This method works well in this case because the plates are bright white and are carrying a tone greater than specular.

The exact highlight starting point can be found using the vignetting tone method. Looking at the gas tank on the right side of the bike, you can see a blue tone vignetting from the specular white of the metal tank. By adjusting the highlight dot percentage until a 4 percent cyan dot prints where the blue tone begins, you set the correct highlight point.

Vignetting tones also can be colors vignetting on other colors. Magenta can go from nothing to a dot in a yellow color. Watch where the yellow color takes on weight in the original. Some magenta printing must be there to help make the weight in the yellow color; when yellow vignettes to a higher dot percentage, the color gets more yellow but not heavier. (We recommend studying a color chart of yellow colors that have magenta in the 5-25 percent range.)

This vignetting tone technique can be applied to many other colors as you get more familiar with CMYK color. Magenta vignettes in a sky from a small dot on the horizon to a large dot as the sky goes to darkest violet. Cyan in flesh even can be used as a highlight point by watching the depth of the flesh vignetting from light to dark. Set a 5 percent cyan dot where the flesh starts to take on weight.

Pastels

Pastel, or light, colors are useful as highlight points if the operator knows their dot percentages. Pastels are made of dots in the 5-15 percent range—perfect for highlight setting.

Beige, which is 5 percent C, 5 percent M, and 8-9 percent Y, is a handy pastel for highlight setting. You can set the cursor or eyedropper in the beige color and adjust the highlight dot percentage until a 5 percent cyan and magenta comes up on the readouts.

Drawing or Unwanted Color

Another highlight setting technique is to use the unwanted, or complementary, color. The complement is the opposing cast of a color. If the complement is added, the result is a darker, less pure (dirtier) color. For this reason, the complementary color also is called the unwanted color. Table 15.3 lists colors and their complements.

Table 15.3. Colors and their complements.

Color in Original	Complementary Color
Red	Cyan
Green	Magenta
Blue	Yellow
Yellow	Blue
Magenta	Green
Cyan	Red
Orange	Cyan
Brown	Cyan
Purple	Yellow

Even though the complement is called an unwanted color, unless a color is pure with no detail, there must be a complementary color in the CMYK makeup of the color. The unwanted color adds shading and detail to the object made of that color. The detail or texture that the complementary color adds to a color is called drawing. Additionally, as mentioned in the vignetting tone section of this chapter, the unwanted color can create light to dark shading in a color.

For example, a ripe orange typically is made of 80 to 100 percent yellow and 40 to 50 percent magenta with a minimum of cyan to make the detail in the skin of the fruit. The yellow printer is near solid and the magenta dots are too large to draw the fine texture on the fruit. The third color, the complement, has to make or draw the detail. In this case, the unwanted color, cyan, is a group of tiny dots around 5 percent in value.

Because the drawing color's dots usually are very small, they can be used as highlight points. Magenta in green plants, magenta and cyan in yellows, cyan in gold, cyan in flesh, and magenta in sky horizons are examples of this principle.

Missing drawing means that the highlight setting is too clean. You always should be on the lookout for lack of fine detail or textures and understand that their appearance (or disappearance) is due to the highlight density selection.

The vignetting tone, unwanted color, and pastel color highlight selection methods take practice and should be done carefully. Apprentices should observe journeymen using these techniques to better understand them. With practice and patience, the experienced operator can select the proper highlight density each time to produce a reproduction with maximum sparkle.

The Shadow Point

After selecting the starting density of the printable detail at the highlight point, you need to select the shadow density point to set the complete tonal range of the reproduction. This is the range of tones in the original to be printed on the press. The length of the tonal range determines the contrast of the reproduction and should match the contrast of the original. (See the section "Tone Reproduction and Contrast" in Chapter 14.)

Finding the Shadow Point

To find the shadow point, analyze the original for the area of maximum density. This is the darkest looking part in the scene. Shadow point density setting also is called black point because the area of maximum density is always black. In a densitometer readout, this would be the area of highest RGB or CMYK percentage.

After taking several readings, select the highest density spot in the copy and adjust the shadow dot percentage until a 95 percent cyan dot comes up on the readouts. This spot should be the largest dot printed in noncolored areas. The density of the original where the 95 percent cyan dot is set is the shadow point.

If your software does not read out in density, use the Set Black in RGB color space to identify and set the Dmax (maximum density) area of the transparency. Subsequent exporting to CMYK files enters in the shadow percentage dot values set in the software's gray balance program.

The scanner is set up in standard program to compare the color and balance of the transparency to its neutral setting. If the original is exposed normally and the proper calibration is set, the resulting reproduction should be a close match.

Figures 15.6a, 15.6b, and 15.6c were scanned with the same highlight points but different shadow points. Figure 15.6b was scanned with normal contrast, setting a 95 percent cyan in the black point. Figure 15.6c was scanned with a 10 percent increase in contrast by setting 105 percent cyan, and figure 15.6a was scanned with a 10 percent decrease in contrast by setting 85 percent. Notice that a shadow point which reads 100 percent or more appears too contrasted and a shadow point in the 80 percent range appears too flat. Figure 15.7 shows graphs of the corresponding shadow point adjustments of the images in figure 15.6.

Fig. 15.6b.
Normal contrast.

Fig. 15.6.
Contrast is changed by adjusting the shadow point dot percentage. Each figure has the same highlight setting.

Fig. 15.6c.
Plus 10 percent contrast.

Fig. 15.6a.
Minus 10 percent contrast.

Fig.15.7
Curves show the shadow point adjustments of 15.7a, 15.7b, and 15.7c.

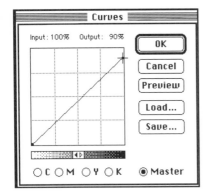

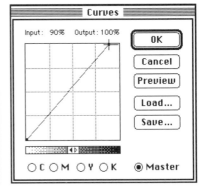

Fig.15.7a.
Minus 10 percent.

Fig. 15.7b.
Normal.

Fig. 15.7c.
Plus 10 percent.

Copy Without a Shadow Point

The Dmax and tonal ranges are standard with reflective copy such as C prints, so setting a shadow point in the last step of a reflective gray scale usually yields a reproduction of matching contrast.

Not all transparencies contain a usable shadow point. The subject matter may not have a dark black object or heavily shaded area. Many washed-out, overexposed subjects lack a good black shadow.

If you cannot find an obvious shadow point in the transparency's image area, the border area makes a good substitute. The border is the unexposed area of the transparency surrounding the image area. Because the border is unexposed, it is the maximum achievable density that film can produce; exposure to light reduces density in a transmissive original. Entering a 95 percent cyan dot in the border usually yields a reproduction of acceptable contrast.

To help compensate for high-key, washed-out copy with no shadow point in the image area, increase the dot percentage set in the border. (For example, set 100 percent cyan rather than 95 percent cyan.) This procedure adds weight and contrast to the overall reproduction.

A similar technique can be used to help low-key, dark originals. Entering a lower dot percentage at the shadow point reduces the overall weight of the reproduction. You must take care to avoid desaturating any areas that should be a rich, dark black because with this method, the darkest areas are not as dark as they can be. Use this method only to help very poor originals.

The Shadow Point and Color Saturation

The shadow point is set with the tonal range and resulting contrast in mind, but the strength of the heavy, saturated colors also depends on the setting of the last printing density. (Note that an inaccurate standard color calibration program also can cause incorrect color saturation.)

Colors such as wine red, apple red, dark violet, and lemon yellow need at least one of the three CMY printers in the high 90 percent range or solid to faithfully reproduce that color. These are colors of high saturation, which means color strength.

If the customer sees a reproduction of a deep red apple with less than 90 percent magenta in the richest part of the fruit, his usual comment is "The apple is not red enough!"

A low-contrast reproduction gives low readings in the saturated colors, usually the 80 to low-90 percent range rather than the accepted 95-100 percent. This problem can clue the operator that the shadow point density is too high.

Reproductions with excessive contrast show saturated colors reading at 100 percent or more, if the four-color readouts can exceed 100 percent. The operator should become suspicious if readouts of 110 percent keep popping up. Colors that should be in the 90 percent range also go solid because of the shadow point selection. These excessively high readings may indicate that the shadow point density is too low and, consequently, the contrast is too high.

Shadow Points in Reflective Art

Reproducing wash art or drawings can be tricky if the colors are not very saturated. Always scan them with a reflective gray scale on the side to have a standard for adjusting your shadow point. Setting up on the last step of the reflective gray scale works well for color prints, but drawings have less range and saturation. You must select a shadow density to yield a contrast in the reproduction that matches the contrast of the drawing.

One way to find the shadow point density is to adjust the density setting to match a known color. Choose a color in the drawing that has the most saturation, and find a match for it in a color chart. (Note the four-color dot percentages necessary to produce it.) For example, say an aqua color is made of 80 percent C, 5 percent M, and 30 percent Y. Go to the gray scale and set the 95 percent cyan dot in the next-to-last step. Now take a reading in the color and note the value of cyan dot percentage. If it is near 80 percent, you have found the correct shadow point. Be sure to take several readings. The texture of drawings can cause the readouts to vary. Readings of less than 80 percent require a shadow point of less density. Therefore, readjust your shadow and try again. Readings of more than 80 percent mean that the selected shadow density is too low and you need to select a higher density.

Handling Shadow Casts

The standard program in a scanner compares the original copy to neutral. If the scanner reproduces the original with all its color casts, it may not always match the original perfectly. The scanner sees the casts in the original, but when you put the original on the viewer, the eye may see it more to the neutral side. (See the section in Chapter 14 titled "Gray Balance.")

When the shadow point is set, you must choose to separate the original as the scanner saw it or neutralize the shadow to achieve a match to how the original looks in the viewer. If the scan appears color casted overall compared to the original, neutralizing the border usually helps. Set Black is a quick way to achieve a neutral border because the software makes the border 100 percent RGB. For example, the readout in a transparency's border is 95 percent C, 93 percent M, and 85 percent Y. Keeping in mind that the gray balance difference in the shadow is 7-10 percent, the neutralized shadow should read 95 percent C, 88 percent M, and 88 percent Y. (See figures 15.8 and 15.9.) Checking any casted neutrals in the subject shows a move toward neutrality. The resulting reproduction should give a cast-free reproduction of the original.

The shadow adjustment has an effect on the whole tonal range except the highlight. Figures 15.9a, 15.9b, and 15.9c demonstrate that the entire printing tonal range except for the highlight moves with the shadow point.

If neutralizing makes a big change in the shadow dot percentages, be careful. Some colors may change and not match. Colors such as chocolate and deep, yellowish wood tones need 95-100 percent yellow, and neutralizing the yellow can hurt these colors. Read certain colors in the image to determine whether they match as is or whether they should be neutralized.

Figure 15.8a looks extremely colorful. The oranges are very orange and appealing compared to figure 15.8b. Without seeing the original transparency, however, most people like figure 15.8a. A trained color separator notices the intense redness of 15.8a from the balance of the four-color readouts. The border of the transparency reads 94 percent C, 96 percent M, and 92 percent Y—hardly a neutral balance. The oranges read magenta in the 60 percent range, which, compared to their appearance in the original, seems oversaturated.

Fig. 15.8a.
An uncorrected scan.

Fig. 15.8b.
Neutralized shadow/transparency match.

Fig. 15.9.
Graphs show the shadow correction curves of 15.8a and 15.8b.

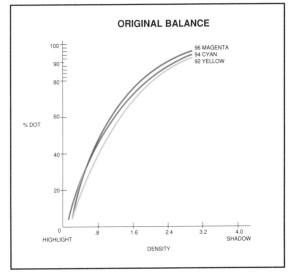

Fig. 15.9a.
Curve uncorrected.

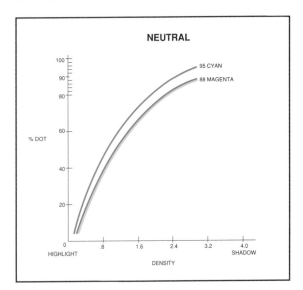

Fig. 15.9b.
Curve corrected.

Using that information, we decided to neutralize the border of the transparency to 95 percent C, 88 percent M, and 88 percent Y. The result is 15.8b, which is not as colorful as 15.8a but which matches the original transparency. Determining shadow casts and how to handle them takes experience. If in doubt about a shadow cast, neutralize it and wait for the proof.

Setting the highlight and shadow points is the most important decision when making a color separation. If you become proficient at locating these important densities, the majority of your work will be sellable.

Correcting Tone and Color

You should sort all originals to be scanned by quality of exposure, cast, emulsion, final size, and grain condition. The main concern is which scans are normal and which need special handling. Subjects that are exposed normally with no apparent cast or grain problems usually reproduce well with just a simple setup of highlight and shadow setting. This is why your color system should be calibrated to faithfully reproduce normal originals.

Tone Corrections

Color separation software should be equipped with controls to modify the contrast of a subject by increasing or decreasing the amount of ink used in reproduction. You can compensate for abnormally dark subjects by printing a lesser amount of ink in the areas of the image that are too dense. Conversely, weak or washed-out subjects can be compensated for

by printing an extra amount of ink in the areas that are lacking in color and weight. In either case, the tone controls can normalize an image's appearance, negating or decreasing the effect of an improper photographic exposure.

The controls that make this compensation are called tone or gradation controls. These controls operate between the highlight and shadow dots and create a visual lightening or darkening effect overall, in the light areas only, or in the dark areas only.

Scanners and some color separation software have what is called five-point tonal control. In other words, these separation systems can affect five areas of the tonal range of a subject: highlight, shadow, quartertone, middletone, and three-quartertone. The highlight and shadow settings are endpoints. The other three affect the interior of the tonal curve.

The middletone moves the 50 percent dot area, causing an overall visual lightening or darkening effect on the reproduction. Using the middletone control to print the 50 percent dot print as a 55 percent dot print, for example, prints more ink overall and creates a reproduction that is darker or stronger in color than the original. Middletone movement corrects most minor exposure problems.

The quartertone operates in the 25 percent area of the tonal curve and brightens or darkens the lighter areas of an image. The highlight works on the lightest tones in an image, with the quartertone manipulating the light tones just past the highlights. Quartertone adjustment usually works well for outdoor shots that are washed out or weak in color. A warning: Many scanners and much software label the quartertone as highlight in the tone control section. This designation is incorrect, but it has been incorrectly used this way for many years. The novice operator should be alert to the proper control selection when using gradation settings.

Three-quartertone adjustments affect the 75 percent area, which is the darker region of an image. Decreasing this control opens up the dark areas and brings out detail that was not easily visible in the original. A warning: Many scanners and much software label the three-quartertone controls as shadow in the tone control section. Again, the novice operator should be aware of the functions of all controls in the gradation section.

The operator should be aware how far the compensation is made for each control in dot percentage. A move of 3 percent is a small visual move; a 6 percent move is a medium step. Moves of 9 percent or more cause a large shift in the reproduction's appearance. This relationship is known as the 3-6-9 rule.

Tone corrections using gradation controls create overall shifts in the lightness and darkness of the original image. These corrections adjust the printing percentage of the yellow, magenta, and cyan printers equally, so they affect only tone reproduction and not gray balance.

Cast Correction

You must correct originals with obvious color casts by adjusting the basic gray balance of the scanner or separation software. You should compensate for the cast of the original by programming in an opposite cast to negate, or neutralize, it.

This step involves using the highlight, shadow, quartertone, middletone, and three-quartertone controls individually for RGB to affect the CMY gray balance. You now must compensate for the non-neutral condition of the image and subdue the color cast in the scan.

You need a good knowledge of gray balance percentages and additive-subtractive color theory to determine which colors to adjust and how much to move them. You also must be aware that adding and subtracting ink to compensate for casts may affect the contrast of the reproduction. Be sure to compensate for any lightening or darkening caused by cast correction with a tone correction.

Color Correction

The variety of color correction tools available is discussed in Chapter 5. To have good color correction skill, you must be able to adjust additive and subtractive color using curves and slider controls. Also, Chapter 14 gives many aimpoints for important memory colors that appear in most images.

The Black Printer (K)

This section examines the black printer's contributions to the separation process.

The scanner does not analyze the original copy separately for its black component because photographic originals have no black dye layer. Instead, the black information is derived from the RGB color input signals. Whenever the three signals are equal—a neutral condition—the black printer information is generated. (This information comes from Gary G. Field's *Color Scanning and Image Systems,* © 1990.)

The purpose of the black printer is to add weight to the shadow areas, increasing the overall contrast of the reproduction. The additional black ink on the press increases the Dmax as much as .5 density in the shadows.

For the color separator, the black printer presents yet another way to create and enhance tonal steps in addition to using the cyan, magenta, and yellow printers.

Setting the Black Printer's Contrast

Just as the highlight and shadow density settings of the cyan, magenta, and yellow printers affect the visual density of the reproduction, the density endpoints of the black printer affect its contrast. A black printer of low contrast is undesirable in most cases because the black ink does not optimize the contrast of the scene.

Highlight Point

After the CMY printers have been set up for their highlight and shadow values, the black printer's end densities must be set too. Unlike the CMY printers, the black printer does not start in the usual highlight densities because it would dirty the bright areas of the reproduction. Instead, the black printer begins to print in the image's middletone range. This middletone starting point explains why the black printer is sometimes called a half-black.

Most separators program a 5 percent black highlight dot to start somewhere between where the cyan's 35 and 50 percent dot prints. (This is usually between .70 and 1.0 density.) The starting position of the black highlight dot in the standard program is a matter of preference with every operator. For ease of setup, novice operators should start their black highlight where the cyan dot prints a 50 percent dot in a neutral.

You can adjust the black highlight to help enhance steps further up the tonal range in the quartertone areas. This is useful if you need to enhance light shadows in the subject or make the detail in a wood grain more visual, for example.

High-key photos or overexposed transparencies are deficient in black because the originals are weak in color; the scanner does not "see" any black in them. In high-key scans, go to a gray scale and set a 5 percent black dot where the cyan printer reads 35 percent. This creates a longer range black printer. For color separation software, it is just a matter of setting the black starting point to a lower highlight percentage number than standard. Always adjust the black highlight for high-key and low-key originals.

The opposite situation holds true for dark, low-key originals. When the scanner analyzes a dark original, it "sees" too much black printing in the scene. You should set the black highlight below (less than) the standard setting to compensate.

Compensate for high-key and low-key subjects with the highlight, shadow, and gradation controls of the yellow, magenta, and cyan printers. These adjustments automatically influence the black printer. Moving the CMY middletone controls shifts the black highlight. Shifting the CMY shadow point moves the black's shadow point also, so set up the black printer after setting the CMY endpoints.

Shadow Point

The many kinds of originals have a wide range of maximum densities. Because the black separation signal is derived from the three-color signal, the amount of black that the scanner places at the scanner point changes with each subject. Transparency Dmax may read anywhere from 2.2 to 3.5 density routinely. The maximum black reading that the scanner gives you is influenced by this Dmax value.

The darkest black shadow point of a reproduction should read between 70 and 80 percent black to reproduce a rich, deep black on the press. You should not exceed these values unless you use some method of undercolor removal.

Many times when the operator reads the dot percentage in the darkest black shadow or border of the original, the black reads below 70 percent. This means deep blacks do not reproduce that way, and the contrast of the black printer is low throughout its tonal range. A flat black printer does not enhance the other printers' tonal steps as much as a black printer of normal contrast can. (See figures 15.10a through 15.10d.)

Fig. 15.10a.
A scan with the black shadow percentage at 50 percent.

Fig. 15.10b.
The black printer only. (50% shadow)

Fig. 15.10c.
The same scan with the black shadow percentage at 80 percent.

Fig. 15.10d.
The black printer only. (80% shadow)

Always be sure to check the amount of black printing in the heaviest shadow point or border of the original. Use the black shadow endpoint control to adjust the dot readout to 75 percent. If the copy is high key, set the dot readout to 80 percent. For low-key copy, set the dot readout to 70 percent or less.

UCR

UCR, or undercolor removal, describes the practice of removing quantities of yellow, magenta, and cyan ink from where black is printing. This is an advantage on press because the black areas print black anyway, so less ink is needed to print black. Less ink means better control, faster drying times, and less expense on long runs that use a lot of ink. Also, blacks and neutrals that print black are not influenced easily by shifts in the undercolors which cause color casts in the shadow tones—there is enough black printing to cover them.

The UCR controls subtract yellow, magenta, and cyan ink individually or together from the shadow areas of the reproduction. This removal can be performed neutrally, or the printers can be shifted individually to make the shadow areas neutral.

These controls affect only neutral areas where black is printing. Saturated colors such as deep orange and red are not affected by UCR. (See figure 15.11a.)

The printer usually gives a UCR specification to the separator. Typical values are 280 percent, 260 percent, or 240 percent. These values are the amount of ink allowed to print in the Dmax of the copy. Because a shadow point on a normally exposed original is around 350 percent total ink printing (95 percent C, 88 percent M, 88 percent Y, 80 percent K), 280 percent UCR means the UCR controls are rolling off around 70 percent of the total ink value. For noncoated paper, use 280 or 260 percent UCR.

If the proper amount of black is used to replace the amount of yellow, magenta, and cyan that is removed, the UCR reproduction should look as good as the same reproduction done without UCR. All separation software that offer UCR automatically boost the black printer to compensate for the undercolor removal of the CMY.

It is very important to use the UCR as a post operation only because the dot percentages in the shadow areas are of no use when determining the shadow point density. The CMY dot percentages would read excessively low, and the black printer percentages would be too high. Be sure to have the UCR off when setting up the highlight and shadow endpoints. The UCR (and GCR) should be the last control turned on before you export the RGB files for separation.

GCR

GCR, or gray component removal, is used to save even more ink than UCR. This function removes yellow, magenta, and cyan ink from neutrals and colored areas.

When the GCR circuit senses equal amounts of all three printers, it totally removes that gray component from the color and replaces that component with black. GCR removes all complementary colors, because they are the third printer, and replaces them with black. (See figure 15.11b.)

GCR saves a lot of ink and reproduces a smoother looking image because the black printer carries most of the tonal steps in the reproduction. The yellow, magenta, and cyan are used mostly for making the purer saturated colors.

Fig. 15.11a.
Image with UCR, black partially removed.

Fig. 15.11b.
Image with GCR, black partially removed.

The control for GCR usually is marked from 0 to 100 percent. Forty percent is a typical amount to use for uncoated paper.

The GCR control automatically increases the black printer to compensate for the amount of undercolor you remove. A GCR reproduction should match a non-GCR reproduction. If there is a big difference, consult the scanner or software manufacturer. Adjusting the GCR program is difficult, so leave that to skilled technicians.

Just like the UCR controls, GCR is a post operation and should be turned off during setup. Turning off the UCR and GCR in some software is as simple as entering 360 percent in a menu area indicating Total Color Printing. The maximum black allowed should be 80 percent for normal printing conditions that do not use UCR. Never give a press house a black separation with dot percent values exceeding 80 percent unless some UCR or GCR is present; the excessive ink causes press/paper problems. Setting the UCR control to 360 percent permits a standard shadow percentage setting of cyan 95 percent, magenta 87 percent, yellow 87 percent, and black 80 percent. Therefore, the UCR and GCR controls are effectively off.

UCR and GCR help make printing color separations more affordable and easier. Some press houses make UCR/GCR a standard requirement; others do not.

However, there is a potential problem with these two ink-saving functions. UCR and GCR black inks usually are formulated specially for better density because of the undercolors being removed.

Most prepress proofs do not have a dense enough black to compensate for large removals of undercolor. Their black does not represent the result on press because the black press ink prints denser and covers undercolor removal better than the black proofing material. The visual result contains weak-looking black shadows, and the overall contrast suffers.

Unfortunately, weak shadows are especially true for 240 percent UCR separations and GCR separations over 60 percent. If the proofs are marked with comments such as "too weak; lacks saturation," tell the customer the separations are good and will print just fine. No amount of adjustment on the separation makes up for weak-looking black proofing material when a 240 percent UCR is required.

The "fourth" printer, black, has a very important role in the color separation process. This printer increases the contrast of the reproduction and improves the printing conditions when combined with UCR and GCR functions. A properly made black printer adds the right amount of weight to give deep rich shadows and enhance the tonal steps in the darker half of the reproduction.

To get the optimum reproduction with a color scanner or separation software, you must use all four printers at their best contrast and balance levels. This means the black printer should be as carefully adjusted as the three color separations.

The printing house that is printing the color normally specifies the UCR and GCR. This information comes in two pieces: the kind of undercolor removal and how much is removed. Typical UCR percentages are 240 percent, 260 percent, and 280 percent. GCR is specified in percentages, with the minimum being 40 percent and the maximum around 80 percent. A GCR of 100 percent rarely is requested and should be questioned.

Trapping

In the printing industry, there are two meanings for the word *trapping*, depending on which area of the reprographic process you work in. For press operators, trapping is the amount of ink that goes on top of another ink. If you are composing a color ad or job on a stripping table or paginating on a screen, trapping is an operation that prevents registration problems.

Perfect registration on an offset press is the capability to lay down the cyan, magenta, yellow, and black printers on top of each other in exact position. The result is a press print reproduction of maximum sharpness and detail. To achieve perfect registration, the substrate, usually paper, must go through the press

and contact each color printing cylinder at exactly the same place as the other colors.

Registration accuracy can suffer because of paper or mechanical press problems. The paper is compressed when it is imprinted by the first color cylinder and has its size changed by the pressure. This changes the positioning of the sheet to get maximum registration through the next colors. Paper also can get hung up while releasing from the feed pile, causing its entry into the first printing unit to be inaccurate. The press can have mechanical play in its cylinders and register guides, which contributes to register errors. An excessively high rate of speed also pushes the press' ability to achieve good register.

The amount of misregister is described by how many rows of halftone dots a color is out of register. Movements of a half row of dots or more generally are unacceptable.

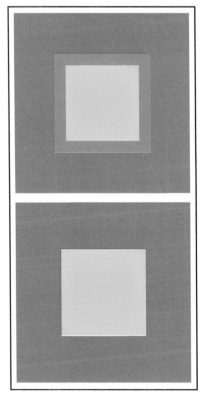

Fig. 15.12.
Microscopic view of trap and no trap.

Besides decreasing visual sharpness, poor registration causes colors to bleed into other colors and white lines of no dots to appear between neighboring process color areas. This is especially evident with four-color halftones surrounded with a black border. (See figure 15.13.)

Fig. 15.13.
Movement of a colored image within a black border. Note white line at right border.

A procedure called trapping prevents bleeding color and white lines. This process involves spreading the ink from neighboring color areas into each other so a registration shift does not create a visible white line. Spreading one color into another is called trap.

Trap dimensions are typically one-tenth or two-tenths of a millimeter (one to three pixels) for good printing conditions and as much as a half millimeter for newsprint conditions.

The spreading is achieved photomechanically in the film contacting stage or on the Macintosh by software command. In either case, the operator must be aware of which areas to trap.

Output Devices

Color separations can be output by conventional color scanners or by high-resolution exposing units called imagesetters. When four-color files are combined with text files, the output device must have adequate resolution to reproduce the sharp edges of the text without jagged breaks and the detail and smooth tones of the color images.

Standard color scanners cannot achieve the edge resolution necessary to output text unless they are modified to do so. The result is adequate quality text at best and a great loss in output speed.

Imagesetters have the resolution to produce sharp, clear text and can produce four-color halftones of excellent quality. The key to getting four-color quality is to provide an image file of proper pixel-to-dot resolution and the correct number of pixels per inch squared. (See Chapter 1, "What Are Pixels?" and Chapter 12, "Preparing Images for Output.")

DPI often is confused with the lines-per-inch ruling of the halftone dot pattern. DPI actually indicates the amount of possible exposure elements per inch that the imagesetter can provide (EPI). The line screen ruling determines how much EPI is necessary to produce a good-looking image. Fine rulings such as 175 lpi and 200 lpi need a higher EPI such as 3600. Coarser screens such as 85 and 100 require only an EPI like 1270 to create a normal-looking image.

This is the same on the high-end color scanner that puts down laser lines per inch to render each halftone dot. A 200 line screen takes 447 lines per inch, and an 85 line screen needs only 200 lines per inch.

Chapter 12 covers the principles of output parameters for digital files.

Post-Scan Analysis

All file output should be double-checked. Whether the output is to film or disk, you should examine your results for the correct printing parameters. This section outlines what to look for.

Checking the Film

After the scan has been made and the separation produced, the separator has one more chance to check his work.

A careful examination of the separation films offers the last chance to detect any reproduction errors before making the prepress proof.

Separation films should be viewed as a set on a light table large enough to hold a full sheet of film so you can look at the film from a macroscopic viewpoint. When you view the films from a distance, you first should look for dirt, moiré patterns, scratches, or bubbles in the reproduction. This is especially true for big enlargements. These problems have nothing to do with color but always result in a rescan. If these problems are present, take the proper actions to fix them, and then rescan. Even if the films are rejected, you should continue to judge the color of the reproduction so you know whether you can reuse the stored color setup for that original when it is rescanned and separated.

Next, look for gray balance and contrast. With negatives, the cyan film should appear lighter than the magenta and yellow films in neutral areas. This difference is because for proper gray balance, the cyan printer should be printing more than the magenta and

yellow. In a negative type film, the lighter an area, the more ink prints there. Be sure you examine any neutral areas in your subject.

Each printer should have a good range of contrast whether in negative or positive form. This does depend on the color and contrast of the subject, but a colorful, normally exposed image should produce four separation films with individual printers exhibiting good contrast from light to dark.

If two or more printers appear flat, the shadow point may be incorrect or there may be an overall color cast. Take a good look at the original and determine whether this might be a problem.

The black printer should be of good contrast, even for high-key images. Use a magnifying loop and check the darkest shadow for a black dot between 70 and 80 percent. Notice where the black highlight comes into the image too.

Look at all four films for relative sharpness from a distance and up close. Check for white and black halos. Is the grain too visible? Is any detail missing? Are the flesh tones and vignettes smooth?

Now it is time to use the magnifying loop to examine the dots. Check to see that the desired dots are at the highlight and shadow points. Are the highlights too big or missing? Are any drawing dots missing in the bright colors that have texture? Is any detail missing in light tones? Is the deepest shadow area holding a 95 percent dot? Are the saturated colors near solid in the proper printers?

Next, check any special colors such as product colors and flesh tones. You may need to use a densitometer to verify certain special colors that were programmed.

Through this examination, the operator can decide whether the color reproduction is ready to proof or needs some adjustment and another scan.

Post-Scan Analysis on the Screen

If the scan is going to disk rather than film, you should check the separation parameters in a program that has a four-color densitometer readout. Mistakes that proceed past this point are very costly because you need to repeat several operations to correct a mistake.

The scan should be viewed the same way each time on the screen, from the same distance with the same background or room lighting. This brings some continuity into the viewing situation. You should get accustomed to these conditions, so they must not change continuously. The scanned original should be nearby for reference.

First, analyze the image for dirt, scratches, bubbles, and moiré patterns. These defects are more difficult to see here than in film, so look closely. Dirt easily can be cloned out. Moirés can be softened too, but the retouching personnel must know that the moirés are there.

Next, stand back five feet or so and look at the contrast of the scan. After you work with the same screen and viewing conditions for a while, you become a very good judge of whether the contrast of the scan is acceptable.

Use the densitometer and check the highlights, shadows, and any neutral areas for proper dot percent. Finally, check the dot percentage of any special colors. Do not expect the screen to tell you whether a red apple is red enough. Use the densitometer—it is your link to the reality of ink on paper. The screen is only an approximation of the color and shows only a low-resolution version of the actual image data.

You must make a decision from the post-scan analysis information to rescan the original with adjustments, keep the scan as is, or keep the scan and do some retouching to solve any problems you have found.

Producing a sellable set of color separations takes the skill of a craftsman as well as patience and knowledge of color and the printing process. This process has been made available to all Macintosh users who have access to digital input devices.

You should not expect to hit a winner the first time every time. But as in all situations, practice makes perfect. Take the time to examine your results carefully and learn from your mistakes. At first, you may have plenty of mistakes. However, patience and practice reward you with color reproductions of excellent quality and beauty.

Now that you are an expert on CMYK color separation techniques, the next chapter brings you back into the RGB color space to look at film recording, or transparency output, considerations. Your digital files can go full circle from being created by scans from transparencies to producing transparencies to scan.

Digital Film Recording

This chapter discusses specific concerns involving transparency output quality. Pixel size, file size, and resolution still apply. Understanding the proper terms and being able to communicate using them makes it easier to get the output quality you need.

Introduction to Film Recording

Reproducing digital image files to high-quality transparencies presents unique conditions for many reasons. For instance, transparencies are a semi-permanent storage medium that is transported easily because of its physical size. You can view the image without any mechanical aids except light. A color transparency is easier to analyze and judge than a digital file. To test this concept, hold up both a digital transparency and a digital file stored on a hard drive, one in each hand, to a light. The transparency gives you an instant display of the image, whereas the hard drive simply shades your eyes. All kidding aside, to view the digital image on the hard drive, you need a separate apparatus such as a monitor, which can have its own bias. You can view a transparency wherever you like. Another consideration is that digital storage mediums are not necessarily the perfect place to store important digital images. Many unusual circumstances can corrupt a digital file on a hard drive, and it is impossible to foresee all of them. A transparency is a physical storage medium that can be scratched, melted, or bleached by excessive sunlight. All of these possibilities easily are avoided with proper care.

A transparency is a familiar piece of source material because most people in the imaging profession work with color transparencies. Relating color that is not dependent on a viewing device (that is, a monitor) is much simpler. Because of transparencies' color-saturated nature and pleasing contrast, they are a popular medium for many print buyers, photographers, and artists. Even if the image eventually is placed in a digital environment, an artist or a retoucher does not need to worry about print production concerns if he delivers a transparency as final work. Because printers and color separators are used to working with transparencies, conversion to CMYK separation film is easy.

In some cases, you can improve digital images in the process of transparency output. If you take a digital image and make a continuous tone transparency first, any subsequent scan is of a continuous image. Scanning a digital transparency may help reduce possible image pixelization.

Production Considerations

After you perform all necessary image manipulations, you want to consider a few concepts before you output to transparency. Film output has its own gamut and range of tones or contrast. It is important to

understand that a transparency contains continuous tone CMY dyes. Because your digital systems are based on RGB values, you can see the natural linkage between a digital image of RGB color and output based on the same system. There is no need for the color conversion that is necessary when creating print color film separations. Because the transparency film is exposed by RGB color, it is easier to judge correct color. This is not to imply that what you see on the monitor is exactly what you get in a transparency, only that the color systems of the monitor and transparency are the same. You still need to make considerations and compensation for transparencies' color output.

In print production, the values on the color percentage indicators in your program determine how to judge the probable color result in transparencies. The color on your monitor should be fairly representative of your ultimate results. It is unwise to rely on viewing color on a monitor at any time; you always should judge your output to the values you read with your software. The most frustrating exercise is trying to adjust a monitor to the colors in print. It is literally painful to see someone run around in this hopeless maze. The calibrating devices many manufacturers offer can keep your monitor's color appearance stable and consistent, however. And although consistency is the key to keeping a monitor close to reproduction color, the real test is to check important values against what you actually get in output. That is the only way to be absolutely sure of color fidelity. Irradiated phosphorous is different from illuminated printing inks and transparency dyes. They are two different items. Different gamuts. Different. Period. You can get them close but that is all. Do not waste time trying to find a monitor that exactly matches your printed output.

Highlight and Shadow Points

Just as in print, the tonal endpoints of highlights and shadows are the two main areas of concern. First, you should identify your highlight point. In a digital image, pure white is 0 percent RGB. This is also the case for output to transparencies. Identify the brightest or least dense tone in the original. If the brightest point in your image is not 0 percent RGB and it should be, you need to set that color. What if there is no spot in the image that is honestly a pure white? You can paint a zero value in the borders of the image and use this point as your 0 percent RGB setting point.

The second process is to determine the shadow point. In most transparency output, the densest black occurs before 100 percent RGB. Typically, this occurs between 87 and 95 percent RGB. Any value of RGB above 87 percent leans toward black. This means that a color value of 87r 87b 87g, in most cases, results in the densest black produced by the transparency output device. This may vary depending on the specific film recorder, so your visual tone range should be between 0 and 87 percent RGB to ensure all desired tonal steps are visible in the transparency. You may be able to identify the tonal steps above 87 percent on the monitor, but the film recorder cannot do the same. The result is a flat black where you may have expected tone and shadow details.

The highlight and shadow points' positions determine the visual contrast of the transparency you produce. For example, if a transparency comes out too heavy overall, you must select lighter densities of the highlight and shadow points. (See figures 16.1a and 16.1b.)

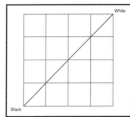

Fig. 16.1a.
Transparency output without correction.

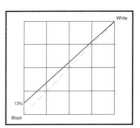

Fig. 16.1b.
File with correction prepared for output to transparency.

The best way to compensate for transparency output is to adjust the endpoints using color correction curves found in most programs (see Chapter 5, "Color").

Correcting for the contrast range bias in a film recorder may make the image look a bit washed out on the screen. If you take these production concerns into account, however, you should achieve an accurate transparency with no loss of detail in either the highlights or the shadows when it is reproduced. Because every film recorder has different amounts of bias, it takes experience to become proficient in compensating for the endpoints.

Table 16.1 illustrates the corrections that might be necessary for transparency output.

Always set the highlight point first and then the shadow point because any subsequent movement of the highlight shifts the position of the shadow. If an incorrect highlight setting has proper contrast, reset the highlight and then re-enter the shadow point at the same value as before.

In images such as snow scenes, which have a great degree of white and in which the more subtle detail could be lost, you may need to increase the first quartertone anywhere from 5 to 20 percent to retain the detail in those white areas. This situation is one of the few exceptions to simply picking endpoints of highlight and shadow.

Film Recorders

Film recording devices actually record pixel information. They are considered direct pixel imaging devices. The elements per inch (epi) the recorder can produce is directly related to the number of pixels in your image. A film recorder with 1270 epi exposes 1,270 pixels for every inch of film. This is very different from imagesetters, whose elements create dots. Remember, for film recording, you do not have dots but a continuous tone image related directly to the number of pixels contained in the image.

A high-end film recorder such as the MacDonald Detwiler produces 50 pixels per millimeter, or 1,270 pixels per inch. An image with 2,540 pixels across and down results in a transparency 2 inches by 2 inches (2,540 divided by 1,270 equals 2).

Because the fine grain in film transparencies requires much more information to reproduce a continuous tone image, this greater amount of information also results in large file sizes—20 megabytes for the 2-inch-square example. These file sizes can be unmanageable or harder to work with depending on your quality needs. Up-sampling an image 200

Table 16.1. Corrections for transparency output.

Condition	Correction Method
Highlight too light, shadow (contrast) OK	Increase highlight percentage, reset same shadow
Highlight dark, shadow (contrast) OK	Reset highlight in denser (darker) area, reset same shadow
HL OK, contrast heavy	Decrease shadow percentage
HL OK, contrast weak	Increase shadow percentage
HL heavy, contrast heavy	Lighten highlight, decrease shadow percentage
HL weak, shadow weak	Increase highlight percentages, increase shadow percentages

percent gives you a greater amount of pixel information resulting in a larger potential output size (see Chapter 1, "What Are Pixels?"). It is recommended you do not increase the amount of pixel information by more than 200 percent because this may result in a seriously degraded image quality in the form of softened edges with interpolation and pixelated edges with replication. In many circumstances, you may disregard this recommendation if you are not concerned with the highest quality possible.

A typical 8-by-10-inch transparency needs 10,160 pixels across and 12,700 pixels down. This file size is nearly 387 megabytes! You seldom see an entire file this size. Rather, you would use a file with half that amount of information with a total size of 90M. This file then would be interpolated 200 percent during output; the resulting transparency would be of the highest quality. Figure 16.2a is a full-size 8x10 transparency up-sampled 200 percent during output. Figure 16.2b shows how even small files when up-sampled properly can produce excellent results.

Fig. 16.2a.
Example of a full-size 8x10 transparency. File size 80M.

Fig. 16.2b.
Example of same image with fewer total pixels and therefore smaller file size.

Text

Combining text with a digital file for output to a transparency is possible in two ways. At very high resolutions, the text does not necessarily need to be anti-aliased. But in most cases, anti-aliased text produces outstanding text in a transparency. "Text" here refers to headlines or display text and not bodies of copy. The reason long galleys of copy are not recommended is that the photographic film reproductions of fine text are not as sharp as standard typesetting procedures. But you achieve dramatic results with text above 14 points. As shown in Chapter 13, "Reproducing Vectors as CT Bitmaps," you can take a PostScript linework file and render the PostScript into the bitmap. When the edges of the text are properly anti-aliased, you get a fine, pleasing edge and the text is appropriate for film output.

Conclusion

In most cases, output to transparency offers fewer production concerns than producing an image out to film separations. The ability to interpolate 200 percent at the output stage without loss of quality enables you to keep images at manageable sizes. Because the artist stays in RGB the entire time, color concerns are fewer and the output is more predictable. In most circumstances, persons trained for CMYK print production would rather make the separations decisions than have an artist guess at the proper figures. This relieves the artist from learning things he or she does not need to know and keeps the print production expert from correcting mistakes that stem from lack of experience. Because all the desired ad or image information is contained in the transparency, separations of various sizes and with various printing specifications can be made easily at the scanner shop. The transparency can be sent to people whose reproduction facilities may not be able to receive digital information. Overall, the options that transparency output can provide make the Macintosh retouching environment much more flexible.

The next chapter discusses the concepts of digital image output to video.

CHAPTER 17

Video Output

his chapter looks at the importance of flicker and color gamut concerns involving video output quality. The function of video output boards and analog versus digital layoff are discussed also.

Video Color

The resolutions of video color are smaller than the 24-bit color systems you have on your Mac, because broadcast video usually operates only with a signal of 8-bit RGB color. Two major types of video color spaces are NTSC and PAL. The National Television Systems Committee (NTSC) of the USA established a video color standard adopted by the FCC for general broadcast use in 1953. The Phase Alternation Line (PAL) video color space was adopted by Great Britain and Germany in 1967. The broadcast systems of NTSC and PAL are similar, but the numbers of total picture elements and color gamuts differ slightly. (See figure 17.1.)

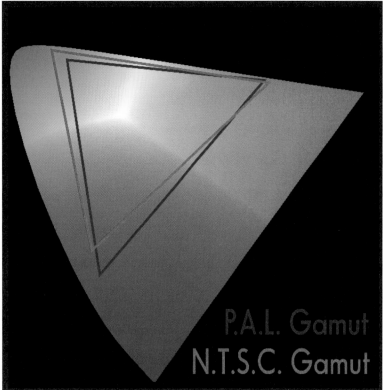

Fig. 17.1.
Color gamuts between NTSC and PAL differ slightly.

A one-pixel-high horizontal line blinks on and off 30 times per second and appears to be flickering more than a two-pixel-high line, which blinks 60 times per second. (The two-pixel line is refreshed alternately by an even and odd field.) You see continuous motion on a video image when the even and odd fields work together. If the title bar lines of Macintosh windows were two pixels thick, there would be no perceptible flicker. When you create or draw images for eventual video output, avoid horizontal or nearly horizontal lines composed of odd numbers of pixels. Because video is projected in horizontal lines, vertical lines have no flicker problem.

The PAL system uses 625-line television standards at 24 frames per second, and NTSC uses 525 lines at 30 frames per second. NTSC video projects alternating horizontal lines (fields) that are one pixel thick. Alternating even and odd fields are displayed on the screen every 1/30 of a second, which refreshes the image every 1/60 of a second.

For example, look at a title bar on a Macintosh window. The black and white lines you see are one pixel thick. If you were to bring in an image from the Mac that had the window title bar in it, the black and white bars alternately would be blinking on and off every 1/30 of second and would seem to jump or flicker on the screen.

The gamut of color for video is not as large as the gamut of color on the Macintosh. Colors that are outside of the gamut of video will bleed into adjoining areas. This bleeding creates an effect of color smearing, also called *bloom*, which usually is accompanied by undesirable noise interference. Working outside the video color gamut also decreases the apparent sharpness of the image. (See figure 17.2.)

Many programs have special color palettes that allow use only of colors within the video gamut. These programs cause the colors on the Macintosh to look duller to compensate for the limited NTSC gamut. Also available are plug-in production filters that filter out any colors outside the NTSC gamut. A filter specific to PAL may be necessary to filter out to the PAL gamut, which differs from the NTSC gamut. In both cases, compensation for video's limited color gamut is necessary to ensure the best possible output.

Fig. 17.2.
An example of bloom.

Video Output Boards

As mentioned in Chapter 2, "Color and Tones," video boards provide for display as well as acquisition and can program for many kinds of output formats. Many video boards can provide full red, green, and blue (RGB) in-out synchronization for video images. This capability means that you freely can import video images into your Mac as well as export to video without special encoding needs. Video boards also may supply an 8-bit alpha channel for overlays and *chroma keying*, which is text and title placement in video.

Out to Video (Layoff)

Getting an image from the Mac to videotape is called *layoff*. There are two types of layoff: *analog layoff* and *direct digital layoff*. You achieve analog layoff by recording the animation from the Mac into a video tape recorder (VTR), which is an analog format. Typically, in the layoff procedure, sync problems from the Mac and tape deck can result in unwanted duplication of frames. This problem is especially common with 24-bit images because these images cannot be moved fast enough from the Mac to keep up with the videotape's frame rate. To solve this problem, a device called a *frame-controller* synchronizes the layoff of the image from the computer to the tape. If you plan on frequent video output, a frame-controller is strongly recommended. (See figure 17.3.)

The direct digital layoff directly imports from the Mac into the digital edit processor. The advantage of this system is maintaining a digital-to-digital link. Direct digital layoff involves less loss of image quality because there is no conversion to an analog signal.

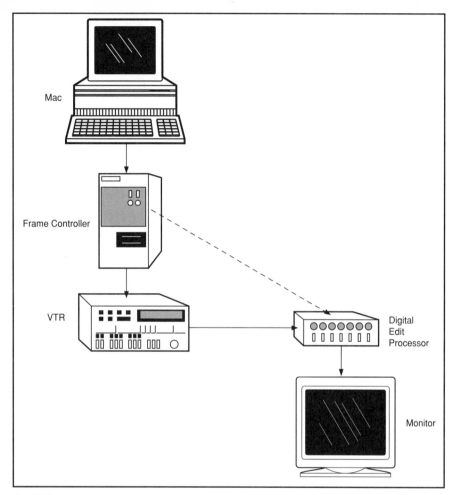

Fig 17.3.
A Mac system set up for video output.

Conclusion

In all color reproduction of digital images, you always should be aware of the conditions and properties of your chosen output. The conditions demanded by the output you are using must be understood and met to achieve the quality level most professionals require. By understanding the properties of your chosen output, you will find it easier to meet the required conditions.

Now that the types of output mediums from the Mac have been discussed, the next chapter looks at storage mediums available to hold your output files.

CHAPTER 18

Digital Files

Storage Medium

I n a production environment, files have three purposes. The first purpose involves working with and processing files. The second involves delivering the files. The third involves archiving the files. Of all file types available on the Macintosh, the TIFF format is the most widely used and the most flexible. TIFF is such a popular format that most service and production centers prefer to have files in this format.

Choosing a file type depends on which stage of the process you are in. The following information examines some file applications—specifically, working files, archiving, and high-end system links.

Working Files

Which file format you choose largely depends on memory space and the image programs you work with. If you are working with Photoshop alone, you may want to use only Photoshop's internal format because that format is quick to load. If you are working with ColorStudio's internal RIFF, you will save space because of the loss-less compression built into that format. But if you are working with both programs as well as others such as Painter, Pixel Paint, and Oasis, to name a few, you may choose more common formats that all the programs use, such as PICT and TIFF.

RGB or CMYK

The only choice you need to make before you deliver a file to output is whether the file needs to be prepared in RGB or in CMYK. Your service center will let you know which it prefers. Be sure the service center clearly explains what color space your image should be saved as.

After you convert an RGB file into CMYK, you should not convert the file back to RGB. Because the color gamut of CMYK is smaller than that of RGB, you will lose RGB color information during the CMYK-to-RGB conversion. Converting CMYK to RGB will not bring back the original RGB information. Always retain the original RGB file if you anticipate the need to make additional corrections. If additional corrections are necessary, discard the unwanted CMYK file and use the original RGB file to make the adjustments; then reconvert the file to CMYK. Using this procedure ensures that you will have the greatest amount of color information with which to work.

The sizes of CMYK files are larger than those of RGB files because of the additional eight bits of information. Saving the RGB information only, until you need to convert to CMYK, also saves valuable memory space.

Archiving

The third option used for digital files is *archiving*. Archiving stores digital information that you may need later. Archiving, which is intended for long-term storage, involves placing large quantities of data on one particular storage device. There are short-term benefits to storage though, such as freeing hard disk space and backing up important working files.

Linking to High-End Systems

Links to Scitex and Crosfield Systems prefer CT files; again, the most common is the TIFF file format. These high-powered electronic retouching stations are expensive to use, so supplying your data in the correct format the first time avoids any extra charges for system time. Ask your service center which file type it prefers.

File Types

File types or formats are like memos in the United Nations. The information being delivered must go to someone who can interpret it. For example, the memos meant for the French ambassador should go to the French embassy. If the French memos went to the Chinese embassy, they would be useless. Digital files are the same way; they must go where the file format is interpreted properly. Many different file types can be used on the Macintosh. Regardless of which format you decide to use, be sure to anticipate whether someone other than yourself will need to use the file and match that person's format preferences as well. Next, we cover the most common file formats and investigate their options.

PICT

PICT is Apple's internal format intended as a standard format for images in the Macintosh environment. Nearly every paint program on the Macintosh reads and writes to the PICT format. This standard enables you to exchange files freely among different Mac programs. The PICT format originally was only a one-bit-per-pixel format for MacPaint files. PICT later was modified to include up to 32 bits per pixel of color information. Sometimes color PICT files are referred to as PICT2 files. But it generally is accepted that when you refer to a PICT file, you mean the PICT format that allows color information. Figure 18.1 shows the various options for saving a PICT file. The relative file sizes are given in Appendix D, "Determining File Size."

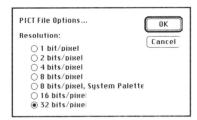

Fig. 18.1.
Options for saving a PICT file.

TIFF

The Tagged Image File Format (TIFF) is the most commonly used format and is one of the most flexible formats. TIFF, which was introduced by the Aldus corporation, is used extensively on the PC platform. Because you can save the file in an IBM PC format, you can pass the files from system to system with relative ease. Since TIFF is so flexible and is used by so many different programs, there are differences in how individual programs create TIFF files. This is becoming less the case as programs move toward a more standard interpretation of the TIFF format. Be aware that images saved in older versions of TIFF may

not work with some programs. Even so, most programs today accept the 5.0 version of the TIFF file format. The Crosfield StudioLink system, a high-end dedicated prepress system, now reads in the TIFF format directly. (See figure 18.2.)

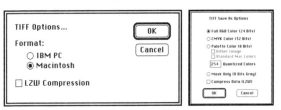

Fig. 18.2.
Options for saving a TIFF file.

The Tagged Image File Format also takes advantage of LZW compression. This compression, developed by the team of Lempel, Ziv, and Welch, results in a smaller file size. But recognize that not all page layout and composition programs read these LZW-compressed files. If ever in doubt, do not use the LZW compression option a program may offer you. Always be aware of where you plan to transport your images because that affects your decisions on file preparation.

EPS

The Encapsulated PostScript file format exports files to page layout programs. EPS originally was developed by Alsys for use in object-oriented PostScript graphics. An EPS or EPSF file is saved as one composite file of RGB or CMYK images for output directly to color PostScript printers. A full 32-bit separated CMYK file is saved as a five-file EPS file. This format saves the color separation information in a separate file for each of the four process colors. The fifth file, also known as a Pict preview, is used as a proxy for placement into a page layout program. The four other files are linked to this proxy; they always need to follow this file wherever the Pict preview is saved. Figure 18.3 illustrates this concept.

EPS Save As Options

○ RGB (1 File)
◉ CMYK (5 Files)
○ CMYK (1 File)

Selecting CMYK requires that a 4 color print selection be made in Printer Setup.

☐ Hex (ASCII) Picture Data
☐ Suppress Dot Gain
☐ Suppress Screen Angles
☐ Include CMYK data in main file

Comp Device [_____]

[OK]   [Cancel]

Fig. 18.3.
Options for saving an EPS file.

EPS files are much larger than files in most other formats. EPS files should be used primarily during the final stages of production to save storage space. The EPS format is used mainly when dealing with full-color images. Because EPS files are very large, if you work with gray-scale images, you should place the TIFF format into a page layout program to save valuable storage space.

TARGA

The TARGA or TGA format was designed for and is a standard for programs using the Truevision TARGA and TrueVista video boards. Primarily used in the IBM PC world, this format is useful if you plan to transport your images into PC systems. Many Macintosh programs enable you to save and read an image in the TGA file format. (See figure 18.4.) When you transport TGA files to other systems, you should remember that the filename must have a maximum of eight letters in the name plus a ".tga" suffix. An appropriate filename would be "maccolor.tga." When reading files from PC systems, be aware that there are several types of TARGA formats, each of which has

special considerations. Refer to the system where the file was created to be certain. Another consideration when you are exporting TARGA-type files to a PC-based system is the pixel aspect ratio mentioned in Chapter 1, "What Are Pixels?"

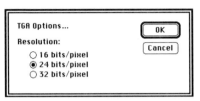

TGA Options...   [OK]
Resolution: [Cancel]
   ○ 16 bits/pixel
   ◉ 24 bits/pixel
   ○ 32 bits/pixel

Fig. 18.4.
Options for saving a TGA file.

Photoshop

This format is the default format used in Adobe's Photoshop image retouching program. Photoshop is a simple format that has no compression associated with the files. You can save the Photoshop format in a number of different color spaces from one to 32 bits. In addition to the 24 bits of color information, this format saves a single alpha channel or multiple 8-bit alpha channels for various image compositing purposes. Photoshop is a clean, quick saving and loading format. But if storage space is a concern, choose a different file format. In most cases, you cannot use this format in a page layout program. If you plan to use the image in other Macintosh retouching programs, save the file in one of the previously mentioned file formats. The Photoshop format also can be read directly by the Scitex Visionary and VIP II system, a dedicated prepress system. The reading of these files can be very time-consuming. You also may want to use the Scitex CT format, mentioned later.

RIFF

The Raster Image File Format is the default format of Fractal Design's ColorStudio program. RIFF, which has been created to work with 32-bit information, also includes options for compressing the file to save storage space. In most cases, you would not use the RIFF format in a page layout program. RIFF is extremely useful in conjunction with ColorStudio because it can save space. But if you intend to use the image in other retouching programs, you need to save the image in one of the previously mentioned formats. See Fig. 18.5.

Fig. 18.5
Options for saving a RIFF file.

Scitex CT (Continuous Tone)

This image file format is not a native Macintosh format. Scitex CT is used to export 32-bit CMYK or gray-scale images into a format that the Scitex prepress workstation can read. Saving files into this format offers a useful way of connecting the Macintosh to a dedicated prepress system used by many professional color separators. Many color separation shops with Scitex systems have an extension to their workstations called Visionary, now known as VIP II. This extension links a Macintosh computer to a Scitex

system and allows the free exchange of files from one system to another as long as the files are saved in the Scitex CT format. If a separator does not have the VIP extension, you still can export the Scitex CT file to a nine-track tape system attached to the Macintosh, which then can be read by the tape drives linked to most Scitex systems. Using a tape drive entry method is less expensive than buying a VIP II extension, but saving to a nine-track tape is time-consuming.

Crosfield CT (Continuous Tone)

Like the Scitex CT, this format enables you to export files that the Crosfield workstations can read. The same options apply except that the dedicated system Crosfield uses to link the Macintosh is called StudioLink.

Knowing which format to use for your specific output ensures that your production goes smoothly and that you avoid spending time resaving files into different formats. See figure 18.6, which was saved in different file formats with the size of each format listed below.

Fig. 18.6.
The image was saved into each file format.

PICT — 3.317K

TIFF — 3.348K

RAW — 3.348K

TGA — 4.49K

SCITEX — 4.49K

EPS — 4.49K

Photoshop — 3.348K

The next chapter discusses some of the guidelines for deciding what type of equipment you should purchase to best suit your needs.

Storage Devices

Working with digital color images means working with extremely large files. The storage devices that hold these files are as varied as the formats you can save them in.

Hard drives offer a great amount of storage space—up to one gigabyte (1,000M) of information. Because hard drives are not very portable, *removable hard drives* are another popular device. Syquest cartridges and Bernoulli cartridges are two common types of removable hard drives used to deliver up to 88M of digital information.

Up-and-coming storage devices are read and write optical drives. Until recently, optical drives, which are based on the same technology as music CDs, could only read information. Called CD-ROMs (read-only memory), these optical devices are popular for multimedia because CD-ROMs have the storage capacity required for images used in interactive video programs. A CD-ROM is considered a write-once, read many (WORM) drive because you cannot change information after it has been written.

Newer optical drives enable you to write to the disk and alter the information as many times as you like. The 5 1/2-inch and the newer 3 1/2-inch optical drives allow the reading and writing of information as freely as conventional magnetic-based drives. Optical drives are considered extremely stable and reliable. The 5 1/2-inch formats can hold up to 268M on each side, and the 3 1/2-inch format can hold up to 128M. Considering that in nearly five years the digital storage capability in 3 1/2 inches of physical space has increased more than 130 times from 800K floppies, you can imagine what possible breakthroughs in storage capabilities will occur in the next five years.

The next chapter discusses considerations you may have when deciding what types of hardware and software are appropriate for your work environment.

CHAPTER 19

Buying Hardware and Software

Many times we have been asked by people, "What kind of equipment and software should we buy?" The answer can be a short recommendation or a complete proposal to research an entire digital color system. Either way, the same questions must be asked. Confusion over what to buy has escalated with the rapid pace of new technology and the increasing number of vendors in the marketplace. Those who have been working with color for a while only need look back just four years ago at the number of vendors and technologies available compared to today. The Macintosh was a rarity in the printing and photographic trades back then. Now the Mac is seen in a majority of print shops in the United States, and digitally produced transparencies are readily available to consumers throughout the country.

This chapter is a guide to help digital color equipment buyers make a good decision about what kind of hardware and software will satisfy their needs. Whether you are producing color presently or are a new entrant into the digital color field, important questions must be answered before you purchase your color gear if you want to get the best pixels for your dollar.

Digital Image Systems

Walking into a desktop publishing trade show or reading a trade equipment publication presents you with an array of new products, old products, state-of-the-art products, and products on the drawing board (*vaporware*). These products perform specialized functions or handle many tasks, such as *workstations*. Software is devoted to both low-end and high-end users. Some products work with specific applications, and others can link up to a wide array of equipment.

This vast number of product possibilities is a wonderful asset for someone wanting to purchase a color system, unless you are a first-time buyer. For first-time buyers, making a decision on what hardware and software to buy can be a frightening experience, especially if you have a limited budget. The many product names, buzzwords, technical specifications, and sheer volume of possible product choices and combinations create much confusion and doubt at purchase time.

If this description applies to you, relax; you've taken a good first step by reading this book and educating yourself about producing color on the Mac. By the time you reach this chapter, you should have a good idea of the various tools available to you, which tools you need to use for the work you plan to do, and what types of input and output devices are available. In other words, a little education about the color medium should be your first step toward buying color system equipment.

For companies with a substantial budget, we recommend using a consultant who specializes in system configurations. The experience of a consultant will be of great value in selecting the best purchase for your production requirements.

The following section contains questions you should ask yourself to help you decide what equipment is right for your particular needs.

Determine a Budget

Usually, the first question any good equipment salesperson asks a customer involves the amount he or she can spend. This question enables the salesman to eliminate choices of products and show the customer what goods are available in that price range.

Make phone calls or shop to get approximate prices of the types of equipment you may need. Examine the products available in your price range and in the next higher price range. This enables you to see what you give up because of budgetary restraints. If the equipment in the next range up appears to have many important advantages over the cheaper gear, you may want to rethink or reorganize your finances in this area to move up to the next price level of equipment.

If you are buying equipment to produce sellable work, determine the daily cost of the equipment (from the payments you will be making on the equipment; the hourly cost of the operator; and the material costs of paper, film, and so on). Divide that cost by the number of jobs you estimate you will do each day. The resulting number is the estimated cost per unit. Subtract the estimated cost per unit from the average price that you estimate you will charge for each job to get the average profit per job. (You also may want to consider training costs or a lesser number of units per shift due to the time it takes to learn how to operate the equipment efficiently.) The calculation is summed up here:

Daily cost (payments + operator hourly rate + material cost) *divided by*

Estimated number of jobs per day *equals*

Estimated cost per unit

Average price per job charged *minus*

Estimated cost per unit *equals*

Average profit per job unit

Or:

Daily cost ÷ Estimated # of jobs = Estimated cost per unit

Average price per job − Estimated cost per unit = Average profit per job unit

What is the production capacity of the equipment? Get an idea of how many units or jobs can be produced per operation shift. Estimate how many jobs you can sell each week of operation. Multiply the number of jobs per week by the average profit per job to get the average profit per week. This number indicates the amount of money you can expect to earn with the equipment for each week of operation. How does the amount of expected weekly profit compare with the weekly payments on the equipment? You need to make enough money selling the work derived from the machine to cover its payments.

Will the equipment bring in new customers, or will it enable you to better service the customers you have? Will the new equipment help keep your present customers? If the answers are yes, consider the actual profits of the equipment to be higher because you are increasing your customer base and current customer satisfaction. After you know the potential profitability of your equipment choice, you have a more realistic view of your budgetary decisions.

For those of you who are just hobbyists, the question of budget is much simpler: you set an amount and live with it. Cost per unit and profit are not part of the picture.

What Do I Get?

When you have decided what you can spend, you must decide exactly what you want to do with the equipment. Look at this decision, first from a basic level of input, image manipulation, pagination, and output. Are you going to work with supplied digitized images? If so, you may not want an input device. If you want to use image-capture techniques, you must plan to buy a scanner or video capture system.

Do you want to do complex image manipulations? How about ad assembly and pagination? Will you use the computer as a design tool? How much is speed a factor in your production needs? These questions determine what kind of software, the power of hardware, and the amount of storage you need.

Will you handle large or small quantities of images? What will your average image file size be? Will you store images for long periods? What kind of storage medium will customers who use their own input devices supply? Your memory requirements are decided by these questions.

What kind of output devices will you produce work for? Will your job time frame demand producing output in your shop, or can you send the job out somewhere else? Can your budget accommodate a specialized output device?

By answering all the previous questions with a knowledgeable salesperson, you arrive at one or two choices of equipment packages. Be sure to collect all brochures and all technical data available for the choices.

Whose Equipment Do I Get?

Locate the people who sell the type of gear you want. Look through all the trade publications available, and pick out which manufacturers produce the types of equipment in which you are interested. Meet with a sales representative to discuss your needs. Trade shows are especially good for meeting manufacturers' representatives because many contacts are in one spot, which saves you much time and travel.

When you meet with the salespeople, tell them of your budget and your needs. Discuss the questions mentioned in the previous section. Get price and specifications for each package they recommend.

After you have decided on a particular equipment system, ask about compatibility with other brands of hardware and software. Be concerned with the capability to upgrade and expand your basic system. Find out how long the equipment has been on the market and when the next upgrade is expected. Can you apply any new upgrades to your planned purchase?

Find out from the salespeople who else makes this type of equipment. Find out their opinions of the competitors' equipment and how that equipment compares. If you have spoken to the competitors previously, bring up any shortcomings that arose about the gear and try to verify the information.

Arrange a demonstration to see whether the equipment operates to the specifications given. Bring in work to do that represents your average and not-so-average job.

Finally, arrange to meet people who have the same equipment. Observe this equipment at work. Ask about productivity and reliability. Ask how long it takes to learn and profitably operate the equipment. See whether other people are happy with this equipment and the manufacturer. Were service and support from the manufacturer good? Would the owners buy more of this brand of equipment?

Choosing Software

Choosing software is not as difficult as choosing hardware. You should follow the same criteria as when choosing hardware. If you have more than one Macintosh, you should buy a copy of the software for each. Although you may be tempted to buy a single copy of a software program and copy it to all your workstations, there are two important reasons not to. First, having a copy for each workstation ensures that each Macintosh has the proper documentation and any future upgrades; second, copying software is illegal. Software does not cost nearly as much as hardware, but when you start buying many copies, the cost runs up quickly.

Regardless, the cost of software is not so much that you should lock yourself into one digital image program. Working with only one software brand eliminates other features and possibilities available from another software product. The basics described in this book enable you to explore any Macintosh image program. The bottom line is that if a program provides an effect that you want, buy it!

A common complaint is that a different program is too hard to learn. If you have a thorough familiarity with the ideas presented in this book, learning new programs is not a problem. The short-term investment of learning the hows of programs other than the one you usually use always is rewarded by increased capabilities. You limit yourself by not exploring the possibilities different software products offer.

Software solutions to color reproduction should be evaluated not only by what the programs decide for you but what reproduction choices you can make independent of the software. Many programs that offer simple solutions to color reproduction are often taking shortcuts that may or may not be appropriate for your needs. A program's true worth and strength is not only how good the program's shortcuts are, but more importantly the software's ability to override these enhancements and apply your own choices based on your personal knowledge, experience and desires.

Most advanced cameras offer, in addition to an automatic exposure setting, the option to manually adjust the exposure. Often the automatic setting is fine but with a manual override the photographer has the freedom to explore and create with only his experience and imagination as boundaries. If a photographer did not have the option of manual settings, many creative effects would not be possible.

Companies that insist upon making everything easier for you often limit your freedom to choose. If a software product offers a simplified way of reproducing color does the software also offer an option to override their choices with yours? All the episodes of Star Trek we've ever watched always have Scotty or LaForge switching to manual override because the computer was not doing what it was supposed to do. If the software doesn't provide you with what you want, the software should allow you to switch to a manual override and let you decide the best course to take.

Conclusion

By now, you should know a lot more about hardware and software than you did before you started. If your detective work is thorough, you now should be an *informed buyer*, someone who can make a logical and practical decision on what kind of equipment to buy. Now you can look at the choices available, weigh the pros and cons, and place your order.

What if you don't feel informed, but instead feel more confused? Because not everyone is good at researching equipment specifications, specialized consultants are available to help you determine your equipment needs. In addition, the consultants are familiar with the latest gear available. Look in the trade magazines for these types of specialists under consulting companies.

Remember that trade magazines also have their own natural specialties and biases; nothing can substitute for seeing the equipment and software at work.

Questions you may want to ask someone who shows you a wonderful-looking image include how long, what total material, and what labor cost did it actually take to produce that piece. Through enough trial and error, and unlimited material and labor, any one piece can be made to look great. Producing the piece under a deadline with fixed costs and profit is quite another story. Make sure that the salesperson knows how the piece was produced and understands your needs and what you want to do.

The next chapter discusses the details of preparing a work environment after you have made your product choices.

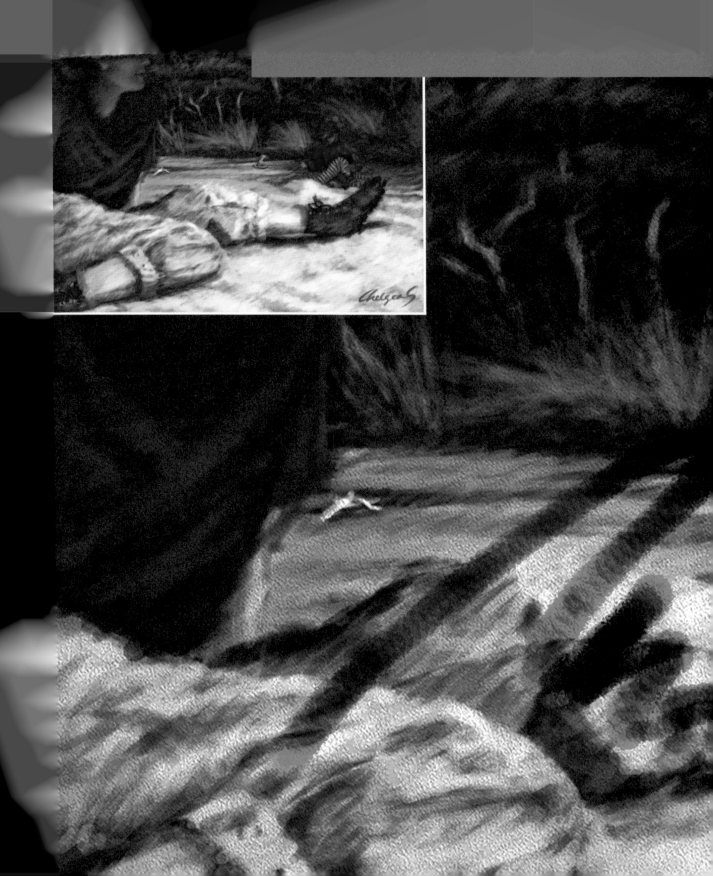

Creating a Work Environment

The important aspects of producing digital images in the work environment are planning and performing a job, viewing the input and output subjects, and establishing your own best methods. This work-environment chapter focuses on the practical side of digital image production. You should make preplanning, proper viewing conditions, and analysis of customers' needs a part of your everyday work routine. The results of adding these disciplines to your work procedures are increased productivity and happier customers because work gets performed correctly the first time.

In this section, the output form of the work is an RGB file for the customer's use, a CMYK file for the customer's use, an RGB file for film (transparency) output, or halftone separation film and prepress proof for color printing.

The job production procedure is outlined in Appendix A, "Producing a Job."

Producing a Job, Step by Step

The most important step in producing jobs on the computer is the first step: preplanning the entire job. In the preplanning stage, you analyze the customer's job information to determine what the customer wants from you, and then you plan the steps necessary to produce a job that satisfies the customer's desires. Preplanning is critical to success because laying out a plan of attack saves unnecessary operations, coordinates all efforts, and discovers potential errors that can result in delivering work the customer does not want.

The Preplanning Stage

Before starting on any production work on the computer or input device, you should review the entire job from end use to production steps, to the basic components and instruction given by the customer. You perform this analysis, (the first part of the preplanning stage), to determine if you can produce the job with the components and information given.

Job Analysis

The first part of the preplanning process involves the accuracy of communication of the customer's wants to the craftspeople who will perform the work. The customer can communicate directly or through intermediaries such as art directors or salesmen. If the customer uses intermediaries, there is a risk of confusion caused by missing information or a misunderstanding about the client's instructions. Many times, this author has been in a situation in which the salesman's idea of a job's composition and the customer's ideas were markedly different. So whenever possible, if you have any doubts about the details of a job, try to speak to the customer or job designer directly.

Nonverbal information from the customer comes in the form of written instructions, photographic images (transparencies, art, photographs), and a drawing of how the completed job is to look. This drawing is called a comprehensive drawing, or *comp*. Comprehensive drawings show the exact position of all job elements: images, text, tints, and headlines. Comps also give all text fonts as well as colors of type, borders, tint blocks, and lines. Images are designated as colored, black and white, or needing special effects.

The accuracy of the comp is critical to the success of the completed job. A poorly made comp does not convey the exact wishes of the client and can send the craftspeople who work on the job in wrong directions. For example, problems such as images not fitting image windows correctly, type going into a person's head, or text disappearing into a background of similar tone are results of poor comprehensive drawings. Many comps are delivered incomplete, lacking all the necessary information to produce the job. Some comps are too rough, lacking accuracy, so when you assemble all the components, they do not fit as shown in the supplied comp.

Images should be shown on the comp with a *stat*, which is a photographic copy of the actual image being used. Stats can be of low quality because their only function is to show an image's position and *crop* (the part of the image being used). It is important that the stat be of the image being used in the job and also be the actual size desired. Simply sketching a representation of an image in a window on the comp may not be good enough; such a sketch may cause a proportionality problem. *Proportionality* problems result in the image not fitting the window in either the x-axis or the y-axis. A sketch does not take into account the actual proportionality of the image, so the subject may end up fitting a window left to right, but not top to bottom (see figure 20.1). Placing crop marks on an image to designate its fit to a window is a poor substitute for using stats and leads to proportionality errors.

Another proportionality error is to ask for a 35 mm slide to be enlarged full frame into a square window. Since a 35 mm slide is a rectangle, this request is impossible.

Fig. 20.1.
Proportionality problem from using a sketch.

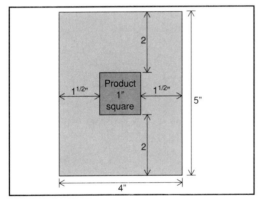

Fig. 20.1a.
Customer's 4"x5" original with product in center of colored background.

If the customer does not supply image stats on the comp, you should check all images to ensure that they fit their prospective windows in both directions to avoid proportionality problems. If an image is being cut out instead of going into a window, check this image's size to see what area it will cover in the layout of the job. Be sure the cut-out image is not covering up other elements of the job. Be on the lookout for image fit problems, which are common.

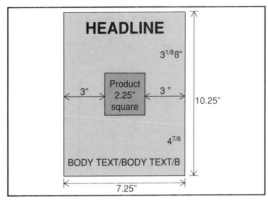

Fig. 20.1b.
Customer's comprehensive drawing shows product in colored background in this position at 8"x10" size with 1/8" bleed of image on all four sides for trim.

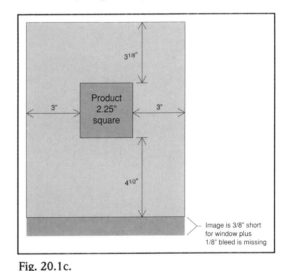

Fig. 20.1c.
Actual result when image is scanned and put in window. There is not enough background to fill the window, a proportionality problem not shown in the customer's sketch.

Besides size and proportionality errors, you also may encounter design errors such as placing text in a background of similar tone or color. Because the text does not stand out from the background, the text is hard to read. Making the comp in full color eliminates this mistake.

Sometimes, the photographic image components of the job are supplied without a comp or stats. Having no comp or stats to check the image size and crop against is inviting disaster in most cases. There must be a stat somewhere! In this case, if the customer wants the work to proceed, any mistakes made because information supplied on the comp is not available are chargeable to the customer. Make every effort to get the comp or a copy of the comp before starting the job to avoid the unpleasant task of collecting extra unnecessary charges from your customer.

Take the time necessary to examine carefully each comprehensive drawing given to you. Be sure to understand every element of the job shown in the comp. Visualize what the final, assembled, full-color result will look like. A craftsman who accurately reads a comp produces work from start to finish with better results and fewer headaches because he detects any omissions of important information.

The next part of job analysis is to inspect the images supplied by the customer. As previously mentioned, you should check all images for size, crop, and proportionality. Look also at the condition of each image. Is it scratched, bent, or stained? Does the image have spots in the emulsion that can't be wiped off? Are there any obvious color casts or exposure problems? Is the image different from the supplied stat?

If the answer to any of the previous questions is yes, some communication with the customer is in order. See whether you can crop the damaged area from the image area. If you cannot crop out the problem area, the image should be replaced, if possible. Sometimes the customer has similar alternative images. If your customer is a photographer, he may be able to reshoot the image.

Always make sure that a customer knows if he supplied you with poor or damaged images for the job. Informing the customer is important because you may be blamed for damaging the images if the customer is not aware of the original damage. You can offer to correct or subdue the damage if that is possible with your color system. Tell the customer you can do a better job if, for example, you remove the dirt from the sky in transparency B. The axiom "garbage in garbage out" may get you a better original to use. This way the customer gets a better job and you earn more profit on the job. (Remember, the customer's happiness is your goal!) Additional benefits of accurate image analysis include impressing the customer with your expertise, gaining the customer's trust, and not spending time on an image that eventually gets rejected because of poor quality.

After you have examined the comp for correctness and the images for quality, you must consider the technical aspects of the job. You need to determine two main technical considerations to produce any job on the Macintosh: what form you want the job delivered in and what the image requirements for output are.

The final form of the digital information you deliver typically can be an RGB file, a CMYK file, an RGB file for transparency output, or separation films with a prepress proof. Make sure the customer knows what forms are available from you, and be ready to help the customer determine which format is best for his needs.

The technical image requirements for output are crucial pieces of information that must be correct the first time. Image requirement information includes image resolution, the file type, and the final form the job will be produced in. The image resolution is dependent on the resolution of the output device being used and determines the number of pixels that are contained in the file being output. (See Chapter 1, "What Are Pixels?") The output device also determines the file type, such as PICT or TIFF. You should be aware of the final form of the job so that you can incorporate any necessary modifications into the job file. For example, transparency outputs need adjustments in contrast for the contrast range of the transparency format. (See Chapter 16, "Digital Film

Recording.") Any job that is being printed must have the following information: film type, emulsion direction, line screen requirement, and any UCR or GCR requirements. If you do not understand the technical requirements for a job, find someone in the reproduction chain of the process who knows, and find out what the requirements are.

Having the wrong technical image requirements results in an incorrect output. The consequences of supplying a job that can't be output properly are schedule delays, extra expense, and an unhappy customer. You can avoid these consequences by getting all needed technical information in the preplanning stage. Don't be pressured to start work on a job that is missing standard required information.

Production Planning

Now that you know from the comp what the customer wants, and your job analysis has confirmed that it is possible to produce the job with the components supplied, you must decide on the steps and order of steps to produce the job. If the job involves many steps, write up a list of all the procedures you must accomplish. Assign tasks to each work station being used, and place the operations in chronological order.

If others are working on the job with you, discuss your plan with them and let them know all your requirements, especially the technical ones. Remember, teamwork takes communication to be successful. The left hand needs to know what the right hand is doing.

After you have planned how to produce the job, examine the equipment you will use. Does it work? Can the equipment satisfy the technical requirements of the job? Is the machine in top working order? Has the proper software been installed? Has the equipment been calibrated? Has standard maintenance been performed? Is there enough open memory for the size of files you will work with?

After you determine that the equipment is ready and able to perform the job, you are set to begin production according to plan.

Producing the Job

As your skill at preplanning improves, you will find that production proceeds according to plan. Ideally, there will be no interruption in the sequence of events you have scripted, and the production stage will travel smoothly from start to finish as planned.

During the production stage, any preplanning flaws come out. Missing information causes the production process to pause or stop because you must determine what information is missing and where to go to get it, and then you must get the missing information. Problems such as proportionality errors also make you deviate from your production script. If you must deviate from your plan and improvise, note whether the improvising is a special situation for the job or if you changed your sequence because of something you missed in the preplanning stage. Add a step to the preplanning procedure to anticipate a recurring problem that causes production delays.

Remember that producing good color is a complex task and that it takes practice and patience to develop your skills to a journeyman level. Make note of your mistakes and learn from them. Expect to have good days and bad days.

Post-Production Analysis

The job is finished and in its final form. Now is the time to see whether the job satisfies all the requirements of the comp, the customer's written requests, and the technical requirements of the job.

Does the job look like you imagined? Did the equipment perform as expected? Is the quality of the job what you expected?

This is your last chance to check for production errors. Look over any areas that were especially difficult. Check that cloning for realism. Look at the vignettes for smoothness. Be sure the edges where the cutouts join have been blurred correctly. Stand back and take a good look. Go over the job ticket and double-check the output requirements. If you are satisfied, go on to the next job. If not, note why and fix it.

As you learn to master the fascinating medium of computer color, you will appreciate the wonderful tools that today's technology makes available to you. Your ability to preplan and use the tools available to you to produce color on the Macintosh will grow as you produce more and more color. Each job is a unique puzzle that you must solve using your experience and skill with the tools of today's electronic color craftsman.

Viewing Conditions

Accurate analysis of the images you are working with is important at all phases of job production. Before starting the job, you and the customer should analyze the images to be used to ensure that everyone involved understands what the customer wants. You must inspect the quality of each original carefully before input to ensure that the images will be acceptable to the client. During production, you may need to stop and take a good look at the image and note special areas you are working on. After production, you carefully must compare the image with its output form (if the form is a transparency or prepress proof) for reproduction accuracy and check the quality of any special changes or modifications you performed on the original subjects.

To achieve the best analysis of the photographic images supplied by the customer, you must standardize the viewing conditions used to analyze the images. Standardized lighting ensures that the original and reproduction images will be seen the same way each time, regardless of the time of day or location. If every viewing station uses the same conditions of illuminance, most perception variables are eliminated. The result is less confusion and better communication of opinions and ideas between customer and craftsman.

For example, say you mail your client a prepress proof of a CMYK file that looks like a perfect match in your viewing booth. The client returns the proof with the comment, "Too red overall." You shift the image's gray balance to reduce the red component, reproof the image, and examine the result. The new proof is a whole step cooler than the previous proof and is a little cooler than the original too. You ship the new proof to the customer, and the customer sends it back marked, "Still too red!" You're in a tough spot. Your viewing conditions show that if you subtract more red, the result will be significantly different (cooler) than the original image the customer wanted to match. Did the client change his mind about matching the appearance of the original? You call the client, who says that nothing has changed, you are to 'match copy.'

The next step is to find out what kind of lighting conditions the client is using to view the original. A visit to the customer's office is necessary. At the client's office, you give him the original and proof and ask to see him where he always views the work you send him. The client goes to a table and viewer by a large window and puts the original transparency on the viewer and the prepress proof on a table by the window. Sure enough, the proof looks too red when compared to the original on the viewer. Why does it look different here when it looked cooler than the original in your viewing booth? The answer is usually the spectral wavelength output of the overhead lighting or viewer the client uses. In this case, though, you happen to look out the window and notice a huge red Coca-Cola ad on the brick wall across from the window. The sun reflecting off the ad into the window biases all the viewing light toward red!

The moral of this story is that everyone involved with making color judgments of images must look at the images using the same lighting conditions. This means everyone from client to Macintosh operator to pressmen. Otherwise, confusion, poor customer relations, waste of time and materials, and lower profit result.

The printing industry uses standardized lighting as prescribed by the American National Standard Institute, No. 2.32. This standard calls for the lighting temperature of the bulbs in the transparency viewers and in the viewing booths to approximate the color temperature of normal daylight, 5,000 degrees Kelvin (abbreviated D5000K). Also, the surround area in the viewer must be a neutral gray. The *surround* area is the adjacent area the viewer is located in. Gray is the best surround color because it does not influence color viewing toward any cast. (As previously mentioned, viewing proofs next to windows with Coke ads is hazardous to your productivity!)

Viewing booths come in large stationary models and portable desktop versions for small working areas and easy transport. If you are working with a printer, discuss his viewing conditions and check with your color buying clients on the methods of viewing they use. Purchasing a portable viewer is handy for clients who do not use standardized lighting conditions.

Get everyone on the same page as far as viewing conditions. Eliminate a guaranteed source of confusion. You will be happy you did!

Room Conditions

The natural tendency when working with color monitors is to turn off all the lights and work in a completely dark, isolated room. The monitor gives a glowing and intense view of an image. This view can be aesthetically pleasing, but there are three reasons why working in a dark, isolated room is highly detrimental to producing good work. The first reason is what is called the isolation factor. Being in an undisturbed area is one thing if you work with many other people, but one of the biggest contributors to understanding how to work with digital imagery is to consult with other people on their techniques and methods. Being isolated cuts you off from any useful interaction. The second reason a dark room is not the best idea is the viewing conditions. You cannot realistically judge color from reflective art illuminated by a single light. Yes, some people actually believe that the monitor is sufficient lighting to analyze the color of original copy. Often a swivel lamp is nearby, but the illumination from this round type of lamp is not sufficient either.

The last and most significant reason for not working in total darkness is eye strain. You know that the pupil in your eye opens and closes to let in light. While you stare at a monitor, your pupil is opened very little. When you look into the dark, your pupil opens wide to let in as much light as possible. When your eyes go back and forth like this constantly, you get eye strain. This strain tires you quicker and makes it more difficult to spend long periods in front of the monitor. This strain also affects your ability to judge color.

Lighting a work area with dim, even lighting is your best bet. Experiment with different levels at first, and find what room light level is the most comfortable for your eyes. From then on, keep the room lighting constant for the benefit of consistency in color viewing.

Don't forget your computer's environment too. Computers have to be worked on occasionally, peripherals installed, cables removed, and so forth. Provide enough room to prevent having to move the system every time something is done with the system. If your space allows, try to resist the urge to put your Mac system directly up against the wall. Allow enough space to step behind the Mac and all the other peripherals you have attached. This will prevent the cursing when you need to move something. The air and ventilation given your system also will ensure that your system does not overheat. You're creative. Make it work!

Establishing Your Own Best Methods

We have discussed the importance of a structured production process using preplanning and a logical production sequence. The novice color craftsman should master a structured procedure and follow it for every job. As the standard procedure is used more, fine-tune it as much as possible for exactness and best results.

After you are comfortable with the standard procedure, you can begin to develop methods of your own that help in special situations, with special clients, or with certain types of equipment. You may have a customer who uses an unusual type of original film or set of paints that need a special color calibration. You may have a client whose quality requirements enable you to process work at lower resolutions that save time and file space. Maybe a certain lab's film recorder

produces transparencies that look as though you could supply more contrast to give a better result. Learn how to ask your client the right questions.

The idea is to watch for exceptions to the rule that become trends. These exceptions are jobs for certain clients or jobs performed on certain pieces of equipment that consistently can be improved even though you followed your standard procedures properly. Be sure that the exception is a trend (happens more often than not), and not just a rare exception. As you deal with color images more, you will find that there are many one-time exceptions. *Do not* be too quick to abandon your standard procedure quickly because of occasional exceptions! *Do* be alert for bad situations with clients that are becoming trends, because most trends of delivering consistently poor work result in customers who go elsewhere to have their work performed.

Once again, experience and alertness will help you adjust to the many production situations you will find while reproducing color.

This final chapter illustrates the importance of planning and preparedness to produce color work. A sound plan of attack and standardized viewing conditions for each job eliminate potential errors and time wasted trying to figure out what the client wants or which production steps to perform next.

Appendix A, "Producing a Job," contains step-by-step procedures of the image manipulation process described in the first part of this chapter. Also, a procedure for input scanning of images for CMYK files is given in Appendix B, "A Step-by-Step Guide to Color Separating by Scanning."

We invite everyone reading this book to enter the world of color on the Mac. Start out slowly and simply. Try some of the tools available. Practice some of the techniques given in this book. Use some good and bad images. Let your imagination go, experiment, and most of all, have fun.

Producing a Job

I. Preplanning

  A. Creative considerations

    1. Image types

      a) Color

      b) Black and white

      c) Special effect (posterize, tritone, etc.)

    2. Image attributes

      a) Size and location

      b) Proportion (fit to window or stat)

      c) Cropping

    3. Text attributes

      a) Size and location

      b) Font

      c) Color

    4. Tints and borders

      a) Location

      b) Color

      c) Trapping

  B. Technical considerations

    1. Type of output

a) RGB file

b) CMYK file

c) CMYK films and proof

d) Film recorder (transparency)

e) Other

2. Type of output device

a) Resolution of device (number of pixels needed)

b) File format required

(1) PICT

(2) TIFF

(3) TARGA

(4) Other

3. Final use

a) Printing on press

(1) Line screen requirement

(2) Type of film

(a) Negative

(b) Positive

(3) Emulsion direction

(4) Special considerations

(a) UCR

(b) GCR

(c) Dot gain

(d) Spot colors

b) Transparency

(1) Color gamut considerations

(2) Contrast range adjustment for RGB

c) Other (special digital use by customer)

C. Makeup of production procedure list

1. List all steps to make job

2. Put all steps in chronological sequence

3. Assign tasks if more than one person is working on job

4. Check equipment

II. **Produce job as planned**

III. **Post-operation**

A. Examine output

1. Satisfies comp and creative considerations?

2. Satisfies technical considerations?

3. Any last-minute changes by customer?

4. Is job clean, dirt-free?

A Step-by-Step Guide to Color Separating by Scanning

I. **Prescan evaluation**

   A. Analyze image quality

      1. Dirt, scratches, spots, etc.

      2. Exposure

         a) Normal

         b) High key (too bright)

         c) Low key (too dark)

      3. Color cast

         a) Neutral appearance (no casts), or

         b) Color cast (pink, green, blue, etc.)

   B. Check image to comp

      1. Size (magnification in scanner range?)

      2. Proportionality (fits window both dimensions?)

      3. Crop (area desired fits comp as shown?)

   C. Technical considerations

      1. Number of pixels needed (height and width)

      2. Type of file needed (TIFF, PICT, etc.)

      3. Printing considerations

         a) Line screen requirement

         b) Film type

         c) Emulsion direction

         d) Special conditions

            (1) UCR

            (2) GCR

            (3) Dot gain

II. **Mount originals**

   A. Select proper input image holder

      1. Template or slide

      2. Drum

   B. Clean originals

   C. Mount originals to image holder

      1. Place in template or slide

      2. Mount on drum

         a) Use anti-Newton ring powder under 400 percent enlargement

         b) Use oil mounting over 400 percent

   D. Examine mounted images for dirt or bubbles

   E. Place image holder in scanner

III. **Scanner setup**

   A. Mechanical considerations

      1. Position scanner optics and focus to original

      2. Set any apertures needed and balance scanner's input

         a) Photomultipliers null to clear drum

         b) CCD run calibration routine

      3. Set the sampling area (crop) of the input copy (format: landscape or portrait)

      4. Focus

      5. Check available memory versus file size

   B. Setting the endpoints

      1. Locate highlight point; set density and dot percentage for YMC

      2. Locate shadow point; set density and dot percentage for YMC

  C. RGB scan

IV. Size scanned image

V. Exporting for CMYK (if going to print)

  A. Check and adjust highlight and shadow points if necessary

  B. Check and adjust black printer

  C. Set sharpness

  D. Make any tone and cast adjustments

  E. Make any color corrections

  F. Set in any UCR or GCR needed

  G. Set output characteristics

      1. PPI

      2. Line screen (if needed)

      3. Imagesetter PPD and characteristics, or film recorder

      4. Dot gain adjustments (if needed)

  H. Export RGB file

  I. Place Image into electronic layout page

  J. Send electronic page to imagesetter and run film

IV. Post-scan analysis

  A. Check for dirt, scratches, and bubbles

  B. Check image size and number of pixels

  C. Check image settings

      1. Highlight

      2. Shadow

      3. Color casts

      4. Any corrections made from standard setup

      5. Examine any special colors

  D. Check all printing condition settings (see I.C.3 of this outline)

CMYK Combinations

Color	Cyan %	Magenta %	Yellow %	Black %
Deep violet	100%	65%-75%	10%	25%
Deep purple	85%	95%	10%	20%
Sky blue	60%	20%-25%	0%	0%
Aqua	60%	0%	25%	0%
Kelly green	100%	0%	100%	0%
Lemon yellow	5%	15-20%	95%	0%
Gold	5%	15%-20%	65%-75%	0%
Orange red	10%	100%	100%	0%
Orange	5%	50%	100%	0%
Deep red	25%	100%	80%	20%
Pink	5%	40%	5%	0%
Beige	5%	5%	15%	0%
Caucasian flesh	15%-20%	45%	50%	0%
Asian flesh	15%	40%	55%	0%
Black flesh	35%	45%	50%	25%-35%*
Chocolate brown	45%	65%	100%	35%-40%
Dark black	95%	87%	87%	80%*
Gray	55%	42%	42%	15%*
Silver	20%	15%	14%	0%

*Recommend 40% GCR for smoother, more neutral result.

The colors listed are approximate values for offset lithography. The hues can differ depending on the prepress proofing system and ink sets used.

Adjusting the amounts of ink in the ratios shown changes the saturation of the colors.

Determining File Size

To determine the approximate file size of a digital file, use the following formula:

TOTAL NUMBER OF PIXELS ACROSS

multiplied by

TOTAL NUMBER OF PIXELS DOWN

equals

TOTAL NUMBER OF PIXELS IN AN IMAGE

multiplied by

TOTAL BITS OF COLOR USED divided by EIGHT

equals

TOTAL NUMBER OF BYTES OF INFORMATION

For example:

A one-bit black-and-white image with 1,200 by 800 pixels would yield

1,200 x 800 x (1 ÷ 8) =
960,000 pixels x .125 =
120,000 bytes (120 kilobytes)

An 8-bit gray-scale or color image with 1,200 by 800 pixels would yield
1,200 x 800 x (8 ÷ 8) =
960,000 pixels x 1 =
960,000 bytes (960 kilobytes)

A 24-bit color image with 1,200 by 800 pixels would yield
1,200 x 800 x (24 ÷ 8) =
960,000 pixels x 3 =
2,880,000 bytes (2,880 kilobytes; 2.8 megabytes)

A 32-bit color image with 1,200 by 800 pixels would yield
1,200 x 800 x (32 ÷ 8) =
960,000 pixels x 4 =
3,840,000 bytes (3,840 kilobytes; 3.8 megabytes)

A 24-bit color image with 1,200 by 800 pixels and
three additional 8-bit mask channels would yield
1,200 x 800 x (48 ÷ 8) =
960,000 pixels x 6 =
5,760,000 bytes (5,760 kilobytes; 5.7 megabytes)

This formula always yields the near-maximum file size
of all digital files. Depending on the file format you
use to save your image file, the size may be smaller.
The formula is a useful method of planning for the
memory storage requirements to accommodate a
project.

E

Hardware and Software Companies

This appendix lists some of the hardware and software available to persons using color on the Macintosh. By no means is this list all-encompassing. As fast as the technology moves, changes are inevitable; you always should keep aware of the latest technology available.

Image Processing Software

Adobe Photoshop
Adobe Systems, Inc.
1585 Charleston Road
P.O. Box 7900
Mountain View, CA 94039
415-961-4400
800-344-3385
415-961-3769 (fax)

ColorStudio
Fractal Design Corp.
335 Spreckels Drive
Aptos, CA 95003
408-688-8800
408-655-9663 (fax)

PhotoMac
Data Translation
100 Locke Drive
Marlboro, MA 01752
508-481-3700

Paint Programs

Color MacCheese
Delta Toa Software
760 Howard Avenue
Sunnyvale, CA 94087
408-730-9336

Easy Color Paint
Creative Software
3213 Annandale Road
Durham, NC 27705
800-367-6899
919-493-9503

MacPaint
Claris Corporation
5201 Patrick Henry Drive
P.O. Box 58168
Santa Clara, CA 95052
408-987-7000
408-727-8227

Oasis
Time Arts, Inc.
1425 Corporate Center Parkway
Santa Rosa, CA 95407
707-576-7722

Painter
Fractal Design Corp.
335 Spreckels Drive
Aptos, CA 95003
408-688-8800
408-655-9663 (fax)

PhotonPaint
MicroIllusions, Inc.
P.O. Box 3475
Granada Hills, CA 91394
818-785-7345

Pixel Paint
SuperMac Technology
485 Potrero Avenue
Sunnyvale, CA 94086
800-334-3005
408-245-2202

Studio/8 & Studio/32
Electronic Arts
1450 Fashion Island Boulevard
San Mateo, CA 94404
800-245-4525
415-571-7171

SuperPaint
Aldus Corp.
411 First Avenue
S. Seattle, WA 98104
800-333-2538
206-628-2320

UltraPaint
Deneba Software
3305 N.W. 74th Avenue
Miami, FL 33122
800-622-6827
305-594-6965

VideoPaint
Olduvai Corp.
7520 Red Road, Suite A
South Miami, FL 33143
800-822-0772
305-655-4665

3-D Programs

MacRenderMan
Pixar
1001 W. Cutting Boulevard
Richmond, CA 94804
510-236-4000

Sculpt 3D
Byte by Byte
9442 Capital of Texas
  Highway N.
Austin, TX 78759
512-343-4357

Strata Vision 3D
Strata, Inc.
2 W. St. George Boulevard
Ancestor Square, Suite 2100
St. George, UT 84770
800-678-7282
801-628-5218

Swivel 3D
MacroMind-Paracomp, Inc.
600 Townsend Street
San Francisco, CA 94103
415-442-0200

Scanners

Abaton Scanners
Abaton Technology Corp.
48431 Milmont Drive
Fremont, CA 94538
510-683-2226

CIS Systems
Barneyscan Corporation
130 Doolittle Drive, #19
San Leandro, CA 94577-1028
510-562-2480
510-562-6451 (fax)

ColorGetter
Optronics, of Intergraph
7 Stuart Road
Chelmsford, MA 01824
508-256-4511

Eikonix
Atex Magazine Publishing
Systems
32 Wiggins Avenue
Bedford, MA 01730
617-276-7195

Howtek ScanMasters
Howtek
21 Park Avenue
Hudson, NH 03051
603-882-5200

HP ScanJet Plus
Hewlett-Packard Company
700 71st Avenue
Greeley, CO 80634
303-845-4045

JX-Color Scanners
Sharp Electronics
Sharp Plaza, Box C Systems
Mahwah, NJ 07430
201-529-8200

Nikon Electronic Imaging
623 Stewart Avenue
Garden City, NY 11530
516-222-0200

Microtek Scanners
Microtek Labs, Inc.
16901 S. Western Avenue
Gardena, CA 90247
213-321-2121

ScanMan
Logitech
6505 Kaiser Drive
Fremont, CA 94555
510-795-8500

Silverscanner
LaCie
19552 S.W. 90th Court
Tualatin, OR 97062
800-999-0143

Thunderscan
Thunderware, Inc.
21 Orinda Way
Orinda, CA 94563
510-254-6581

Video Frame Grabbers

Color Capture
Data Translation, Inc.
100 Locke Drive
Marlboro, MA 01725

ColorSnap 32
Computer Friends, Inc.
14250 N.W. Science Park Drive
Portland, OR 97220
800-547-3303

ColorSpace
Mass Microsystems
550 Del Rey Avenue
Sunnyvale, CA 94086
800-522-7979

ComputerEyes
Digital Vision, Inc.
270 Bridge Street
Dedham, MA 02026
617-329-5400

DigiView
NewTek
115 W. Crane Street
Topeka, KS 66603
800-843-8934

Eikonix
Atex Magazine Publishing
Systems
32 Wiggins Avenue
Bedford, MA 01730
617-276-7195

Frame Grabber 24STV
RasterOps
2500 Walsh Avenue
Santa Clara, CA 95051
800-468-7600
408-562-4200
408-562-4065 (fax)

MacVision
Koala Technologies
70 N. Second Street
San Jose, CA 95113
408-438-0946

NuVista+
Truevision, Inc.
7340 Shadeland Station
Indianapolis, IN 46256
317-576-7700

Radius TV
Radius, Inc.
1710 Fortune Drive
San Jose, CA 95131
800-527-1950

VideoSpigot
SuperMac
485 Potrero Avenue
Sunnyvale, CA 94086
800-334-3005
408-245-2202

Still Video

Canon Xapshot
Canon USA
1 Canon Plaza
Lake Success, NY 11042
516-488-6700

Nikon HDTV 1920 x 1035
Nikon Electronic Imaging
623 Stewart Avenue
Garden City, NY 11530
516-222-0200

Sony Mavica
Sony Corp. of America
9901 Business Parkway
Lanham, MD 20706
301-577-4850

Stock Images

Comstock Desktop Photography
Comstock, Inc.
30 Irving Place
New York, NY 10003
212-353-8686

Darkroom CD-ROM
Image Club Graphics
1902 11th Street S.E., Suite 5
Calgary, AB T2G 3G2 Canada
800-661-9410

PhotoFiles
GoldMine Publishing
4994 Tulsa Avenue
Riverside, CA 92505
714-687-3815

PhotoGallery
NEC Technologies, Inc.
1414 Massachusetts Avenue
Boxborough, MA 01719
508-264-8000

Professional Photography Collection
discImagery
18 E. 16th Street
New York, NY 10003
212-675-8500

The Right Images
Tsunami Press
275 Route 18
E. Brunswick, NJ 08816
201-613-5533

Graphics Tablets

Calcomp
14555 N. 82nd Street
Scottsdale, AZ 85260
800-458-5888

Kurta
3007 E. Chambers
Phoenix, AZ 85040
800-44-KURTA
602-276-5533

Wacom, Inc.
W. 115 Century Road
Paramus, NJ 07652
201-265-4226

Prepress Systems

Freedom of Press
Custom Applications, Inc.
900 Technology Park Drive,
Bldg. 8
Billercia, MA 01821
508-667-8585

SpectreSeps
Pre-Press Technologies, Inc.
2441 Impala Drive
Carlsbad, CA 92008
619-931-2695

StudioLink Crosfield
Crosfield Systems
65 Harristown Road
Glen Rock, NJ 07452
201-447-5800

Visionary
Scitex America Corporation
8 Oak Park Drive
Bedford, MA 01730
617-275-5150

Printers and Imagesetters

Birmy Setter
Birmy Graphics Corp.
P.O. Box 420591
Miami, FL 33142
305-633-3321

Chelgraph
Electra Products, Inc.
1 Survey Circle
N. Billerica, MA 01862
508-663-4366

ColorMate
NEC Technologies, Inc.
Printer Division
159 Swason Road
Boxborough, MA 01719
800-632-4636

ColorPoint
Sieko Instruments
1130 Ringwood Court
San Jose, CA 95131
800-873-4561

ColorQuick
Tektronix, Inc.
Graphics Printing & Imaging
Division
P.O. Box 500, MS 50-662
Beaverton, OR 97077
503-627-1497

ColorSetter 2000
Optronics, of Intergraph
7 Stuart Road
Chelmsford, MA 01824
508-256-4511

Compugraphic Imagesetters
Agfa Compugraphic Corporation
90 Industrial Way
Wilmington, MA 01887
800-622-8973

4CAST
DuPont Electronic Imaging
Systems
300 Bellevue Parkway, Suite 390
Wilmington, DE 19809
800-654-4567

HP LaserJets
Hewlett-Packard Company
P.O. Box 60008
Sunnyvale, CA 94088
800-538-8787

Kodak XL 7700
Kodak, Inc.
Rochester, NY
800-44-KODAK

Lasersmith, Inc.
430 Martin Avenue
Santa Clara, CA 95050
408-727-7700

Linotronic Imagesetters
Linotype Company
425 Oser Avenue
Hauppauge, NY 11788
516-434-2000

Mitsubishi Thermal Printer
Mitsubishi Electronics America
991 Knox Street
Torrance, CA 90502
213-515-3993

QMS ColorScript
QMS, Inc.
One Magnum Pass
Mobile, AL 36618
800-631-2693

RasterOps
2500 Walsh Avenue
Santa Clara, CA 95051
800-468-7600
408-562-4200
408-562-4065 (fax)

Varitype Printers
Varitype, A Tegra Company
11 Mt. Pleasant Avenue
East Hanover, NJ 07936
201-884-6277

Image Pixel Resolution Requirements

As mentioned in Chapter 12, "Preparing Images for Output," the number of pixels per inch for halftone printing depends first on the halftone line screen ruling (lpi/dpi) and then on your output device's elements per inch (epi) capabilities. Simply doubling the value of the line screen ruling gives you an appropriate pixels-per-inch value. Considering the epi of the output device and the angle of the black film separation as well alters the required pixels per inch (ppi) to a more precise number. The following list provides the ppi required for the most common epi output settings. To determine the number of pixels per millimeter, simply divide the number of pixels per inch by 25.4, and that gives you the required number of pixels per millimeter.

For 300 EPI Printers

LINE SCREEN # of dots per inch (dpi) lines per inch (lpi)	Pixels per inch (ppi) Sampling rate 1.5:1	Pixels per inch (ppi) Sampling rate 2:1
45 lpi	68.2 ppi	90.9 ppi
53 lpi	79.5 ppi	106.1 ppi
65 lpi	95.5 ppi	127.3 ppi
85 lpi	119.3 ppi	159.1 ppi
100 lpi	159.1 ppi	212.1 ppi

For 1200 EPI Printers

LINE SCREEN # of dots per inch (dpi) lines per inch (lpi)	Pixels per inch (ppi) Sampling rate 1.5:1	Pixels per inch (ppi) Sampling rate 2:1
45 lpi	70.7 ppi	94.3 ppi
65 lpi	106.1 ppi	141.4 ppi
85 lpi	136.4 ppi	181.8 ppi
100 lpi	159.1 ppi	212.1 ppi
110 lpi	173.6 ppi	231.4 ppi
120 lpi	190.9 ppi	254.6 ppi
133 lpi	212.1 ppi	282.8 ppi
150 lpi	238.6 ppi	318.2 ppi
175 lpi	272.7 ppi	363.7 ppi
200 lpi	318.2 ppi	424.3 ppi

For 1270 EPI Printers

LINE SCREEN # of dots per inch (dpi) lines per inch (lpi)	Pixels per inch (ppi) Sampling rate 1.5:1	Pixels per inch (ppi) Sampling rate 2:1
45 lpi	72.2 ppi	96.2 ppi
65 lpi	101.0 ppi	134.7 ppi
85 lpi	134.7 ppi	179.6 ppi
100 lpi	155.4 ppi	207.2 ppi
110 lpi	168.4 ppi	224.5 ppi
120 lpi	183.7 ppi	244.9 ppi
133 lpi	202.1 ppi	269.4 ppi

LINE SCREEN # of dots per inch (dpi) lines per inch (lpi)	Pixels per inch (ppi) Sampling rate 1.5:1	Pixels per inch (ppi) Sampling rate 2:1
150 lpi	252.6 ppi	336.8 ppi
175 lpi	288.7 ppi	384.9 ppi
200 lpi	336.8 ppi	449.0 ppi

For 2400 EPI Printers

LINE SCREEN # of dots per inch (dpi) lines per inch (lpi)	Pixels per inch (ppi) Sampling rate 1.5:1	Pixels per inch (ppi) Sampling rate 2:1
45 lpi	72.0 ppi	96.1 ppi
65 lpi	103.2 ppi	137.6 ppi
85 lpi	136.4 ppi	181.8 ppi
100 lpi	159.1 ppi	212.1 ppi
110 lpi	173.6 ppi	231.4 ppi
120 lpi	190.9 ppi	254.6 ppi
133 lpi	212.1 ppi	282.8 ppi
150 lpi	238.6 ppi	318.2 ppi
175 lpi	272.7 ppi	363.7 ppi
200 lpi	318.2 ppi	424.3 ppi

For 2540 EPI Printers

LINE SCREEN # of dots per inch (dpi) lines per inch (lpi)	Pixels per inch (ppi) Sampling rate 1.5:1	Pixels per inch (ppi) Sampling rate 2:1
45 lpi	72.2 ppi	96.2 ppi
65 lpi	103.6 ppi	138.2 ppi
85 lpi	134.7 ppi	179.6 ppi
100 lpi	161.6 ppi	215.5 ppi
110 lpi	175.7 ppi	234.3 ppi
120 lpi	192.4 ppi	256.6 ppi
133 lpi	212.7 ppi	283.6 ppi
150 lpi	237.7 ppi	317.0 ppi
175 lpi	269.4 ppi	359.2 ppi
200 lpi	310.9 ppi	414.5 ppi

Glossary

additive primary colors   Red, green, and blue, which make white or gray when added together in equal amounts.

alias   An immediate transition from one area of color or tone to another. Describes the edge effect possible for various tools.

alpha-channels (or mask layers)   Specialized channels of control information for image masking or collaging.

anti-alias   An averaging or softening of the transition of one color area to another. For jagged lines, anti-aliasing smooths out the stairstep effect.

archiving   Storing digital files for long-term or backup purposes.

automatic selections   Selecting pixels within a variable range of hue, saturation, and/or value.

banding   A breakup of a smooth blend or vignette into bands of color.

binary   Digital data system based on 0 and 1.

bitmap   The pixels of an image all are assembled in a binary bitmap, or grid, which gives each pixel its location on the x-y axes.

bleed   The excess area outside the final trim of an image which ensures that the image goes off the sheet in full color with no white paper around it.

blend   A smooth gradation of tone or color from light to dark, or the smoothing of the demarcation of two neighboring color areas.

blur   The averaging of pixel values.

brightness   The amount of light emitting from or reflecting off something.

buffer   A digital holding area in which to store pixel data temporarily.

byte   Eight bits of digital data that represent a digit, character, or special value.

C print   A color print, reflective-type subject.

CCD   Charge coupled device, a light-sensitive array of sensors used to sample color data used in scanning devices.

channel   A layer of a color image. A 24-bit image has 8 bits of color information in each channel of RGB.

chroma   Hue, color information.

chroma-key   A video overlay system that allows for special effects and text to be added to video programs.

chrome   A transparency, transmissive-type subject.

clipboard   A buffer holding area the Macintosh uses for text and digital color information.

clone   To copy from one source point of pixel values to another area. Cloning also is called pixel copying.

color casts   An imbalance of color from neutral, "unreal" color appearance.

color curve   A graphic method of color correction using a 45-degree line as a point of reference to gauge change.

color key   A prepress proofing system manufactured by 3M composed of separate CMYK acetate overlays.

color separation   The breaking up of the visible spectrum into the subtractive colors of cyan, magenta, and yellow into black-and-white film halftone records of the original copy. A black separation is added for extra detail and depth in the darkest areas.

color space   A system used to describe all available colors graphed on a set of axes. RGB, CMYK, and HSV are examples of color spaces.

complementary color   The color that moves (dirties up) a pure color toward gray.

comprehensive drawing (comp)   An exact representation or drawing of what a finished job will look like with all elements to size, color, and exact position. Also called a comp.

contacting   Copying the dot values of one film to another photographically.

contrast   The difference between the lightest areas and the darkest areas in a reproduction and an original.

convergence   The focusing of RGB electron signals onto the surface of a video display screen.

cool colors   Colors on the blue side.

copy   Items or images to be scanned.

creative filters   Filters used primarily for visual effect.

Cromalin™   A prepress proof made of toner powders representing CMYK all laminated into a single sheet.

crop   The area of an image to use in a reproduction.

crop marks   Lines on a comp indicating where the finished page is to be trimmed.

cropping tool   A tool to select and size an area of an image.

cross curve   An original that has two opposing casts in the same scene, such as a magenta cast and a green cast.

CRT   Cathode-ray tube.

CT file format   Continuous tone file such as TIFF, PICT, and Scitex CT.

CT prints   Hard-copy reflective images that are continuous tone photographs.

densitometer   A device that reads the density of transmissive subjects or the reflective capabilities of reflective-type subjects. Readouts of the densitometer can be in density values or dot percentages.

density   The light-stopping power of an original subject or film.

density range   The gamut or range of tones from the lightest printing tone in a scene to the darkest printing tone in a scene. The range of tones that carry a printing dot.

depth of field   The range of focus from front to back.

digital still camera   A fixed-resolution image capture device that digitizes a scene as a single frame of pixel information.

direct digital layoff   Importing a digital Mac signal directly on an imaging device to digital video processor.

direct pixel imaging   Outputting one pixel for every pixel in a digital file.

dithering   A randomizing pattern that redistributes pixels.

Dmax   The maximum density in an original subject.

dots per inch   The number of halftone dots in an inch or the number of analyzing or exposing elements being used; a device resolution measurement. See *EPI*.

duotone   A full-range black-and-white image combined with a second color of lesser tonal range to create an image of greater tonal depth.

drawing   Creating fine detail using small printing dots.

dye sublimation process   Process of printing color images using a thermal dye process in which the amount of heat determines the amount of dye transferred to a carrier sheet.

dynamic effects   Image processing procedures that include sizing, rotating, scaling, flipping, and distortion.

8-bit color   A binary system that assigns 8 bits of information for each pixel in an image, making possible 256 colors or shades of gray.

elements per inch (epi)   The number of exposing or analyzing (sampling) elements in one inch. A measurement of device resolution.

emulsion   The light-sensitive coating on photographic film that creates the photographic image.

endpoint   Relating to the tonal range, the highlight and shadow points set the beginning and ending of the tonal range.

EPS or EPSF   Encapsulated PostScript file, the CMYK files made from an RGB file. Also included is a lo-res file for image placement.

equalizing   Making all RGB color curves equal or neutral at a particular density or location in an image.

eyedropper   A color sampling or choosing tool.

file compression   Reducing the amount of space used to store a digital file. See *lossy* and *lossless* types.

fill tool   Also known as paintbucket, a tool that replaces selected areas with flat colors, blends, or patterns.

film recorder   An output device that produces digital images in transparency form.

filter   A formula that modifies the pixel matrix of an image to create a visual effect.

5000 degrees Kelvin   The recommended color temperature of viewing lights that approximates daylight. A standard designation for fluorescent viewing lamps.

flicker   The visible blinking of the alternating scan lines of video displays.

flipping   Creating a mirror-image representation of an image.

floating selection   A selected group of pixels that floats above the image until deselected and dropped onto the desired position on the image.

gamma   The slope of the line that represents output value versus input value. Also a description of the contrast of a monitor.

gamut   A range of possibilities, such as the range of colors a color film can produce.

Gaussian distribution   The bell-shaped curve distribution of pixel value information.

GCR   Gray component removal, replacing the gray component of a CMYK reproduction with black ink.

gigabyte   One thousand megabytes.

gray balance   The balance of cyan, magenta, and yellow ink that will reproduce as a neutral gray.

gray scale   A tonal scale graduated from white to gray to black. Used for calibration and setup of color systems.

gray-scale mode   A selection mode that enables you to assign more than one bit per pixel to a black-and-white image.

half black   The black halftone printer that starts printing at the reproduction's middletone and ends at the shadow point.

half-cast method   Removing half of a color cast from the white areas in a reproduction.

halftone   A dot pattern that represents a continuous tone image, white to black with shades of gray in between.

halos   Surrounding lines of white or black around lines of detail or between contrasting areas. Halos should be felt, not seen.

high key   An original subject that is composed of very bright subject matter or that is improperly exposed so the color is abnormally weak and washed out.

highlight point   The density in an original subject where the smallest printing dot of cyan, magenta, or yellow starts to print.

histogram   The distribution of pixel value information shown visually in a special type of chart or graph.

HSB   Hue, saturation, and brightness.

HSL   Hue, saturation, and lightness.

HSV   The hue, saturation, and value color space.

hue   The color of something. Hues can be specified by wavelengths of light or CIE coordinates.

image aspect ratio   The horizontal versus vertical size of an image.

image processing programs   Programs that specifically process image manipulation data, as opposed to image creation programs, which create images from scratch.

imagesetter   An output device that produces separation halftones and text on film or paper.

informed buyer   Someone who knows what he needs and what is available in the marketplace to satisfy his needs.

interpolation   A sampling method used to create more pixel information by averaging the existing pixel information.

jaggies   Lines that, because of missing information, are staircased or jagged rather than straight. The result of low resolution.

JPEG   Joint Photographers Experts Group. A compression-decompression standard for digital files.

kilobyte   One thousand bytes.

landscape   Horizontal orientation of an image, as opposed to portrait orientation, which is vertical.

lasso   A selection tool that allows free and arbitrary selection of pixels.

layoff   The transferring of digital data to video format.

LED   Light-emitting diode, an exposing element.

lines per inch   Refers to the number of halftone dots in an inch. Used as a halftone screen designation such as 150 lpi, which is 22,500 (150 squared) halftone dots per square inch (dpi).

loss-less   Nondestructive file compression that keeps all original pixel information regardless of how many times it compresses the data.

lossy   Destructive file compression.

low key   An original subject that is made up mostly of dark subject matter or is an abnormal exposure causing the image to be darker than normal.

LZW compression   Method of loss-less compression used with TIFF files.

marquee   Tool for creating rectangular selections to be altered or cropped.

mask   A mask designates an area that is to be changed or protected from change.

matchprint™   A prepress proofing system by 3M that is made of laminated pigments.

megabytes   One thousand kilobytes.

memory colors   Colors that people can create without seeing an original to compare the color to, such as food, flesh, and blue sky.

middletone   The 50 percent dot printing area.

mixing palette   Area in a program where colors can be blended and chosen for use in an image.

moiré pattern   A halftone dot pattern that doesn't look continuous in tone. The dot pattern is becoming visible due to incompatible screen angles or a pattern in the original copy.

montage   To combine separate images to become one image, also called a composite image.

motion blur filters   Filters used to create a sense of movement.

neutral   An area of no color bias: white, gray, or black.

neutralizing   Changing the existing color balance to a neutral, noncasted balance.

NTSC   National Television Standards Commission. The U.S. television standard.

object images   Images based on vectors and points connected by formulas.

opacity   The degree of apparent density, or the amount of background a graphic element shows through itself.

original copy   Photographic subjects and art that is to be reproduced.

PAL   Phase alternation line. The European video standard.

palette   A selection of colors available in a color system.

Pantone Matching System (PMS)   A color identification and matching system.

pastel   Light colors that contain printing dots in the 5 percent to 15 percent range.

photo-realism   Images that resemble actual photographs.

photomultiplier   A light-sensing, photosensitive device that transforms light intensity to a stream of electrons. The eyes of a color drum scanner.

PICT   The standard Apple file format.

pixel   A picture element that is a discrete unit and has a location-area and value.

pixel aspect ratio   The horizontal versus vertical size of a pixel. Square pixels have an aspect ratio of one.

pixelization   A condition of too-low resolution that allows individual picture elements to become visible.

pixels per inch (ppi)   The number of pixels that occupy one inch. A measure of a file's resolution.

plug-in filter or module   A third-party vendor-developed software that provides an extra function not available in the standard software application.

portrait   A vertical image orientation, as opposed to landscape.

posterize   Limiting the gamut of color values to create an intensified visual result.

PostScript   A page description language by Adobe Systems, Inc., that describes text and graphic elements. Files made with PostScript can be used with any PostScript-compatible output device regardless of resolution.

process inks   Cyan, magenta, yellow, and black are process inks or subtractive colors. When they are combined on the printing press, they make a complete printing color gamut or range of colors.

production filters   Filters that are used primarily for enhancing color reproduction quality.

proof   A sample representing the finished result.

proportionality problem   The horizontal and vertical dimensions of an original must be properly scaled to fit both dimensions of a window. For example, a full-frame 35mm slide will not fit into a rectangular window.

quartertone   The 25 percent dot printing area, a bright area of the reproduction.

Quickdraw   A set of drawing routines for the Macintosh trademarked by Apple.

RAM   Random-access memory.

raster lines   Lines of pixel data used to image bitmap and object data.

RAW   An image of raw pixel data not corresponding to any particular file format type.

real time   A term used to indicate little or no waiting for computer processing to occur.

reflective copy   Subjects that do not pass light through them but reflect light, such as color prints and art.

register marks   Marks on a separation in the same spot for each of the four colors. When the negatives are assembled, the register marks are positioned on top of each other to ensure accurate positioning of colors.

registration   The exact positioning of a color on top of other colors.

render   The process of interpreting vector image information into bitmap image information.

replication   A sampling method used to create more pixel information by duplicating existing pixel information.

resampling   Changing the resolution of an image by adding or discarding pixels. Also known as "resing."

rescreen   To reseparate a subject that already has been separated as a halftone.

resolution   The number of discrete elements that make up an image or the number of imaging or sampling units used in a device.

resolution independent   Object-oriented files that are composed of points and vectors are not dependent on resolution, so they do not lose edge quality with enlargement. Being resolution independent is desirable for text. Bitmapped images are not resolution independent.

resing-up (or down)   See *resampling.*

RIFF   Raster image file format used by ColorStudio.

RIP   Raster image processing, a device that breaks an image into lines of pixel data. (See *raster lines.*)

RLE   Run-length encoding.

rods and cones   The light receptors in the human eye that sense hue, saturation, and value.

rosette pattern   A dot pattern of CMYK that should look continuous, not screened.

rotating   Turning an image from its original axis.

rubber stamp   The name of a cloning tool. See *clone.*

sampling   Making a copy of something.

sampling rate   The number of copies made in a specified area, such as 200 lines per inch.

saturation   The strength of a color, or the amount of gray in a color.

scaling   Changing from one size to another.

scan line   The basic unit of sampling used by a color scanner created by a sampling spot on a rotating drum.

scanner   A device that samples analog images and converts them into digital form.

Scitex Visionary   A color system that links the Scitex workstation to the Macintosh.

screen   To break up a continuous tone image into halftone dots.

screen angle   The direction of the lines of dots for each of the process colors. Proper screen angles place the halftone dots next to each other on the printed page to make an invisible rosette pattern that looks continuous tone to the eye.

selection   An item or location isolated for manipulation.

shade   A pure color mixed with black.

shadow point   The area of greatest density in an original where the 95 percent printing dot is set.

sharpen   To enhance the edge contrast in an image to make the scene appear sharper, more in focus.

skewing   Distorting an image as if it were being italicized.

sliders   Controls that increase or decrease an effect by moving the control from right to left.

special colors   Colors that are critical to the customer in a reproduction, such as product colors.

specular highlight   An area of a reproduction that carries no dots, being paper white. These areas include reflections on glass, water, and metal that are extremely bright and carry no color.

spot color   A single ink color applied to a specific area, such as a product color.

stairstepping   See *jaggies*.

stat   A low-quality reproduction of an image on a comprehensive drawing that represents an image's position, cropping, and sizes.

subtractive secondary colors   CMY (cyan, magenta, and yellow) when added together subtract all light and make black.

surround color   The color that is around a featured color and has an effect on how the featured color is perceived.

TGA   TARGA file format.

three-quartertone   The 75 percent printing dot area.

TIFF   Tagged image file format, an image file format that works on both IBM and Macintosh.

tonal range   The range of printed densities in an original or a reproduction.

tone   Any color or neutral that is denser than specular white.

tone reproduction   The reproduction of all the tonal steps from an original that also matches the contrast or dimensionality of the original.

toolbox   The area on the screen where the working tools are assembled for easy access.

transmissive subjects   Subjects that allow light to pass through them; transparencies. Also called transmission copy.

transparency   A photographic transmissive color subject in various format sizes such as 35mm and 4"x5".

trapping   Making two neighboring colored areas overlap into each other to prevent white gaps.

tweening   Creating intermediate steps between objects, with the steps metamorphosing from one to the other.

24-bit color   A binary system that assigns 8 bits of information for red, green, and blue in an image, making more than 16.7 million color possibilities.

UCR   Undercolor removal; subtracting CMY under black areas and replacing the undercolor with additional black as a means of saving ink on long press runs.

undo   A function that takes you back one step or command, erasing the previous command.

unsharp masking (USM)   The circuitry in a scanning device or software that enhances the sharpness of a screened reproduction.

up-sampling   Increasing the number of pixels in a file.

value   The degree of lightness or darkness.

vaporware   Hardware and software that is still on the drawing board and in development but not available.

video tape recorder (VTR)   A device that samples visual data on videotape for playback to a video display.

vignetting tone method   A method of highlight density locating that involves looking for tone coming off a specular area.

vignetting tones   Densities that go from light to dark.

virtual memory   Memory space allocated for an image being worked on (working file) so that any changes made to the portion of the image seen on the screen are made on the entire image regardless of the actual image size.

visual spectrum   The range of visual light from 400 to 700 nanometers of light wavelength.

warm colors   Colors that are on the red-orange side.

workstations   Computers set up primarily to perform a group of specified functions with added speed and efficiency.

WORM   Write-once, read many.

zoom   To change the size of the viewing area to examine a larger area or to examine a smaller area at greater detail.

Index

pixels, 3
zero point, 6
see also x-axis; y-axis

B

balance, 33
   gray, 227
   white, 216
banding, 142, 304
base (separation film), 189
beams, light, 43
   see also drum scanners
Bernoulli cartridges, 258
best eight, 38
biases, 64
bicubic interpolation, 15
binary
   code, 304
      pixels, values, 7
   numbers, picture elements, 44
bit resolution, 10
bitmaps, 9, 180, 304
   images, 6, 9, 20, 88-90, 125-126
   pixels, 6-8
bits, 7
black (K), 32
   channel, 8
   component, 227-228
   highlight dot, 228
   point, 220-222
   printer, 227-229, 234
   set black, 75-76
   shadow endpoints, 229
bleeds, 233, 248, 304
blends, 99, 304
   noise filter, 142
   objects, 180, 184-185
   patterns, 142
   pressure, 108-109
blocks, pixels, 58

bloom, 248
blur filters, 136, 139
   Gaussian distribution curve, 140
   motion, 140
blurring tools (drawing), 94, 304
boards
   video, 35-36, 249
   video capture, 48
border, neutral, 224
bright whites, 216
brightening highlights, 216
brightness, 32-33, 304
   see also value
broadcast video, 247-248
brushes
   airbrushes, 92-93
   paintbrushes, 92-93
   see also paint tools
buffers, 46, 115-116, 304
bytes, 304
   kilobytes (KB), 52
   megabytes (MB), 52

C

C print, 304
C prints, 42, 223
calculating file size, 290
calibration
   monitors, 207-208
   scanners, 204-208
   software, 206
Callier's Q factor, 205
camerals, digital still cameras, 41
cameras
   digital still, 48
   electronic, 48
capture video, 41
captures, 48
Cartesian coordinate system, 6
cast removal, 217

cut option, 115, 116
cyan dot white, 215

D

dark stroke filter, 144-146, 148
default file format, 55, 256
densities, 217-222
　see also highlight point
densitometer, 205-206, 211, 214, 220-222, 234, 306
density, 223-227, 306
　endpoints, 75
　　black printer, 228
　low, 213-214
　range, 306
　tone, 33
depth of field, 122-123, 306
design errors, 269
desktop scanners, 45
　see also CCD scanners
destructive compression, *see* Lossy compression
device resolution, 10-11
devices, storage, 258
digital
　masks, 113
　file formats, 51
　files, combining with text files, 244
　image files, 51-60
　　blank, 87
　information, converting to output, 180
　pixel format, *see* pixels
　pixels, 4
　signals, scanners, 45
　still cameras, 41, 48, 306
digitizing images, 41
direct digital layoff, 249, 306
direct pixel imaging, 171, 180, 240-241, 306
direct pixel output, 174
Discrete Cosine Transform (DCT), algorithm, 58-59
discrete units, pixels, 4-8
Disk Doubler file compression program, 58

disks, floppy, recording images, 48
displaying, RGB, 32
displays
　24-bit, 35
　convergence, 36
　screens, curved, 36
distortions, 19-20, 35
dithering, 306
Dmax values, 223, 228-229, 306
documents, Control Panel, Gamma, 38
dots
　50 percent area, 226-227
　75 percent area, 227
　angling, 192
　contacting, 189-190
　drawing color, 220
　halftone, 13
　　registration, 232-233
　highlights, 213, 226-227
　　black, 228
　　specular, 190-191
　ink, 191
　moire pattern, 192
　none (specular highlights), 213
　percentages, pastels, 219-220
　rosette pattern, 192
　shadow, 226-227
　shape, 191
　sizes, ink, 190-191
　values
　　densitometer, 211
　　minimum, 214
　see also halftone dots
dots per inch (dpi), 12-13, 306
　resolution, imagesetter, 12
down-sampling, 13, 20
drawing, 306
　aliasing, 88-90
　anti-aliasing, 88-90
　complementary color, 220
　dots, 220

more option, 138
mosaic filter, 144
mosaics, 4
motion blur filters, 140, 308
mouse, drawing, 108

N

nanometers, 23
negative color separation film, 189
neutral, 308
neutralized white, 215-216, 308
neutrals, 24, 28, 194-199, 224-227
    monitors, 207-208
    scanners, 204-206
    software calibration, 206
noise, 248
noise filters, 142
    blends, 142
    Gaussian distribution curve, 142
non-align (clone tool), 95-96
nonproportional scaling, 129
normal exposure, 217
normalizing dark originals, 216
NTSC (National Television Systems Committee) video
  color space, 247-248, 308
numbers, Pantone, 39

O

object images, 20, 308
object points, 20
object-based graphics, 185
object-based langages, 21
objects
    blends, 180, 184-185
    converting for output, RIPing, 181
    masks, 184
    points, 179-180
    rendering, 181
    aliasing, 182-183
    masks, 184
    resizing, 180
    spot color, 180
    transitional processes, 184-185
    tweening, 184-185
    vector-based, *see* vector-based objects
one-bit images, 7
one-bit pixels, 7
one-image buffer, 46
opacity, 108, 308
opaque subjects, 43
optical drives, 258
optical receptors, 23
options
    copy, 115-116
    cut, 115-116
    filters, more, 138
    paste, 115-116
    Set White, 215
    tools, 86
oranges, 202
orientation, 189-190
    landscape, 127, 308
    portrait, 127, 309
original color, x-axis, 67
original copy
    normalizing, 216
    scanners, 42
original filter, 144, 146, 148
outlines (workflow)
    production, 277-278
    scanners, 282-283
    separations, 282-283
output, 169
    checklist, 175-176
    continuous tone (CT) printing, 171-172
    drum scanners, 42
    final size, 170
    halftone printing, 172-173